What Others Are Saying about This Book . . .

"A chilling narrative about the abuses of state power. Intriguing. Compelling. Important."

—Michael Reagan, radio talk show host, author, commentator and political strategist

"An unprecedented first-hand look into the chilling world of Libyan leader Muammar Qadhafi by the man who risked it all to resolve the dispute between the United States and Libya over the Lockerbie bombing. This is sure to be an unforgettable motion picture."

—Tom Brown, producer

"Intensely personal and perceptive. You'll never forget this book, nor the up-and-coming film."

—Donal Bailey, president, Forrest Motion Pictures, London

"A remarkable book—for a lot of reasons."

—Ron Russell, author, *Don Carina: WWII Mafia Heroine*

"A captivating story of international intrigue and conspiracy at the highest levels of the U.S. Government that led to one man's devastating fall from grace. Most amazing of all—this story is true."

—Al Stoffel, producer, *Misdirection*

"Read this book, and don't forget its message when you're at the polls."

—Mary Jeffries, psychologist

"A somber tale, a thrilling read."

—Gary Chafetz, author, *The Perfect Villain: John McCain and the Demonization of Lobbyist Jack Abramoff*

"A book we must all take to heart."

—John Rixey Moore, author, *Hostage of Paradox*

TRUTH NEVER DIES

William C. Chasey

Disclaimer: This is a true story, and the characters and events are real. However, in some cases, the names have been altered, but the overall chronology is an accurate depiction of the author's experience. Some excerpts in this book may have appeared in some of Dr. Chasey's previous writings.

Cover design by Bartej Jizkiwski
Photo of William C. Chasey by Bartek Kozlowski
Except for chapter image all photos © William C. Chasey
Text design by Jane Hagaman

Bettie Youngs Books are distributed worldwide. If you are unable to order this book from your local bookseller, online, or Espresso, you may order directly from the publisher.

Bettie Youngs Book Publishers
www.BettieYoungsBooks.com

ISBN: 978-1-936332-46-5
Library of Congress Control Number: 2012934495

1. Chasey, William. 2. Government. 3. Gadhafi. 4. Lobbyist. 5. Law

10 9 8 7 6 5 4 3 2 1

Printed on acid-free paper

Printed in the United States of America

Dedication

To my beloved Virginia and Katie,
for their faith in God,
their courage under pressure,
and their unwavering trust in me.
It is through their love that God's blessings abound.

CONTENTS

Acknowledgements

I want to express my sincere appreciation and thanks to my wife Virginia and my daughter Katie for their unwavering love and devotion to me during this trying period of our lives. I also want to thank them for their courageous willingness to share our personal story with the world.

I would like to extend my special appreciation and love to my family and friends who were there for us through this ordeal and contributed, each in their own unique way, to our ability to always move forward: my dearest friend, Richard Schubert, my sister and her husband, Gene and Georgianne Chomicky, Virginia's brother and sister, Henry Borys and Mary Coro, along with their respective spouses, Dolores and Don, and our long-time California friends, Bill and Barbara McColl. Some others mentioned in this book have since passed, but remain in our hearts and prayers.

I owe a sense of great indebtedness to my lawyer, Brian Shaughnessy, who always told it straight, but with complete loyalty and compassion. Together, we fought the good fight and I will never forget his belief in me.

All of this work would have not have taken shape but due to the wonderful enthusiasm and support from my Warsaw friend and colleague Donal Bailey, who from the very first time he heard the story, said, "We've got to tell it!" With the help of his staff, especially George Zervakos and Daniel DelPercio, we were able to get this book rolling. Thanks for those great brainstorming TND breakfasts at the InterContinental Hotel Warsaw, and your continuous encouragement.

I express my profound sense of appreciation to Natalie Marciniak, the operations manager of our foundation, but more than that, truly my "Girl Friday and friend" when it comes to getting things done and problems solved. Thank you for always having a great attitude and being there for our foundation and for me and my family.

Last, but not least, a very special thanks to Bettie Youngs of Bettie Youngs Book Publishers. Your total professionalism, true concern and persistence in getting this story out never faltered and kept me motivated throughout. Thanks, as well, to the BYBooks most talented staff for all the ways they nurtured this book and brought it to light.

Introduction

Some may wonder why it has taken me so long to write this book. It was over sixteen years ago that I wrote *Pan Am 103: The Lockerbie Cover-up,* an investigation into the most vicious international terrorist attack on Americans before 9/11.

Over the years, I've thought long and hard whether to make public the nightmarish saga of my personal life during that period. After all, it was all water under the bridge. But something happened that changed my mind. I was recently diagnosed with multiple myeloma, an incurable blood cancer. I realized then that if my story is to be told, I must tell it now.

This will not be a rehash of the controversy over who was responsible for the destruction of Pan Am 103. Instead, it will focus on the abuse of power by the CIA, FBI, IRS, and Justice Department, which conspired to prevent me from helping to normalize relations between the United States and Libya, and to blackmail me, a private American citizen, into participating in a sordid and illegal state-sponsored assassination.

Over a six-year period, the government methodically destroyed my career, along with my financial well-being. I went from one of the most successful and well-connected lobbyists in Washington D.C., to federal inmate 42938-083.

I fully expect that the U. S. government will reject or ignore what I have to say, but now that my story has been written, I am confident it will never die, because truth never dies.

Prologue

In the middle of June 1998, I was sitting alone, minding my own business, eating lunch at a long dining table. Two inmates—carrying trays full of food and dressed like me in khaki prison garb—casually sat down directly across from me.

For the past few days, I had chosen this empty table in the rear of the dining hall, because it afforded me a lovely view of the Allegheny Mountains. It was my only pleasure in this godforsaken place. A few feet away, there was an unlocked door to the outside patio. If I wanted to, I could exit and stroll onto the pastoral road, which ran next to this minimum-security federal prison camp, and walk all the way to those alluring mountains in the distance.

This facility had no perimeter walls or fencing of any kind. Indeed, there were no iron bars on the windows. I hadn't seen a single strand of barbed wire. There were no search lights or guard towers, and no armed guards with attack dogs patrolling the grounds. If I had wanted to flee, and I didn't, I could have easily done so. And if I had timed it just right, nobody would have known I was missing for several hours. Who knows? I might have actually reached those green mountains only twenty miles away.

But around dinnertime, there would have been a "count," in which all prisoners were accounted for. I would have been declared missing. If I'd been captured, which I surely would have been, my unauthorized departure would have been deemed a "violent escape," punishable by an additional ten years tacked on to my sentence.

Obviously, I wasn't going anywhere . . . that is, I needed to serve my sentence and then put my life back in order.

I continued to pay no attention to the inmates sitting across from me, although I could tell they were staring at me. Actually, I was a bit miffed that they had sat down at my table. There were plenty of empty seats at other tables. I avoided all eye contact with them. I was enjoying a little peace and serenity and just wanted to keep to myself. I wasn't in the mood to chat, make friends, or hear their tales of woe. All I wanted to do, as I took an occasional bite of my tasteless food, was to stare out the window at the serene central Pennsylvania landscape.

Finally, one of the men across from me, cleared his throat, leaned forward, and whispered.

"Are they treating you well in here, Dr. Chasey?"

Stunned, I immediately recognized the voice. Give me a break! It was the CIA agent I had dubbed, "Mr. DuPont." And now, he was here in the Allenwood Federal Prison, posing as an inmate!

Several years ago, I had first noticed him coming and going from the U. S. Embassy in Costa Rica, and then later we'd "bumped into each other" on an elevator in the Noga Hilton Hotel in Geneva, Switzerland. What's more, we had also met three months ago at Dulles Airport, where he had propositioned me. He asked for help in murdering Abdelbaset al-Megrahi and Lamen Khalifa Fhimah. Sounds like I'm making this stuff up, doesn't it? They were the two Libyans that the attorney general of the United States and the Scottish Lord Advocate had indicted for blowing up Pan Am flight 103 over Lockerbie, Scotland, on December 21, 1988, resulting in the deaths of 270 innocent people.

DuPont reached across the table, shook my hand, and introduced me to his companion. "This is Mr. DuPont too," he said with a sheepish look on his face, like he had just made a very clever joke. "You mean Mr. DuPont also?" I asked. He raised two fingers, chuckled, and said, "No, he is Mr. DuPont 2. You will now have two DuPonts to kick around in your next book," he laughed! DuPont explained that he was here to follow up on our recent conversation at Dulles Airport.

"It's imperative we bring this case to a close," he said. "The political situation has changed. We must act immediately. When Megrahi and Fhimah are gone, Lockerbie will no longer be an issue, justice will have been served, and the world can move on. I am asking you one more time. Will you reconsider our offer?"

With my best poker face, I sat there, staring at him, saying nothing.

He waited a moment and continued. He pointed out that my relationship with Col. Qadhafi would get me back into Libya and then I could surreptitiously direct our intelligence forces to the two men responsible for the Lockerbie bombing. Finally, I spoke up. "So how exactly would it work?"

He explained that I would have to ask my old friend, Youssef el-Debri, the head of Libyan intelligence, to arrange for me to meet again with Megrahi and Fhimah.

"You would claim to be writing a new book exonerating them. You would conduct several interviews and clandestinely plant an electronic homing device in their residence for our planes to lock on to."

He paused again. When I didn't respond, he continued.

"We will safely get you out of Libya," he said, "and no one will connect you to the attack. If you agree to help us, you will be released from prison this afternoon, and we will see that your criminal record is expunged. We will make you and your family whole again. As far as the public and press are concerned, you were working on our behalf all along for reasons that can't be divulged."

For the past three months, I had mulled over DuPont's offer at Dulles Airport. The CIA was right. I was the only American with access to Qadhafi and his inner circle. If they wanted to assassinate Megrahi and Fhimah, I was the only one who could help them do it.[1]

I thought about everything that had been done to me. In order to pressure me into cooperating, the government had destroyed my reputation, bankrupted me, and sentenced me to federal prison on trumped-up charges.

Again, DuPont was waiting for my response.

The warm summer breeze coming from a nearby screened window carried the faint aroma of manure from nearby farms. It made me smile. It reminded me of the horses that we used to keep in the corral of our Rancho Santa Fe home, and the many times my daughter Katie and I had ridden them into the canyons and across the hills near our home. I hadn't smiled in weeks.

My life was in ruins. Most of my friends were now shunning me. I was destitute and a convicted felon. I would never vote again. Upon my release, there was the distinct possibility that my wife, my seventeen-year-old daughter, and I would end up homeless. I had little left to lose.

DuPont wanted my answer . . .

ONE

How It All Began

Eleven years earlier, the ski conditions at Vail, Colorado, could not have been better. I can say that with certainty, because I had skied there almost every Christmas week for the past two decades. The clean brisk air of the Rocky Mountains was filled with excitement in anticipation of the joyful Christmas holiday.

It was December 21, 1988, a day that would change my life forever.

After hours of vigorous skiing, we were comfortably nestled into our small, cozy condo, just steps from the main chair lift. My wife and ski buddy, Virginia, and I were relaxing and sipping a glass of California Merlot as I channel surfed between CNN and the Vail ski report. I didn't think I could have been happier at that very moment, watching our six-year-old daughter, Katie, playing quietly with her Barbie dolls on the floor in front of the fireplace.

Gifts were neatly arranged beneath our small Christmas tree in the corner of the living room. This was our third tree of the holiday season. There were two others, larger and meticulously decorated with special family ornaments, in our La Jolla, California, home.

We had decorated them in early December for our traditional open-house party, which we had just hosted the previous Sunday afternoon, for our personal, business, and political friends. While the adults had been sipping wine and eggnog upstairs, a rent-a-Christmas elf had been performing magic tricks downstairs for Katie and her friends. We had been throwing this annual party since moving our main residence five years ago from Washington, D.C., to La Jolla, in north San Diego County.

Despite the commute of 6,000 miles every week, the move had opened up vast business opportunities and contacts I never anticipated. More importantly, Virginia and I felt it was a better environment in which to raise Katie. Every Monday morning I would fly to Washington, D.C., and then fly back home every Thursday evening, always in the same first-class seat. I was undoubtedly American Airlines' most frequent flier.

Christmas in Vail was one of the highlights of our year but, as usual, there was little distinction between work and play. While Aspen attracted the Hollywood set at Christmas, Vail was a political town at that time of year.

It probably started with former President Gerald Ford, as a result of his well-publicized Christmas ski vacations. Ford had become the unofficial mayor of Vail, and Christmas wasn't complete until he had lit the community Christmas trees at Beaver Creek, Lions Head, and Vail Village.

Many political names and faces of the past and present were often seen mingling in the quiet little haunts of this pristine village during the holidays. Of particular interest to me were the members of Congress who came to Vail. As a registered lobbyist, I had to know and influence these people in the course of my daily business life.

We had started the day skiing with Minnesota Sen. Rudy Boschwitz and his wife, Ellen. Sometime during that Christmas week, I could count on exchanging pleasantries and some political talk with Ohio Sen. John Glenn, the first American to orbit the Earth, who usually skied with his good friend, composer Henry Mancini.[2] I often represented Mancini's wife, Ginny, and her Society of Singers in Washington.

(The following year, my wife and I would attend a memorable Hollywood dinner party in the Mancini's Oscar- , Emmy-, and Grammy-laden Beverly Hills home, honoring the 100th birthday of Irving Berlin. After dinner we sat around as Mancini played the piano, singing Berlin tunes with Andy Williams, Jack Jones, and Dionne Warwick.)

This year, I knew I wasn't going to have much time to talk to Indiana Sen. Dan Quayle, whom I had known since his days in the House of Representatives. He would now be returning to Vail as the vice president-elect, along with a large contingent of staff and Secret Service agents.

Our dear friends, Jack Kemp (R-NY) and his wife, Joanne, were also at Vail. Like us, the Kemps were committed Christians. Virginia often attended Joanne's home Bible study when she was in Washington.(A star quarterback for thirteen years, much of it with the Buffalo Bills, Kemp was about to be named the Secretary of Housing and Urban Development by President George H. W. Bush. In 1996, Kemp was the running mate of Republican presidential candidate Bob Dole.) That afternoon, we had skied with the Kemps and with New Jersey Sen. Frank Lautenberg. Before parting, we made plans to get together for dinner at the Lodge later that evening.

As I continued to channel surf, I heard something unsettling on CNN. "We interrupt our scheduled programming to bring you this special news bulletin." A jumbo jet had just crashed over Scotland.

We stopped talking and listened, sickened by the thought of a major air crash, especially just before Christmas.

Soon, we learned that just after 7 PM, Pan Am Flight 103—on route from London's Heathrow Airport to JFK in New York—had crashed into Lockerbie, a village in southern Scotland. An unknown number of people on the ground had been killed, along with the passengers and crew. Many were American exchange students from Syracuse University, returning home to celebrate Christmas with their families.

We shuddered to think of the terror these people must have felt as they plunged to their deaths from 31,000 feet.

TWO

First Attack in the War on Terrorism

Pan Am 103 had taken off earlier that day from Frankfurt, Germany, on a Boeing 727.

At Heathrow Airport, passengers and baggage had been transferred to a bigger Boeing 747, named "Maid of the Seas," for the trip over the Atlantic Ocean.

The plane was the fifteenth 747 that Boeing had built. At the time of the crash, it was one of the oldest jumbo jets flying. Since 1970, the plane had flown 72,000 hours and taken off and landed 16,500 times. This was well below the number of takeoffs and landings considered high for this type of aircraft, normally around 50,000.

A number of new passengers boarded the plane at Heathrow. Pan Am 103 was scheduled to stop at JFK in New York and then continue on to its final destination, Detroit Metropolitan Airport.

On board were 259 people, including a sixteen-member flight crew. Fifty-five-year-old Captain Jim MacQuarrie was an experienced pilot who had flown this route frequently. His copilot was Ray Wagner. Both men were married and had two children. The flight attendants on board came from many countries, including Sweden, Spain, the Philippines, and the United States.

The passengers were also diverse. They included university students, business people, and military personnel from U.S. bases in West Germany. It was a very young passenger list with an average age of twenty-seven years. Most were going home for the holidays, so the overhead compartments were bulging with Christmas gifts.

Thirty-five students from Syracuse University were returning home that evening. They had just completed a study-abroad program in London. Many of the business passengers had wrapped up meetings and projects in time to travel for the holidays. Flight attendants served drinks and handed out headphones for the movie. At the same time, in the tranquil town of Lockerbie, people were taking care of last-minute preparations for the holidays.

The 740,000-pound jumbo jet pushed back from Heathrow's newly remodeled Terminal 3 building. A few minutes later, at 6:25 PM— nearly a half hour after its scheduled departure time—"Maid of the Seas" lifted off runway 27 Left and climbed into the slate-gray skies. There was a slight drizzle falling at Heathrow. The winds-aloft report predicted that Pan Am 103 would encounter steady headwinds of nearly 100 miles per hour when it reached cruising altitude. Because of the huge size of the Boeing 747, the strong winds would go unnoticed by the passengers and crew. Nothing suggested that this was anything but a routine flight.

Thirty-five minutes later, the plane leveled off.

"Clipper One-Zero-Three," MacQuarrie radioed from the darkened flight deck. "We are level at three-one-zero."

Pan Am 103 had reached its cruising altitude of 31,000 feet.

Alan Topp, an air traffic controller at the Scottish Air Traffic Control Center in Prestwick, on the southwest coast of Scotland, was tracking the plane's progress. He requested that Flight 103 identify its position by squawking identification code "zero three five seven" on the jet's transponder. He checked the identification code on his radar screen and confirmed the plane's position and altitude. Topp directed Captain MacQuarrie to fly a route direct that would take the plane directly over Lockerbie.

Topp, a twenty-three-year veteran air traffic controller, tracked the plane, a bright green box about 2 millimeters across on the radar screen, as it moved in the appropriate direction following his instructions.

It was just another routine night.

In a split-second, the bright green box was gone. In its place were five little blinking green boxes that reminded Topp of a Christmas tree. Almost immediately, those boxes also vanished from the screen.

He thought that it had to be a computer glitch.

"Clipper One-Zero-Three," Topp radioed. "Clipper One-Zero-Three."

There was no response.

He now realized something was very wrong.

He screamed into his microphone, as if it might somehow trigger a response. "Clipper One-Zero-Three!"

In desperation, Topp shouted across the room to Adrian Ford, his shift supervisor. Ford was intently listening to the pilot of a London-to-Glasgow shuttle, who reported that he had just seen a fiery explosion on the ground ahead of him.

"I've got a report of an explosion on the ground," Ford shouted back.

"You've got to be kidding," Topp said, half to himself.

His stomach began to churn. "I've lost the Clipper, One-Zero-Three. That must be him."

Topp knew there was no need to keep trying to raise MacQuarrie on the radio.

What Topp and Ford could not possibly know was that a bomb had just blown Pan Am 103 out of the sky—sending bodies, plane parts, baggage, and blazing debris raining down on the village of Lockerbie.

At exactly 7:03 PM, seismographers at the Earthquake Monitoring Center in Dumfriesshire, about 14 miles from Lockerbie, reported a 1.9 reading on the Richter scale. The tremor was caused when a major portion of the Boeing 747 fuselage hit the ground in Sherwood Crescent in the southwest end of town. The impact gouged a deep crater in the earth and sent an exploding fireball 300 feet in the air. A gas main ruptured as the debris landed, adding fuel to the already roaring fires. The flames engulfed everything—buildings, cars, trees and bushes—into a raging inferno.

Rubble and airplane wreckage were strewn everywhere. What moments before had been a peaceful hamlet was now a horrific scene of death and destruction. Corpses still strapped into their airplane seats were found scattered about the town. Seventy-one dead passengers were found in one destroyed home.

Sherwood Crescent was the part of the village most devastated by the crash. There, the jumbo jet's huge engines and wings, containing the fuel tanks with 200,000 pounds of jet fuel, had crashed to earth.

The human carnage and damage to property seemed ubiquitous. Bodies were wretchedly dismembered. Feet were missing from some. Others had been horribly compressed by the impact of the fall from five miles above. At that altitude, the victims would have experienced a two-and-a-half-minute free fall, reaching speeds of nearly 120 miles per hour before impact.

According to pathologists, who later testified before a fatal-accident inquiry in Dumfries, Scotland, it was unlikely that any of the passengers could have survived. The victims had been grouped into three categories. The majority had been killed immediately. A smaller number had suffered less-severe injuries, but due to extensive damage to vital organs, had died almost immediately after hitting the ground. However, two passengers with less-severe injuries might have survived had they received immediate medical attention.

At the center of the explosion, where the heat was most intense, homes and their occupants had vaporized, vanishing without a trace. In the first hours after the crash, the extent of the destruction made it impossible to tell how many townspeople had lost their lives.

The police attempted to account for those who lived in the most badly damaged parts of town. They went door to door, registering the names of residents still alive and those thought to be missing. At 10 PM, they posted lists of the known survivors on the doors of the town hall, adding names throughout the night. Anxious friends and relatives of the missing gathered outside the hall, scanning the lists for the names of their friends and loved ones.

The whereabouts of many of those missing were determined over the next few days. Some had been away on vacation or visiting friends in town. Some had fled their homes in panic. But others had not been so lucky. Eleven had been killed on the ground.

The plane had landed within yards of the A74 highway, the main road running through Lockerbie and connecting Scotland to England. The fiery crash stopped traffic and ignited cars. Wreckage from the plane also reached the outskirts of Lockerbie.

The cockpit section of the plane, with "Maid of the Seas" inscribed on its side, was found in a farmer's field three miles from town. MacQuarrie's body had been ejected and lay outside the cockpit. Three crew members' bodies remained inside. Despite all the damage, the cockpit lights glowed on, powered by an emergency generator. It was the only life remaining on Pan Am 103.

The plane had been blown up by a massive explosion right under the cockpit, in the most sensitive area of the plane. The force of the blast and resulting depressurization caused it to break up into thousands of pieces, throwing its human cargo into the blackness of the night. It was a secondary shock wave, however, that caused the deaths of the crew and passengers. This secondary shock wave burst a large jagged hole in the side of the aircraft, causing it to start disintegrating.

Within seconds the skin panels peeled backwards and the entire nose section fell away. As the shattered aircraft plunged into a vertical dive, the Pratt & Whitney turbofan engines were torn off and baggage and passengers were propelled into the freezing atmosphere. The wings, heavy with a full complement of aviation fuel, crashed at a speed of more than 200 miles per hour into Sherwood Crescent. The resulting fireball was visible more than six miles away.

As the bodies fell, the force of the air rushing past them

ripped clothing away from the limbs, and pieces of human anatomy were stripped of tissue by the friction. Most landed in the fields stretching out from Lockerbie, the force of the impact making them sink inches into the ground softened by the heavy rain of the previous few days. Fathers, mothers, sons, and daughters, and whole families were wiped out in an instant.

About an hour before Pan Am 103's scheduled arrival time, friends and relatives began arriving at JFK in New York. Word of the disaster began to spread quickly. Some rushed to the airport after seeing news reports on television. On the other side of the Atlantic, shocked relatives began arriving at Heathrow Airport.

Social workers and chaplains offered comfort to the anguished families of the victims. Pan Am knew there were no survivors, but before they could contact relatives, they needed to verify the names of the passengers. Communications between Lockerbie and the airports made this difficult. It was 10:30 PM (EST) before Pan Am officials could confirm the fate of loved ones for anxious relatives and friends.

The search for remains and clues to the cause of the disaster would be a daunting task. Because the airplane had been traveling at 550 miles per hour when it broke apart, the wreckage was spread far and wide. A ten-foot-high piece of fuselage was found in a field five miles from Lockerbie. A body still strapped to a plane seat was found ten miles from town.

Strong winds carried lighter items from inside the plane even farther. Mailbags from the flight were found 30 miles away in the town of Northumberland. Debris scattered in a wide arc across the border area between England and Scotland and as far as the North Sea, 70 miles away. A watch torn from a body that fell in a Lockerbie field was discovered in a village 80 miles away. In the beginning, the search area included locations over

100 miles away. Later, the search for answers would extend much farther.

One point seemed clear from the outset. Investigators suspected foul play. The crash of Pan Am 103 had not been an accident. Huge 747's did not just fall from the sky. The nature of the damage suggested that a bomb brought the plane down, but investigators would have to find solid evidence that could be tested in a crime lab to be certain. If it turned out the disaster had been the calculated work of a terrorist organization, the authorities would have a criminal investigation on their hands.

For that reason, the search had to be thorough. Everybody had to be treated as a potential murder victim. Every piece of debris was a vital clue to be documented. Every body was invaluable evidence for a possible future trial. All those involved with the investigation felt that if this was murder, it was murder on a massive scale. Those responsible must be brought to justice.

The biggest manhunt in the history of Western civilization was now underway to find those responsible for this heinous act.

THREE

Life Changes

As the years drifted by, I felt somewhat detached from the events of that terrible night. I hadn't known anyone on the plane, but I did know some of the basic facts.

There had been a major investigation that initially focused on Syria and Iran as the perpetrators. I remembered being mildly surprised in 1991, when, after a long and extensive investigation, the focus shifted. Libya was now the target of the investigation. Indeed, the United States and Scotland had indicted two Libyan intelligence officers for mass murder. Libyan leader Col. Muammar al-Qadhafi, had refused to extradite them for trial, much to the anger and frustration of the West. As a result, the United States and the United Nations had imposed sanctions on Libya for harboring the two alleged terrorists.

In the intervening years, I had flown the Pan Am 103 route several times without a thought of the tragedy. It wasn't until one dark and stormy night in October of 1992, as I was flying over Lockerbie, that I began to think about the nightmarish catastrophe that had struck this sleepy little town 31,000 feet below. By then I had done some homework, because I was on my way to meet some of the Libyan leaders accused of harboring the terrorists who had purportedly perpetrated this horrific crime.

Even though I had carefully crossed all the t's and dotted all the i's and had gone out of my way to make absolutely certain I was well within the law, my life was about to change forever.

It all began quite innocently on the evening of September 23, 1992. I was schmoozing at yet another Washington, D. C. fundraiser. It's what you do if you're a lobbyist. I had attended hundreds over the past twenty-one years. In fact, it was not unusual for me to receive as many as twenty such invitations in a single day.

This one happened to be a $1,000-a-person fundraiser for my friend Arizona Sen. John McCain.

McCain hardly needs an introduction. He was a POW in North Vietnam for five and a half years, after being shot down over Hanoi in 1967. (In 2000, he would run against Gov. George W. Bush for the Republican nomination for president, and in 2008, he would be the Republican presidential nominee, losing to Sen. Barack Obama.)

McCain and his wife also owned a home in La Jolla, just across the street from the La Jolla Beach and Tennis Club. We often had a chance to visit with them, while sharing a stroll along the beach.

It had been a rather long day, starting with an 8 AM breakfast fund-raiser at the La Coline Restaurant for Rep. Norm Dicks (D-WA). Dicks was a key member of the Defense Appropriations Subcommittee and was sponsoring some language for me in the Appropriations Conference Committee on behalf of my client, Titan Corporation, a San Diego Defense Contractor. I had arranged to have $35 million added to two appropriations bills for Titan. Dr. Gene Ray, the company's president and CEO, was in town for the fundraiser. I had also set up two days of meetings for him with six congressmen and five senators, including Senators Conrad Burns, John McCain and Larry Pressler.

I also invited Dr. Ray to the historic Marine Corps Barracks at 8th and I Streets for a farewell parade and reception for three former Marines, who were retiring at the end of the 102nd Congress in January 1993. They were Sen. Steve Symms (R-ID), Rep. Larry Coughlin (R-PA), and Rep. Larry Hopkins (R-KY). As an ex-Marine, I had remained active with the congressional Marines for many years, and Dr. Ray enjoyed mingling with the Commandant of the Marine Corps[3] and the various other congressional and military dignitaries in attendance.

At his fundraiser, McCain thanked those assembled for their contributions, and introduced his Senate colleagues who had dropped by to show their support for his reelection campaign.

As I was about to depart for my next fundraiser, longtime friend Sen. Larry Pressler (R-SD) buttonholed me. He said he had been looking for me in the Capitol during the day. He wanted to introduce me to his "good friend," Gerrit P. Van de Bovenkamp, president of International Communications Marketing or ICM.

Bovenkamp, a naturalized American citizen born in the Netherlands, was a six-footer with a full head of dark hair and a very captivating smile. He was wearing a navy-blue blazer, a white shirt, a blue silk tie, and brushed-cotton khaki pants.

The McCain fundraiser was in a reception hall of the Phoenix Park Hotel a block from Union Station. Pressler told me that he'd persuaded his friend, who would be taking the Metroliner back to New York later that evening, to stop by in hopes of meeting me.

After the usual introductions and pleasantries, Pressler told me that Bovenkamp was involved in an unusual cause and needed my expert advice. Whispering in my ear, Pressler also informed me that Bovenkamp was a wealthy New York socialite who had contributed handsomely to his reelection campaign. Pressler said that the issue his friend wanted to discuss with me was far too hot for him to handle in his public role.

I had known Pressler since he was first elected to Congress in 1974. Although he'd received an M.A. from Oxford University, where he was a Rhodes Scholar, and a law degree from Harvard, those on the Hill generally considered him a bit absentminded and dull.

Pressler had been a frequent guest in our home in California. Very often, he'd call ahead and we'd arrange to play some tennis or golf together. Virginia and I had hosted a fundraiser for him in our home, and Pressler had even attended services with us at the La Jolla Presbyterian Church. In spite of his reserved demeanor, Pressler had a big heart. For example, at Katie's request, he spoke to her third-grade class at the Evans School in LaJolla, and followed up by sending the school a flag that had flown over the U.S. Capitol (The Capitol Flag Office runs hundreds of flags up and down special flag poles on the roof of the Capitol each day, so there is a sufficient supply of flags for congressmen and senators to give to their constituents and friends).

After Pressler left us alone, Bovenkamp whispered that he wanted to talk about Libya. I suggested we move outside to a noisy part of the hotel lobby where we couldn't be overheard.

"Would you like to get involved in helping me with this country?"

Since time was slipping away, I suggested that we ride together to the Mayflower Hotel, where the next event on my dance card was being held. I told him that my longtime driver and personal assistant, Paul Williams, would then take him back to Union Station in time for his 10 PM train.

Bovenkamp expressed concern about talking openly in the presence of Paul. I assured him that he had overheard just about everything from his front-seat perch and could keep secrets.

I tried to ease Bovenkamp's mind by telling him how Paul and I had to sneak Sen. John Kerry (D-MA) up the back steps of the Sheraton Grand Hotel in Washington to secretly meet with President-elect Oscar Arias of Costa Rica in 1986. And Paul had never told a soul about it.

Bovenkamp looked impressed, which is what I wanted him to be, because I could always use another paying client.

"What was that all about?" he asked.

I explained.

In the spring of 1986, President-elect Arias planned a visit to the U.N. in New York City and to Washington, D.C. President Reagan's State Department had made all of the arrangements, but had not set up any meetings with the Democratic leadership on the Hill. I was asked to correct this "oversight."

The Reagan administration was not enamored of Arias because of his willingness to negotiate with Nicaraguan President Daniel Ortega, who was allied with the Soviet Union.

The night before Arias' arrival in Washington, the Costa Rican ambassador-designee to the United States, Guido Fernandez, called and asked me to arrange for Arias to meet with Majority Leader Sen. Robert Bird (D-WV), and other key Democrats. At the time, I was representing the Coalition for the Promotion of Costa Rica Abroad, so I was very familiar with Costa Rica and its new government's desire to bring peace to this region.

For a number of reasons, Sen. Kerry and Arias wanted to meet first. I arranged the secret rendezvous the following evening in the president-elect's Sheraton Grand hotel-room suite. There, Kerry, Arias, Fernandez, and I met for two hours, during which we hammered out the outline of what would later be Arias' Central American Peace Plan.

The following morning, Arias attended a State Department meeting with the House Minority Leader, Bob Michel, and a dozen other Republicans, in Michel's conference room in the Capitol.

And that afternoon, Arias met with Senate Democrats, including Bird, Illinois' Paul Simon, my skiing friend Frank Launtenberg, and Rhode Island's Claiborne Pell, chairman of the Senate Foreign Relations Committee. Other than personal staff, I was the only other person in the hour-long meeting that I had set up.

President-elect Arias proceeded to outline the preliminary plan for peace in Central America that we had designed the night before. The assembled senators were transfixed by the discussion. Arias stated that the Reagan Administration was doing all it could to keep him away from meeting with congressional Democrats and he thanked me in front of everybody for arranging the meeting.

Two years later, Arias received the Nobel Peace Prize for the peace plan that Sen. Kerry and I had helped him create.

Later, Kerry and I often joked that we should have shared in the prize; and National University, headquartered in La Jolla,

California, with a branch in Costa Rica, recognized my contribution by awarding me an Honorary Doctor of Humane Letters.

When I was finished, Bovenkamp seemed duly impressed by my ability to bring disparate parties together.

Good, except that now, time was running out.

"What about Libya did you want to talk to me about?"

Bovenkamp told me that he was involved in an effort to facilitate contacts between Libyan and American officials. He asked if I would be willing to discuss the project further with him and his business partner, Brendan Kelly.

Like most Americans, I felt a deep mistrust of and disgust for Col. Qadhafi. I said I'd think about it and get back to him later in the week. Bovenkamp assured me that Sen. Pressler would be pleased if we ended up working together.

After Paul whisked him off to the train station, I doubted I'd ever hear from Bovenkamp again. In my business, I ran into all kinds of people with a cause, but very few with substance.

Much to my surprise, early the next morning my phone rang. It was Bovenkamp. "Have you had a chance to think about our discussion last night? I think you are the man who can help us do the job we discussed."

Before I could respond, he asked if I could come to New York the following day. "I'll get you a plane ticket and a hotel. We need to get moving on this right away."

I explained that I would be shepherding an important client around the Hill, and that later that afternoon I would then be flying home to California.

"How about next week? We will only need one day to complete our business."

I told Bovenkamp the earliest I could meet with him was in two weeks.

On Wednesday, October 7th, Bovenkamp, Brendan Kelly, and I met in the coffee shop of the New York Hilton Hotel. I immediately took a liking to Kelly. He was a delightful, slow-talking Irishman. We got right down to business. Kelly informed me that Bovenkamp and he had just returned from Geneva where they had met with Youssef el-Debri, chief of Libyan intelligence, and Dr. Omar Mustafa al Muntassir, Minister of Economy and Finance, who was about to be named Libya's foreign minister.

Bovenkamp and Kelly said they expected to sign a huge contract with Qadhafi and they wanted my help. The assignment, a daunting one, had changed. The goal was to normalize Libyan-American relations. Good luck!

After breakfast, the three of us walked the two blocks to the ICM offices at 666 5th Avenue.

I am not alone in judging people by the way they dress, talk, eat, and by the elegance and size of their headquarters. Thus I was rather shocked that the ICM operation proved to be a single small office. Since all three of us couldn't squeeze into this room, Bovenkamp had arranged for us to meet in a borrowed conference room nearby. There was no question that if Sen. Pressler hadn't given him such a strong recommendation, I would have found a polite way to cut the meeting short and return to Washington at once.

What Bovenkamp and Kelly wanted from me was to provide them with access to key members of Congress, who might be willing to talk to and meet with representatives of the Libyan government. They claimed to have seen correspondence in which Qadhafi had attempted to open a dialogue with the United States, but he had been rebuffed. They also alleged that people in the (first) Bush administration had already taken large fees from the Libyans under the pretense of helping to normalize the relationship between the two governments. Bovenkamp and Kelly were convinced that the United States was part of an international conspiracy to unjustly blame Libya for the Pan Am 103 disaster.

"The Libyans will spend whatever it takes to resolve the Lockerbie issue, so why not make some big money while we help them?" Bovenkamp asked.

After careful consideration, I agreed to represent ICM on the condition that I conduct all my activities in accordance with American law, and I would have to register with the Justice Department as an agent for a foreign government. The First Amendment does guarantee the right to petition Congress for redress of grievances. In other words, ICM, had every right to lobby the Congress and all other federal agencies.

I promised to open doors for them, but I would take no position on who was responsible for blowing up Pan Am 103.

They wanted me to fly to Geneva as soon as possible to meet with several Libyan officials. We would be joined by Mohammed Bukhres, a Libyan-American living in Washington, D.C.

If there were a problem, I assumed the Justice Department would deny my foreign agent application. I was comfortable that ICM was an American firm established in Delaware, because Kelly had shown me its incorporation papers. In any event, at that point ICM had no formal relationship with Libya, so I signed a twelve-month contract with ICM for $120,000. I made it clear that I could not receive any money from the Government of Libya or their agents.

Upon returning to California, I immediately filed my registration papers as a foreign agent pursuant to Section 2 of the Foreign Agents Registration Act (FARA) of 1938, (as amended), with the Justice Department.

ICM directly began making arrangements for me to travel to Geneva to meet Col. Youssef el-Debri, the Libyan intelligence chief, and a member of the Libyan Committee to Resolve the Lockerbie Dispute. El-Debri and I were scheduled to meet in his suite at the Noga Hilton Hotel on Tuesday, the 27th.

On the morning of October 25, an American Airlines first-class, round-trip ticket to Geneva, Switzerland, was waiting for me at the San Diego airport.

And so, I flew off to meet Col. Youssef el-Debri, whose CIA code name I would later learn was "Uncle Ben."

FOUR

Chief of Libyan Intelligence

Two days later, Col. Debri opened the door to Suite 600 of the Noga Hilton Hotel in Geneva, shook my hand, and invited Bovenkamp and me to come in. Gerrit began to fidget. He explained that he was to have met his Libyan consultant, Mohammed Bukhres, the previous evening at London's Heathrow Airport. Gerrit had searched for Mohammed at the airport to no avail, and continued on to Geneva alone.

I was surprised that Col. Debri was black. I'd assumed all Libyans had yellowish-brown skin. He later told me his ancestry was Kenyan.

Col. Debri rented this suite by the year. He used it to get away from the stresses of Libya and to conduct governmental and personal business. He was wearing an African robe, tied around his waist. The robe barely covered his rotund body. He wore no shoes or socks. A lit, unattended cigarette burned in an ash tray next to the large picture window, overlooking a spectacular view of Lake Geneva and the Jet d'Eau, the famous fountain that shoots water 459 feet into the air. Dirty dishes, awaiting room service, were stacked against the walls. Empty wine and beer bottles were scattered everywhere. And a glass dining table with several chairs around it was covered with the remains of a late-night card game.

Bovenkamp had mentioned that Col. Debri, who had never been to the United States, desperately wanted to visit it, but he was barred because of his alleged terrorist activities.

"Nice to meet you, Dr. Chazzy. Did you have a good trip?"

"Yes, thank you very much," I said. "May I call you Youssef?"

"Yes, as long as you don't mind me calling you Chazzy," he replied.

"Please, sit down."

He picked up the telephone and in French ordered sparkling water, wine, and beer from room service.

"I will order lunch later," he told us.

I glanced out the window. It was fall and the trees lining Lake Geneva had started turning colorful. The last remaining flowers of the season were still visible on the balconies of homes and businesses. A fleet of small boats, called "Mouettes Genevoises," was still shuttling passengers from one place to another, among the usual aquatic population of ducks, sea gulls, and swans.

I had walked past the Noga Hilton many times on previous trips to Geneva. However, this was my first as a guest. Bovenkamp had insisted that I not register under my name. He had obligingly made arrangements so that I didn't need to check in when I arrived. I simply picked up an envelope containing my key from reception. He thought it best that there be no record of this trip, and I was assured that I wouldn't get stuck with the bill.

"Why do you think you can help me, Chazzy?" asked Youssef. "We have been paying big money to your elected officials for a long time, and what do we have to show for it? Nothing! I have paid hundreds of thousands of dollars to people right inside of the White House. I have filled their Swiss accounts and never heard from them again. My people are hurting badly from this embargo. We need medical supplies! We can't talk to anybody in the United States. We have tried for months to talk to someone in power."

Youssef paused, lit another cigarette, and continued.

"Bovenkamp says you know lots of congressmen and can get someone of authority to talk to us. What do they want from us? I have sent letters to the secretary of state, the president. What more can I do?"

Youssef became angrier as he spoke.

"My leader is tired of no action. It makes me crazy, Chazzy. He wants something to happen now. He can't wait. My leader blames me for this. I need your help now."

I had always found it interesting that Col. Muammar al-Qadhafi had no official title such as president or prime minister, nor does he have any statutory executive power in Libya. He is referred to simply as the "Leader" of the Great Socialist People's Libyan Arab Jamahiriya, which is the country's official name. However, for those in the cloak-and-dagger business, he was simply referred to as "Charlie."

Youssef seemed to calm down somewhat as two room-service waiters knocked, entered, delivered drinks, and began to tidy up the suite. The bed was made and the dirty dishes were removed as the three of us made small talk. Frankly, I was relieved that this brief interlude gave Youssef a chance to collect his emotions. After all, I was meeting with one of the world's most sought after terrorists. I wanted him to calm down.

Youssef wanted to know about my family and asked if I had a photo he could see. I showed him one of Virginia, Katie and me sitting on a corral fence with Katie's horse looking over our shoulders. I told him about my daughter's riding prowess and all the championships she had won.

Youssef grew excited as he told me how much his own daughter loved to ride horses and that our daughters had a lot in common. He talked with fatherly affection about his three children—two girls and one boy.

"Maybe someday our children will ride horses together. When our countries are friends again, our children can be friends."

He became very introspective, almost sad.

"It will be my pleasure to have you and your family come to my home in Tripoli, Dr. Chazzy."

My anxiety diminished as he seemed to morph from a ranting international terrorist to that of a tender father. He actually became a rather pleasant fellow, and it was hard to imagine a guy like this committing terrorist acts on behalf of any cause

I had a similar feeling when I had the opportunity to meet and spend some time with one of the PLO's top officials, Mr. Bassam Abu Sharif, during the summer of 1989.

Virginia, Katie and I were invited to Cap Antibes, in Southern France by Roger Edde, a wealthy Lebanese, who was running for the Presidency of Lebanon. Roger wanted me to consider representing him in Washington as his liaison to the U.S. Congress.

Roger and his wife Alice, an American, were impressed with my work and the exciting life that I led. I had dinner with

Roger and Alice at the Dancing Crab in Northwest Washington a couple of weeks after we first met.

Roger and Alice would be leaving for their summer home in France in a few days. I told them that Virginia, Katie and I were planning to be in France at the same time. They invited us to visit with them to discuss my involvement with Roger further in a more relaxed environment.

We were among some thirty house guests staying in the main residence of the Edde estate. Virginia and I were provided with a lovely room next to a tree-lined court yard. Katie had her own room just down the hall. I had never seen such a villa. It was beautifully situated on a hill with expansive views of the enormous white yachts cruising along the rocky coast.

We had left Paris that morning by train and arrived at the Cap Antibes Train Station about 4:00 PM. We were travel weary and therefore very happy to join the festivities. We sipped champagne as Queen Farah, the wife of the late Shah of Iran, and her partner, David Sandbar, a wealthy industrialist from London, were crowned champions of the small tennis tournament the Edde's hosted each summer.

Lunch the next day was set out on a long table under an olive tree facing the Mediterranean. The guest list consisted of Israelis, Lebanese, PLO representatives, the Eddes, Virginia and me. The language of the day was Arabic with a bit of French interspersed. The years I spent learning the Spanish language for my work in Central America didn't help much. We felt a little left out, but fortunately Alice sat close by and translated for us. She did her best to make us feel comfortable in a difficult situation.

At one point between courses, the table erupted into laughter. An Israeli had been engaged in a discussion with Bassam Abu Sharif, Yassir Arafat's top lieutenant. Sharif seemed to be a very nice man. I can admit now that I had no idea at the time what a powerful force he was within the PLO. We had first met the night before at the "Grand Evening." Sharif was not easy to forget—his face was badly scarred, and he was missing fingers from his hand.

At dinner that night I asked Roger's brother what had been the cause of the laughter earlier in the day. He explained that Sharif had been the victim of a letter bomb a few years earlier. The Israeli he met for the first time at lunch was the man who had sent the letter bomb to Sharif. I guess in a very strange way, only those personally immersed in the Middle East situation could fully appreciate the special bond that the two men shared.

As the room service crew was leaving, Youssef got up and handed each of them a $100 bill taken from a large grocery bag full of U.S currency situated next to his bed. He smiled, and said "*Merci beaucoup.*"

Before Youssef could sit back down, there was another knock at the door. He opened it with one hand as he picked up the telephone with the other to call room service again. I couldn't see who was at the door, but I heard Youssef talking to him in Arabic. Bovenkamp looked over at me from across the table and whispered, "It's Mohammed Bukhres. The S.O.B. did come after all. Better late than never, I guess."

Now Bukhres fit my preconception of what a Libyan should look like, except for the expensive Italian suit he was wearing. Bovenkamp stood to greet him as he entered. The moment was full of confusion. Bukhres tried to communicate with Youssef in Arabic, who was trying to order lunch in French, while Bovenkamp was trying to find out in English why Bukhres was so late. I just stood there, patiently waiting to be introduced.

When we were finally introduced, Bukhres seemed to have difficulty looking me in the eye as we exchanged pleasantries. He seemed agreeable, but devious at the same time. He claimed to have gotten a phone call from "Charlie," just before leaving Washington and as a result missed his flight. He had just arrived in Geneva and hadn't even checked into the hotel yet. He needed a shave and seemed quite frail. His suit was loose fitting as if he had recently lost weight. He wore dark, stylish, horn-rimmed, tinted glasses. I guessed his age to be about forty.

We all sat down at the table. Youssef was obviously upset again, this time at Bukhres. He raised his voice and waved his arms, scolding him in Arabic. They exchanged words and then became silent. Youssef had the last word as he mumbled under his breath in English, "Mohammed, you make me crazy."

Youssef turned toward me and started asking questions.

"Chazzy, tell me how you can help. What does lobbying really mean? You Americans like to take our money but we never see results. My leader asked me to tell our story to the decision makers of your country. He has set up the Committee to Resolve Lockerbie. I am a member of the committee, and we want to make our leader happy."

Bovenkamp began to talk before I could respond.

"Dr. Chasey is the best lobbyist in Washington. I have been to Washington with him and I am very impressed with whom he knows. I was introduced to him by our mutual friend Sen. Larry Pressler, a member of the Foreign Relations Committee, and the ranking Republican on the Committee on Terrorism, Narcotics, and International Operations."

I was impressed that Bovenkamp had remembered all of this. I had briefed him earlier on the key committees he would need to lobby.

He continued. "Mr. Chasey is the best man to help us resolve this Lockerbie problem. He has represented many foreign governments and clients in Washington for over twenty years. We are lucky to have him here!"

I finally launched into my standard sales pitch. I told Youssef and Bukhres about my life as a lobbyist for domestic and foreign clients.

Most people knew little about what a lobbyist did, except for what they had learned from the 1992 presidential campaigns of Ross Perot and Bill Clinton. Perot called us those "awful foreign lobbyists," and Clinton said that if elected he would put us out of business.

FIVE

The Lobbyist

I explained to Youssef that a Washington lobbyist was required to register with both the clerk of the United States House of Representatives and the secretary of the United States Senate for any work done on a client's behalf.

The lobbying profession dates from the earliest days of the republic as a logical expression of a citizen's constitutional right to "petition the government for a redress of grievances." Lobbyists work both the executive and legislative branches of government, dealing directly with lawmakers, policy makers, and staff in Washington's corridors and cocktail parties of power.

A lobbyist's personal charm and persuasive powers are major assets. However, most important is the ability to collect and present, factually and fairly, vital information, which allows a member of Congress to make the most informed decision when voting. I prided myself on being well educated in the industry I represented and I had a reputation for complete integrity. And I also knew how the game was played. Campaign contributions—from the lobbyist and his clients—provided access so one could plead one's case.

Despite the intense criticism lobbying has come under—especially due to the recent Jack Abramoff lobbying scandal—it is important to remember that all Americans belong to "special interest groups" of one kind of another. Today, every worker from mechanic to physician, every cultural group from Native Americans to retired senior citizens, every issue from cigarettes to gun control, are represented by lobbyists in Washington. The White House has a large staff of lobbyists who roam Capitol Hill every day.

The American public has been misled on the role of Washington lobbyists. In fact, while a congressman represents his constituents, very often it is the lobbyist who gives voice to the "special interests" and concerns of those very constituents.

Many foreign governments, foreign businesses, and other foreign organizations retain lobbyists in Washington. When you are hired by any foreign entity, you must register as a foreign agent with the Criminal Division of the Justice Department. This is exactly what I did, the day after I signed the $120,000 contract with Bovenkamp's International Communications Marketing Company on October 8, 1992. The Justice Department assigned me the foreign agent registration number, 4221.

Although it was debatable that I even needed to register with the Justice Department, I did so to go beyond the letter of the law, because the government of Libya might benefit from my activities on behalf of ICM, a company incorporated in the state of Delaware. In any event, I wanted to be very careful, because my connection to a highly visible and controversial country like Libya was bound to attract attention. And, I was right.

On December 7, 1992, *O'Dwyer's Washington Report,* a newsletter that keeps the public relations and lobbying professions abreast of current activities, carried the following front-page story.

"Chasey Organization gets $120,000 pact to push Libya ties with the United States."

> The William Chasey Organization (TWCO) registered a $120,000 one-year contract to help Muammar Qadhafi's Libya establish normalized relations with the United States. This newsletter made two attempts to reach TWCO President, Bill Chasey, at his Washington Office, seeking comment on his work for the terrorist state. Neither call was returned.
>
> According to the November 12 Foreign Agent Registration Act (FARA) filing, Chasey plans to write letters and arrange meetings with members of Congress on behalf of the Libyans.
>
> His goal is to "assist in the development of normalized relationships between the U.S. government and the government of Libya." The contract runs through October 7, 1993, and calls for TWCO to receive six $20,000 payments every other month.
>
> It is signed by Chasey and two managing partners Brendan Kelly and Gerrit P. Van de Bovenkamp—of International Communications Marketing Inc., a New York outfit.

Fortunately, no one of any importance reads the O'Dwyer newsletter and there were no immediate repercussions that resulted from this article.

SIX

Libya's Offer

I didn't know how much of what I explained to Youssef he understood. I'm not really sure he even cared. He just sat, smoked, and listened.

Bukhres, however, seemed especially interested in my little lecture on lobbying. He said he was an American citizen, who represented a group of American citizens interested in resolving the Lockerbie situation. Bukhres confirmed that the sanctions against Libya were having the desired effect. For example, he was deeply concerned for his mother. She was desperately ill, but her doctors said she might not survive the long trip by boat and train to get the specialized medical treatment she needed in Switzerland.

We were soon joined by two Libyan men—one large and

one small. They made a grand entrance but sat quietly during our discussion. The first man was rather hefty with a thick black mustache. I didn't catch his name and he proffered no business card. Youssef mumbled that he had been Libya's ambassador to Switzerland. I suspected the smaller man was a secret agent working for Youssef. I would later realize that there always seemed to be undercover agents strategically placed in close proximity to him. He ignored them most of the time.

I asked Youssef to give me his government's version of the Lockerbie incident. Bovenkamp had told me earlier that Youssef would prove to me that Libya was not responsible for the bomb that blew up Pan Am 103.

My only concern was to get these two countries to start talking to each other again, so they could get to the bottom of the stalemate, resolve the dispute, and move on. Obviously, it wasn't fair that hundreds of thousands of poor, hapless Libyans, who had nothing to do with Lockerbie, were suffering.

During an unusual lunch of "cow's scalp stew," with a good bit of the cow's hair still attached to the scalp, Youssef appealed to me to bring a member of Congress to Libya to meet with the Libyan Committee to Resolve Lockerbie. I explained that it would be almost impossible to get a member to go to Libya. He then asked if I could get someone to come to Switzerland or Malta for a meeting. I agreed that that would be easier, although it would still be a daunting challenge.

I suggested it might be easier to persuade a small group of American lawmakers to participate, if the Libyans could organize an international conference on Pan Am 103, say, under the auspices of the International Red Cross or some other organization. Libya might consider making a major donation to the sponsoring organization as a token of good faith. I told him I was certain I could get congressional participation to such a conference.

I further suggested that Youssef's Libyan Committee to Resolve Lockerbie could join forces with Bukhres' U.S. Committee to Resolve Lockerbie and jointly sponsor such a conference. Youssef liked the idea, but he didn't want to wait that long.

"Can you bring a member of Congress to Geneva next week? I will pay all the expenses. He can fly here one day and fly home the next. I don't care who comes. I just need someone right away. You know how my leader is. He wants action now. It will only take a few hours."

Bukhres took up the cause. "Yes, he could fly the Concorde from New York or Washington and be here in three hours. Or you can bring an entire delegation and I'll charter a jet. A G-4 can carry ten people across the ocean with no problem. They can even bring their wives, who can shop in Geneva while we're meeting with their husbands. It should only take a few hours."

Bovenkamp jumped in. "Do you think we can get our good friend Larry (Sen. Pressler) to come for a few hours? I know he likes to travel. He can bring his lovely wife along. It would be a very private meeting. No one would have to know it took place. What do you think?"

They badgered me for more than an hour. I tried to explain the political realities of the situation and how it would look for a member of Congress to meet with Libyans. I suggested another scenario.

They might invite Sen. John Kerry's Subcommittee on Terrorism, Narcotics and International Operations to do an official congressional site visit of Libya. There would be a lot for them to investigate, including the presence of training camps for terrorists, chemical and biological warfare factories, etc.

This would give these senators a chance to investigate Libya and take back recommendations to the entire Congress and the executive branch.

"Another great idea, Chazzy, but we don't have that much time. The United Nations will be meeting again in a couple of weeks to discuss further sanctions against us. We need to show them that we are not the world's bad guys. We need to move fast. Bovenkamp says you can do anything with the U.S. Congress. Why not this simple request? How much will it cost? Money is no object. Just get someone here," pleaded Youssef.

I explained that a member of Congress could not accept any type of remuneration or gifts from a foreign entity. All travel expenses would have to be paid by a U.S. citizen or a U.S. corporation.

Bukhres jumped in again. "I'm an American citizen. My company could pay or I can get the members of our Committee to Resolve Lockerbie to pay for it. They have lots of money. You just arrange to get someone to a meeting, and I will see that the payments are made legally."

This first meeting with Youssef broke up after about four hours. I needed a break. Youssef said that he wanted to join us for dinner, but that something had come up for that evening and he wouldn't be able to make it. He apologized.

I left and got on the elevator to escape to my eighth-floor room.

An American gentleman in his forties got on with me. I recognized him immediately as a CIA operative I had often seen going in and out of the U.S. Embassy in Costa Rica. I never forget a face. What a remarkable coincidence that the two of us would end up in the same elevator in Geneva, Switzerland!

I confronted him directly. "I know you from Costa Rica, don't I?"

He replied that he had never been to Costa Rica.

"What brings you to Geneva?"

"I work for DuPont in Delaware. You may have seen me in Washington."

"How did you know I'm from Washington?"

Before he could respond, the elevator doors opened on the seventh floor. He nervously exited and said, "Have a good day."

Mr. "DuPont's" visit brought me back down to earth rather quickly. I had a feeling I would be seeing him again. At least I was relieved to know that the CIA didn't take me too seriously. If it had, it would have sent a professional, not someone whose face I would recognize.

Late that night, Bovenkamp, Bukhres, and I dined in the restaurant on the hotel's second floor. My companions continued to pressure me to get a congressman to Geneva as soon as possible. Suddenly, Youssef walked in. He seemed surprised to see us, nodded, and walked by. He proceeded directly to his reserved table in the back of the restaurant.

I left the restaurant about 11:30 PM and went directly to my room.

I was just about to doze off when Bovenkamp and Bukhres knocked on my door. I let them in. Again, they pleaded with me to persuade a Washington lawmaker to meet Youssef, who was in real trouble with "Charlie." This meeting was needed for Youssef to save face, and perhaps his job.

Bovenkamp pulled out a handwritten contract. He and Bukhres, both U.S. citizens, would pay me a $200,000 bonus if I could deliver a member of Congress to meet Youssef in Libya, Switzerland, or Malta within the next seven days. I said I would do my best. Bovenkamp and Bukhres signed the agreement, and I took it with me.

I asked Bovenkamp to provide me with official letters signed by Youssef, which I could hand deliver to three key senators. I was leaving early in the morning for New York and then on to Washington. Since time was of the essence, I would need these letters before I left for the airport. I asked that these letters be addressed to the following: Sen. John F. Kerry, chairman, Subcommittee on Terrorism, Narcotics and International Operations; Sen. Hank Brown, ranking member, Subcommittee on Terrorism, Narcotics and International Operations; and Sen. Larry Pressler, member, Senate Committee on Foreign Relations.

During the night, a package was slipped under my door.

The next morning, I noticed that Mr. DuPont was up early. He was sitting alone in the lobby. He looked away as I walked by, but in the reflection of the front windows I could see him watching me leave the hotel. I left the Noga Hilton for the Geneva Airport.

I had arranged to have breakfast at the airport with my good friend Ralph Wright, Director of Public Affairs for the International Red Cross. He was an American who began his Red Cross career in the United States and was now assigned to Geneva where he had been living for the past few years.

In the strictest confidence, I shared with him what had happened over the past two days. Wright warned me to be careful. He knew that the Libyans played rough and said our intelligence forces could play rough as well.

As we leveled off over the Atlantic, I opened the package.

It contained three very official-looking, identical letters. The letter to Senator Kerry read as follows:

Senator John F. Kerry
Chairman of Subcommittee on Terrorism,
Narcotics and International Operations
421 SROB
Washington, D.C., 20035 U.S.A.

October 28, 1992

Dear Senator Kerry,

The Secretariat of the Libyan People's Congress on behalf of the Libyan people is pleased to address you with respect to a prospect for improvement of bilateral relations between the American and the Libyan people, as well as relations between the U. S and the Libyan governments.

It is the view of the Libyan Arab Jamaheriya that, as long as contacts between our two nations are suspended and the means of communication virtually nonexistent, the specter of distrust between our nations will never be far from the surface. Separation can generate accusation and accusation may eventually lead to conflict.

Such has been the atmosphere which has pervaded our countries' relations for almost a decade.

In fact we neither wish nor desire such mistrust. On the contrary, we honestly and seriously are seeking an opportunity to dialogue and negotiate through your good offices of Foreign Relations, a positive change toward better relations between our peoples and nations based on mutual respect and understanding a new page in our history marked by good and honorable intentions.

It is in this spirit that we are willing to discuss and come to an agreement on:

1) Libya's willingness to renounce all world terrorism;

2) Libya's willingness to pledge not to engage in anti-government or destabilization tactics;

3) Libya's willingness to open its borders to United

Nations inspection teams in order to assure that weapons of mass destruction are not being manufactured;

4) Libya's willingness to deliver its two citizens accused of the Pan Am 103 disaster provided that an international acceptable neutral country will be used for the trial.

Libya further extends an invitation to you and your Committee on Terrorism, Narcotics and International Operations to visit Libya, in your official capacity and to experience firsthand our recent accomplishments. I will personally work with you through our representative, Mr. William C. Chasey, to arrange this fact finding mission. Hopefully we can meet face to face to plan your agenda.

These accomplishments are decisive proof that Libya has never intended to threaten anyone and in particular your country, the United States of America, whose great assistance in our fight for independence we shall always remember.

It is our appreciation for your kindness, honesty and integrity which has led us to extend this invitation. We are sure that what you will witness in our country will prove to you that the moral philosophy of our system is deeply rooted as well.

We are confident that you and your committee will return with the firm belief that the time has come, to mend the sorrowful rift between our two countries.

We initiate with this letter a dialogue for the road to better relations.

Sincerely yours,

Youssef El-DEBRI
Head of Libyan National Security
Member of the Committee to Resolve
the Dispute of Lockerbie

I was amazed by the concessions that Libya was willing to make, especially agreeing to send for trial the two accused Libyans who had allegedly blown up Pan Am 103. I was sure I could get one of these three senators to respond favorably to this conciliatory invitation.

After checking into my hotel in New York City, I began making phone calls. First, I called Ramona Gustafson, Sen. Pressler's scheduling secretary. I began with him, because he was the one who had gotten me into this deal in the first place.

To my surprise, Gustafson said that Pressler was in New York serving as a United Nations Special Representative for the month. I quickly arranged to meet him at his office on the fourth floor of the United States UN Mission the next morning.

On October 29, at 10:15 AM, I arrived at my destination. After passing through a metal detector, a squared away Marine Lance Corporal, sitting behind a wall of bulletproof glass, waved me into the reception room. I was escorted into Sen. Pressler's office.

Pressler appeared delighted to see me and asked what had brought me to New York. I told him that Bovenkamp and I had just met with the head of Libyan Intelligence in Geneva. He became a bit uneasy and suggested we walk to his hotel, a few blocks away.

At the Waldorf Astoria, we went directly to his suite on the twenty-third floor. The remnants of the contents of the mini bar were strewn about the room. The maid hadn't gotten there yet. He laughed when I noted that his perpetual diet had once again gone astray.

Pressler listened attentively as I described the meetings in Geneva and told him of Col. Debri's invitation to meet with him.

"How can we make such a meeting happen?" he asked. "No one could ever know that I met with Qadhafi's people. What do you think the voters of South Dakota would think if they found out? It is probably a worthwhile thing to do, but the fallout would be devastating."

We continued to talk as we walked back to the United Nations. At first, Pressler was reluctant to meet with Libyan officials, but he finally warmed up to the idea when I suggested it could take place in Malta.

Malta is a Mediterranean island country sixty miles south of Sicily, not far from Libya. Its mild climate in November might be just enough incentive for Pressler to accept.

He became more enthusiastic when I suggested that he take his wife and daughter on the trip.

We devised a plan for the Presslers to travel to Malta as guests of the Knights of Malta, a Catholic men's organization of which Pressler was an active member. I would arrange to have Col. Debri and Omar Muntassir, the new Libyan foreign minister, meet secretly with Pressler sometime during his stay.

I told him I was pretty sure I could persuade the Libyans to make a $1 million contribution to the Knights of Malta for their assistance in this matter. The money could be used for their hospitals located in Third World countries around the world.

Pressler also asked if I could arrange for him to get an honorarium from the University of Malta, if he were to give a speech or to meet with faculty and students. He reminded me that I had done just that for him at the National University (CA) campus in Costa Rica.

Given Libya's pressing interest in resolving the Lockerbie impasse, and the discomfort the UN sanctions were creating for the country, I didn't think that any of these requests would be unreasonable. Desperate to meet with any U.S. official, the Libyans would thank me profusely if I could arrange for a senator on the Foreign Relations Committee to meet with them. I remember what Youssef had said: "Do whatever it takes to get a meeting."

I handed Pressler Col. Debri's letter.

Without comment, he slid the letter into his inside coat pocket and said, "I will read it in private."

We agreed to talk again early the following week. Pressler wanted time to discuss the trip with his wife. He suggested that I call him directly at the Waldorf to avoid his Washington staff, and he reminded me that our discussion was strictly confidential.

He would not be able to make the trip until after Thanksgiving, which was more than seven days away. According to my contract, I couldn't collect the $200,000 bonus, even if Pressler did decide to go to Malta, because the bonus was predicated on my supplying a senator or congressman within seven days. I would have to call Bovenkamp and get him to extend the deadline by a week.

I said goodbye to Pressler and called Sen. Kerry's office in Washington. Pat Gray, his appointment secretary, told me that the senator was chairing a subcommittee hearing on American MIAs and POWs in Vietnam, and that he would then be rushing to Dulles Airport to fly to Vietnam that very afternoon. He would be out of the country for a week.

I quickly caught the next Delta shuttle to Washington. When I arrived, my trusted driver Paul whisked me to the Capitol. I rushed to his office. He was just leaving with his luggage in hand. As we walked to the elevators, I quickly explained that I had a very important letter for him about Pan Am 103 from the head of Libyan Intelligence. As the elevator doors began closing, Kerry said that he wanted to read the letter when he had time to give it his full attention. He apologized for his haste, but asked that I give the letter to David Leiter, his administrative assistant, to review.

I gave the letter to Leiter, who read it immediately with great interest, but he said that Kerry's Subcommittee on Terrorism, Narcotics and International Operations had no immediate plans to discuss Libya. He did say, however, that the schedule for the new congressional session (beginning January 3, 1993) had not yet been set and that he would discuss the possibility of a visit to Libya with his boss. He suggested that I arrange a meeting with Kerry. However, there was nothing more I could do until his return from Vietnam.

Next, I telephoned Sen. Hank Brown's office. Brown was the ranking Republican on the Terrorism Committee, and one of the Senate's most conservative members. His secretary said he was back home in Colorado.

That evening, I talked with Brown by phone for quite some time. Since I really didn't know where he stood on the issue, I made rather broad references to Lockerbie in our discussion. I wanted to avoid pushing any hot buttons or turning him off altogether. I wanted to give him Col. Debri's letter in person. I even offered to fly to Colorado immediately. Finally, we agreed to meet in his Washington office the following week.

I had known Hank Brown since he first represented the fourth district of Colorado in the House of Representatives. He was elected to the United States Senate in 1990, filling the seat that had belonged to my very dear friend, Bill Armstrong. Armstrong, a true Christian and man of his word, retired from the Senate, because he had promised his constituents that he would serve two terms and then return to Colorado to live under the laws he had helped pass. Like so many of his friends, I had tried to get him to change his mind but he said, "A promise is a promise."

A week later, I was sitting in Sen. Brown's office, watching him read the letter with great care.

"Amazing!"

He carefully read it a second time.

"Amazing," he repeated.

"I would say this was some kind of a joke, if I didn't know you so well, Bill. How did you get this letter?"

I told him about my meeting with Col. Debri in Geneva and gave him a little insight about the Libyan Committee to Resolve the Lockerbie Dispute.

"Do you believe this guy, Debri? Does he really speak for Qadhafi? What is your take on this situation? Have you shown this to John Kerry? He chairs the Terrorism Committee, you know."

"Yes, I know," I responded quickly.

"I gave John a similar letter last week. He was rushing off to Vietnam and didn't get a chance to read it. We did discuss it briefly. His staff has the letter. I plan to talk with him this week."

"Kerry is focused on the POW/MIA situation right now," Brown said. "He has the attention of the national press and is not about to give that up without milking it for all it is worth. It's hard to get him to think of anything else. The Special POW/MIA Committee he chairs is scheduled to disband at the end of the year. He is rushing to get to the bottom of the situation while he still can."

Brown skimmed the letter again.

"I want to talk to John about this before I respond to Mr. Debri. Kerry and the Terrorism staff may have something on this that neither you nor I know about. They play it pretty close to the chest. If you control the information, you control everything."

His voice reflected the frustration I have heard so often from minority party members on Capitol Hill. Democrats controlled all the congressional and senate committees, because they were in the majority. In the House, it had been this way for forty-three years. In the Senate, for all but two of the past twenty-six years.

Committees are the engines that make law. The sixteen Senate and twenty-two House standing committees assume initial jurisdiction over legislation. They can move, stall, or stop it. Without committee approval, a bill has little chance of reaching the full House or Senate for consideration. These committees also have the power to create a multiplicity of subcommittees, each often vying for power and money with the others. Because of this vast decentralization of power, it's hard to get anything done in Washington, which tends to perpetuate the status quo.

Sen. Brown discussed the possibility of Col. Debri coming to Washington to deliver his message in person. This, of course, would have been my first choice, but the State Department wouldn't issue him a visa. I explained that Debri was on the State Department's short list of international terrorists and a visa for him was unlikely. I suggested, with a little chuckle, that this could change if a powerful senator on the Foreign Relations Committee were to intervene with the Republican-run State Department.

I had already represented some twenty-three different foreign governments and businesses during my lobbying career, and I always preferred my clients come to Washington to deliver their own sales pitches. First, no one knows the pertinent issues better than they; and second, heads of state make great lobbyists. This is especially true when they can lavishly entertain members of Congress in their own Washington embassies.

Sen. Brown continued. "Why would Libya make such a magnanimous offer? The only real hang-up over the Lockerbie situation has been where to try the two suspected terrorists. Why shouldn't we agree to a trial in a neutral country?"

I was about to respond, when he added, "Does the president know about this offer from Qadhafi?"

"I have been told that numerous letters had been sent to President Bush, Secretary of State Baker, and various members of Congress, with no response."

"I don't know how you got involved in this situation, Bill, but I hope you know what you are doing. I have learned a great deal about the terrorist world since joining this committee. You may know something about traditional warfare from your Marine Corps days, but there are no rules with these guys. Have you registered with the State Department on this?"

"Yes, I registered with the Justice Department," I gently corrected him. "It's under their jurisdiction."

He looked down at the letter again and said, "I am going to talk to Kerry and I will get back to you when I know something. In the meantime, be very careful, my friend."

As I left his office, he offered me four seats to what was expected to be the Clinton Inauguration. (Clinton was way ahead in the polls.) I graciously accepted. Sen. Brown said he had no interest in attending the ceremonies, and I had clients who would have given anything to go.

(By January 20th, I had rounded up an additional eighteen tickets for clients and friends to see William Jefferson Clinton sworn in as the forty-second president of the United States.)

SEVEN

I Got My Man

I paged through my handy, pocket Congressional Pictorial Directory on my flight back to California. I had a feeling that my good friend, Larry Pressler, would probably change his mind about the trip to Malta, and I needed a ready backup. Pressler was always first in line for a free trip, speaking fee or fundraiser, but he rarely helped out on a legislative issue.

I laughed under my breath. I was about to start calling my congressional friends with an "offer they couldn't refuse." The coward's approach would have been to send them an invitation by fax. I jokingly composed one in my mind:

> Dear Joe:
>
> You are cordially invited to join me on an overnight trip to Geneva, Malta or wherever, to meet in a hotel

room with two Libyan agents. One agent is high on the list of the world's most sought after terrorists. These Libyans represent the most hated man in the world, Muammar Qadhafi. I just want you to come and hear what Libya has to say. It will only take a "few hours" of your time. Since we need to depart in the next four days, please cancel all of your pending appointments, speeches and fundraisers. By the way, we don't want anybody to know that you're making this trip. I look forward to our time together.

Regards, Bill

I had taken on challenges before, but this one would qualify me for the "Lobbying Hall of Fame." Still, there had to be one of the 535 members of Congress who would be available, interested, and crazy enough to make the journey with me.

First, I considered asking some of my closest congressional friends, especially those who owed me a favor. Since Bovenkamp and Bukhres didn't stipulate any specific individuals or committees, my hand was free to select any member I could persuade to go.

I made a few phone calls and, as expected, ran into various obstacles.

Rep. Duncan Hunter (R-CA), said that he wanted nothing to do with that "madman" Qadhafi. Rep. Floyd Flake (D-NY), also a minister, had to preach to his 5,000 member Allen A.M.E., African-Methodist-Episcopal Church in Jamaica-Queens, New York on Sunday morning. Others declined because they were still on the campaign trail with the election only a few days away.

The pending meeting with Youssef and Muntassir was now only one week away and I was feeling the pressure. Then, a light bulb went off. Perhaps my best bet would be to target members who would not be returning for the 103rd Congress, either because they had lost their primary races or would be retiring.

I would still be meeting the requirements of my contract. These individuals were still members of Congress and would remain so until the following year. Of course, it would have been better to take a member who would be returning next year, but that option didn't look promising at this point. With the elections coming the following week, there was no sure way of knowing who would be returning anyway.

I called three close friends who met my new criteria. Rep. Bill Lowery (R-CA), had announced his retirement. He was forced out of his own district by a fellow Republican, Randy "Duke" Cunningham, and also found himself in the middle of the House banking scandal. Unfortunately, Lowery told me that he needed to stay in San Diego.

Rep. Bill Alexander (D-AR) had lost his primary fight to his former Washington receptionist, Blanche Lambert. Alexander said that he had vacation plans that he couldn't break, but that if I needed his help later, he would be available as a Washington lawyer for a hefty hourly fee.

Rep. Beryl Anthony (D-AR) had also lost his primary race. He was reluctant to leave the country, because his good Arkansas buddy, Gov. Bill Clinton, would most likely be elected on Tuesday, and would need Anthony's help as he prepared for his move to Washington.

My next call hit pay dirt! I phoned my good friend, and primary-election loser, Rep. Carroll Hubbard (D-KY). He was not in his office, but his secretary said that he had nothing on his schedule the following week. Carroll Hubbard and his wife, Carol (no joke), were scheduled to vacation back home in Mayfield, Kentucky. I left a message that I wanted him to go to Geneva with me the following week. His secretary promised to give him the message.

We were having dinner at home in California when the phone rang. I immediately recognized Hubbard's slow, deliberate Kentucky drawl.

"What does my good friend Bill Chasey want me to do, go to Geneva? Next week? Well, that sounds great!" Without even knowing the purpose of the trip, he asked, "Can Carol come with us?"

"Of course," I replied.

"Are you in your beautiful home in La Jolla overlooking the Pacific? La Jolla, Wow! La Jolla is one of my favorite places in the world. I want to thank you again for letting me use that beautiful home. I will never forget the two weeks I stayed there. Tell Virginia and Katie thanks again from me. People in Mayfield, Kentucky, only see homes like yours in the movies."

In 1987, I had mentioned to Representative Hubbard that the Chasey family would be spending the month of August in England. He jumped at this opportunity in a flash and asked if he and Carol and their two children could use our home for a week during the August recess. I agreed, and thus Hubbard made plans to vacation in Southern California.

A few days after our arrival in England, I was shocked to receive a phone call from our longtime Vietnamese housekeeper. She reported that Congressman Hubbard had arrived, but not with his family. There were three young women staying in the house with him. He had told her that they were members of his congressional staff. Hubbard then called me a couple of days later to ask if he could extend his stay for another week. I agreed.

Well, now I was about to find out if he would return the favor.

"I'm not on the Foreign Affairs Committee," Hubbard responded when I told him the nature of the meeting in Geneva. "I'm a real good friend of Congressman Lee Hamilton, the new chairman of the committee, though. I can report the results of our meeting to Lee when I get back to Washington."

I explained that Col. Debri's primary interest was to meet with a member who would champion his cause of normalizing relations between the two countries. Committee membership was not that important.

I suggested that we maximize our time in Geneva by flying over on the Concorde.

"The Concorde? Wow! You sure do things right my friend, Bill Chasey. We have never been on the Concorde. It's real expensive I hear. Can you afford to pay for the tickets?"

I told him that all expenses would be paid by a public-relations firm in New York. No Libyan monies would be used.

Hubbard agreed to the trip! I couldn't have been happier! I had my man!

Youssef el-Debri, Bovenkamp and Bukhres would be delighted with the news. Regrettably, I did have a problem. I called Bovenkamp in New York and asked him to change the time limit on my contract from seven to ten days. I also asked for permission to have a congressman in place of a senator. When he heard that I actually had a congressman willing to go to Geneva, he immediately made the changes and faxed me a copy.

I was feeling pretty smug. It was hard to imagine anyone else in my business able to cajole a sitting member of Congress to take this trip in such a short period of time.

It had been almost a month since I had registered as a foreign agent for ICM, and the Justice Department had not contacted me. I assumed that all was well on that front. No news was good news. However, I would be required to report the forthcoming trip when I filed my next Justice Department supplemental report, which was due in about sixty days.

These reports are rather exacting. You must list all of the contacts that you make on behalf of a foreign principal. You are also required to report all monies received and spent on behalf of a client. All political activity has to be reported, along with political contributions. And all forms must be filed in triplicate!

Hubbard called in a panic several times in the following week. Each time my heart stopped, sure that he was calling to cancel. As it turned out, most of his anxiety was generated by his wife's questions about what to wear, what clothes to take, how much free time would there be to shop and sightsee. Despite all of the infamous congressional junkets, apparently the Hubbards had not been abroad very often.

Carol Brown Hubbard, a former Miss Kentucky in the Miss America Pageant, was far more politically astute than the average Washington political wife. However, she had just been defeated in a Kentucky Democratic congressional primary. If she and her husband had both won their primary and general elections, it would have been the first time a husband and wife had served concurrently in Congress.

I was convinced that Hubbard had lost his primary reelection, because he had gotten caught up in the House bank scandal. He had 152 overdrafts at the House bank from July 1988 to October 1991. Another factor was voters' perception that, as a senior member of the House Banking Committee, he had not been vigilant in monitoring the savings and loan industry.

However, his losing the election would prove to be the least of his worries.

EIGHT

The Adventure Begins

With everyone's tickets in hand, I departed San Diego for Washington, D. C., on Friday, November 6, 1992. I had planned to be there the night before our departure for Geneva, in case any problems arose.

The next day, our flight from Washington National to JFK was scheduled to depart at 6:35 AM I had arranged for Paul to pick up the Hubbards early that Saturday morning. And I was pleased and relieved when they arrived at the airport in plenty of time to make our flight. I knew that once they were in my car, they were mine.

I hadn't seen Carol in some time. As a former Miss Kentucky, she still possessed a very pretty face, but controlling her weight had always been a problem. She was wearing jeans and a turtleneck sweater, both of which did nothing to conceal her plumpness. Her husband, who had always been heavy set, had also put on weight. My guess was that they had suffered from political-defeat syndrome and had eaten their way out of the doldrums. Oh well, my contract said nothing about how trim or fit they needed to be, only that I land them in Geneva. Although there's many a slip between the cup and the lip, my prospects looked promising.

At JFK, we transferred to the British Air terminal, where we were graciously escorted to the Concorde Lounge. The fact that free breakfast was being served didn't go unnoticed by the Hubbards. I checked us in at the reception desk, as they fortified themselves for the three-hour transatlantic flight.

Traveling faster than a speeding bullet over the Atlantic in the Concorde's cramped quarters was uneventful. As we prepared to disembark at Heathrow Airport, British Air employees handed each passenger a small silver pill box with the Concorde logo embossed on the lid, neatly wrapped in a little gift box. Most passengers left the empty boxes behind on their seats. As I made my way down the aisle behind the Hubbards, I watched with amusement as they stopped to open each little gift box in case some absentminded passengers had left a pill box behind!

We left Heathrow at 8 PM on Swiss Air, arriving in Geneva at 10:30 PM. Waiting for us at baggage claim was Bovenkamp with Youssef's Swiss chauffeur. Always the gentleman, Bovenkamp warmly welcomed us to Geneva and briefed us on our schedule as we rode to the Noga Hilton Hotel.

It was almost midnight when we all sat down in the lobby cocktail lounge to discuss plans for the following day's meeting. Bovenkamp suggested that we rendezvous in the lobby at 10 AM and go to the meeting together. At my insistence we would be using a small hotel conference room, since I didn't want to risk having a possible mess in Youssef's suite. Tired, the Hubbards went to their room.

Bovenkamp then dropped the first bombshell. The Libyan Foreign Minister, Omar Mustafa al-Muntassir, had just telephoned Youssef to say that he would not be able to come to Geneva as planned. He asked if we would mind flying to Djerba the following morning on Youssef's jet and we could hold our meeting at the Djerba airport.

"Where in the world is Djerba?" I asked.

He said it was an island, connected by a bridge to the mainland of Tunisia, where scenes from the first *Star Wars* movie were filmed.

"It will only take a few hours," he said.

Secondly, Bovenkamp told me that Bukhres, the guy who was to host our get-together, hadn't arrived yet and he had not heard from him in a couple of days.

I was starting to get upset.

"Why wasn't I told about Muntassir? How am I going to explain this to the Hubbards?"

They were nervous as it was. I could feel their tension growing on the last leg of our flight from London to Geneva, when they asked me a lot of questions about Debri, Muntassir and Bukhres. Now, I was going to have to face them in the morning and tell them that two of the three people we came to see would be missing. I didn't like the way this smelled.

Bovenkamp apologized profusely as he tried to ease my anxiety, claiming he himself had just learned that Muntassir wasn't coming. Youssef, however, wasn't concerned at all, so why should we be concerned? As for Bukhres, he was always late. He would probably still show up before the meeting in the morning.

I spent a rather uneasy night collecting my thoughts. How

would all this look to Congressman Hubbard? Would he be willing to fly to Tunisia? Come to think of it, would I be willing to fly to Tunisia? I had told him that Bukhres represented the U.S. Committee to Resolve Lockerbie and now he wouldn't even be showing up for his own meeting. On a more personal note, Bukhres was supposed to pay me $200,000 within forty-eight hours of our meeting. Tomorrow would be a telling day.

Bovenkamp and I had an early breakfast together. We had one hour before the Hubbards were expected. Bovenkamp gave me some more bad news. Youssef wanted to meet in his suite instead of the conference room, and Bukhres still hadn't checked into the hotel. It seemed he had disappeared again. While there wasn't anything I could do about Bukhres, I strongly protested the meeting place. Bovenkamp agreed to call Youssef and see what he could do.

At ten, the Hubbards punctually appeared in the dining room neatly dressed in business attire. They looked fresh and quite striking. Since they had already breakfasted in their room, they joined us for coffee. Bovenkamp immediately excused himself to call Youssef. Carol said she was hoping there wouldn't be any delays because she wanted to get some shopping in before dark. I had decided to let Youssef break the news about Muntassir and to let him make the suggestion that we fly off to Tunisia.

We were caught off guard when Bovenkamp reappeared accompanied by Youssef. At this point, no one was quite ready to meet the chief of Libyan Intelligence. This ramped up the tension at our table as he approached.

This was not what I had envisioned. What happened to the formal introductions of Col. Debri and the Libyan Foreign Minister over the neatly prepared conference table? What about the writing pads and sharp pencils? Where were the pitchers of ice water and the green table cloth? There was no chalkboard. It was time for foreign agent 4221 to become creative.

Col. Debri, it is so good of you to join us for breakfast," I improvised. "We are honored to have your company."

I made the introductions and waited to see what would happen next. Much to my delight, Youssef took charge. He was neatly dressed in a tan, short-sleeved leisure suit and seemed completely relaxed as he graciously welcomed Congressman and Mrs. Hubbard to Switzerland. They were obviously charmed and I could feel the tension evaporating.

I could almost read their minds. "This was no way for an international terrorist to behave."

They must have had low expectations, because they seemed seduced by his charm. Everyone began to relax, and suddenly we were like a group of new friends sharing a lovely Swiss brunch.

In fact, they were so charmed that the Hubbards readily agreed to spend the rest of the day in Djerba, Tunisia. All of my worrying had been for naught. Youssef explained that Muntassir had been detained in Tripoli, but would meet us in Djerba. As the man said, it would only take "a few hours."

Youssef looked directly at Bovenkamp and asked, "Will Bukhres be coming with us?"

With some embarrassment, Bovenkamp explained that he had had no contact with Bukhres in the past two days.

Youssef grumbled under his breath as he left the table, "Mohammed makes me crazy."

Youssef's driver was waiting for us outside the hotel in a brand new Mercedes 600 SEL.

Suddenly, out of the corner of my eye, I spied Mr. "DuPont" talking to and trying to hide behind the doorman just outside the hotel's revolving front door!

Since we took no belongings with us, we simply stepped

into the car and were off to Geneva's General Aviation Airport. When we arrived, we were greeted by two male pilots and two female flight attendants. We boarded a Falcon 500 jet that, unbeknownst to us at the time, was about to take us on the adventure of our lives.

The plane was like a Hollywood movie set. The interior was beautifully appointed with magnificent works of art and lavish furnishings. There were two cabins, each with four large and comfortable seats. There was a modern kitchen with all the conveniences. Some seats in the second cabin had been removed to accommodate Youssef's personal belongings and gifts. A red toy electric car, destined for his eight-year-old son, was strapped securely to the starboard bulkhead. Since the imposition of the 1991 United Nations air embargo, such items were scarce in Libya.

I sat directly across from and faced Youssef. The Hubbards were seated across the aisle facing each other. Bovenkamp sat aft in what I jokingly referred to as "coach class." He sat with a mysterious man in a black leather jacket named Zouhair Chirif. His business card said that he was in the construction business in Beirut, Lebanon. Youssef had introduced Chirif as his longtime friend, who was just "hitching" a ride to Libya. Chirif, however, indiscreetly told Bovenkamp that he was actually head of Syrian security on a secret mission to Libya.

The flight attendants served drinks, Russian caviar, and a delicious choice of roasted lamb, Chateaubriand, or salmon. I focused on the caviar. It was a beautiful, clear day, affording us a magnificent view of the Swiss Alps, the Italian coastline, and the Island of Malta.

Our casual conversation turned serious when Youssef began discussing Libyan-U.S. relations. I was surprised by how much he knew of the political situation in America.

"Libya has been the victim of a major U.S. disinformation program brought against our leader, Col. Qadhafi. In 1986, President Reagan approved a strategy of disinformation and deliberate deception against Qadhafi and our people. We are still the targets of this campaign, and Lockerbie is the latest attempt to discredit us in the eyes of the world."

As Youssef spoke, I took notes. I would try to confirm as much of his story later, when I had the chance to do some research. It turned out that Geoff Simons' book, *Libya: the Struggle for Survival*, was very helpful in providing me with much solid background material.

"Did you know that your National Security Advisor, Admiral Poindexter, advocated a plan in 1986 that was a combination of real and illusionary events through a disinformation program? The basic goal was to make our leader think that there was a high degree of internal opposition to him within Libya, that his key trusted aides, like me, were disloyal, and that the U.S. was about to move against him militarily. I have seen this memo. It was reported in *The Wall Street Journal*, August 25, 1986, and by Bob Woodward in *The Washington Post.* This was just a few months after the United States bombed my country. I wish I could take you to see the destruction the bombs caused."

I did remember that the memo had been leaked to the press. It had caused quite an uproar. The White House had lamely tried to draw an absurd distinction between practicing deception toward Qadhafi and using the American press for disinformation. The White House admitted deception, but denied disinformation!

At one White House briefing in mid-November 1986, I recall that President Reagan confirmed Poindexter's memo, but said he simply wanted to keep Qadhafi off balance.

Poindexter had insisted, "We did not intend and did not plan or conspire to mislead the American press in any way."

The problem was that many White House reporters felt, with good reason, that they had already been duped over a phony crisis with Libya. In other words, they had been lied to.

A high State Department official said that some of Poindexter's national security aides fed false information to the American press about Libya, believing that such a story "might be smiled upon" by Reagan. On August 25, 1986, *The Wall Street Journal* asserted that Qadhafi "has begun plotting new terrorist attacks" and that "the U.S. and Libya are on a collision course again." And yet, Poindexter's mid-August memo had said there was no evidence of any imminent terrorist attacks by Libya.

Sometimes, it's hard to know whom to trust and whom to believe. For many Americans, their government had left a bad taste in their mouths over the official lies that triggered the Gulf of Tonkin resolution, ramping up our involvement in the Vietnam War.

Two hours and ten minutes after our departure, we landed in Djerba. Youssef said that Muntassir was really looking forward to meeting us at the airport.

A group of plainclothes Libyan secret agents greeted us as we debarked. They had the familiar "Secret Service" look right down to the dark sunglasses and hand-held radios. Youssef was obviously their boss, because they obsequiously tried to anticipate his every move. His agents escorted us toward the side door of the small terminal building, as Youssef began a rather animated radio conversation with someone. It was very hot outside, so the terminal's air conditioning was quite refreshing.

A few minutes later, Youssef, hot and sweaty from standing on the tarmac talking on the radio, seemed upset as he joined us in the terminal.

"That was Muntassir on the radio. He can't get here. He wants us to come to Tripoli to meet with him in his office. He is very sorry and sends his sincere apologies."

This was not good news. I began to wonder if we were being duped. It was as if they had thrown out a net and were slowly reeling us in. Now, we were being asked to actually set foot in Libya!

We had two very clear choices—return to Geneva or go on to Tripoli. Unfortunately it wasn't that simple. To be perfectly frank, I knew nothing about travel restrictions for U.S. citizens to Libya, not to mention registered foreign agents. Of course, I did know that under the international sanctions, no flights were permitted into or out of the country, which is why Youssef had to fly in and out of Djerba, Tunisia.

We were told that it was only a three-hour drive to Tripoli. But if we decided to go, we would have to spend the night. There would not be enough time to reach Tripoli, meet with Muntassir, and return to Djerba in time to fly back to Geneva before its airport closed at 11 PM. Mrs. Hubbard quickly pointed out that we had no luggage and spending the night would create a hardship for her.

Youssef was still quite upset, but suggested that we drive to Tripoli as quickly as possible. He brightened when he said he would call his wife and have her prepare a very special dinner at their home in our honor. He would arrange for us to spend the night at the El Mahari Hotel in Tripoli and he would provide whatever items of clothing or personal effects that we might need.

It would be best to arrange our meeting with Muntassir for the early morning so we could return to Geneva in plenty of time. Most importantly, he guaranteed that our passports would not be stamped. No one would know we'd traveled to forbidden

Libya. The trip would remain a secret. I remember thinking that no one knew where we were anyway. Those who cared about us thought we were still at the Noga Hilton in Geneva.

Youssef made it sound very inviting and I hoped Congressman Hubbard would agree to the plan. I was intrigued by the idea of visiting Libya. After all, as Youssef had said, "It will only take a few hours."

I huddled with the Hubbards and Bovenkamp, and discussed our options. Congressman Hubbard's first concern was safety. He wondered if we might be the target of a Libyan kidnap plot.

"Why not?" he asked. "Look what they went through to get us this far."

I wondered out loud how the president would feel about launching a military raid to rescue us from Libya, just as President Carter had disastrously done in his failed attempt to rescue fifty-two American hostages from Iran in 1980. Hubbard didn't think my comments were particularly funny. He started getting a little testy with me, almost as if I was a part of this plot. I sincerely apologized.

I think everyone in our party was also intrigued with visiting Libya. However, we knew that we would be traveling without the benefit of diplomatic relations between the U.S. and Libya. We couldn't expect help from our own government if we got into a jam.

"Let's do it!" Congressman Hubbard suddenly declared to the group.

Maybe I should have been more suspicious that he had agreed so impulsively, but no hairs stood up on the back of my neck. All I felt was adrenaline surging through my body.

I was reminded of how I'd felt two years earlier on July 16, 1990. I'd been invited to fly on a reconnaissance mission on a Salvadorian Air Force helicopter, which flew over a guerilla-controlled region in the northern part of the country. Virginia and I had been the guests of President Cristiani, of El Salvador, because he wanted to thank us for creating a foundation that supplied over a thousand prosthetic legs to Salvadorian children, who were the innocent victims of landmines. The helicopter wasn't shot at or shot down. It returned and landed safely. But, it was very exciting. All's well that ends well. I was sure that would be the case with this little excursion.

Youssef looked pleased with the decision. He made a couple of phone calls, while shouting instructions to the men unloading the Falcon 500. We got into our designated limos and hastily departed the airport.

Believe it or not, we were about to venture into the heart of darkness.

NINE

The Caravan

As I peeked through the curtain of the black Mercedes limousine, I wondered, "What is the son of a milkman from Trenton, New Jersey, doing here?"

There were two other men in the limousine with Bovenkamp and me. The driver, who spoke no English, was in his late 40's. Next to him in the front seat was Khaled, a handsome young man wearing an Armani suit and a silk shirt open at the collar. The bulge under his neatly tailored suit jacket was an automatic 9 mm pistol. He had spoken to us in fairly decent English at Djerba airport, where he barked orders in Arabic from his car window to his JSO subordinates.

A short time later, Khaled was once again loudly engaged in an animated discussion outside of our car, but this time it was with armed Tunisian border crossing guards. We were just a few hundred feet from the Libyan border and there seemed to be a problem with our leaving Tunisia.

Bovenkamp was like a little kid in the back seat of our car as the commotion continued outside. He said, "This would make a great book." He asked repeatedly, "What's going on out there? Why are we being delayed?"

Our car was part of a three-car caravan. The black Mercedes directly behind ours contained the Hubbards. They were also assigned two Libyan security guards, one driving and the other in the front seat. The third black Mercedes contained Youssef and his Lebanese friend.

Khaled turned around and said, "They want to see your passports."

"I thought our passports weren't getting stamped," I said.

Irritated, Bovenkamp and I got out of the car. The border guards watched us as we walked back to the Hubbards' car. He joined us and we walked away to an area where we couldn't be overheard. Carol remained inside. She was extremely tense and was obviously afraid of all the commotion. We had a rather long discussion about giving up our passports to the Tunisian guards. After all, we had been told earlier that afternoon by Youssef that our visit was to be secret. A passport stamp would be irrefutable evidence of our travels.

None of us was sure about the legalities of a trip to Libya, so we were somewhat apprehensive.

Congressman Hubbard was traveling on a diplomatic passport with very few stamps. This indicated that he had not traveled very much or that it was a new passport. I checked page two of my well-worn passport to see what it said about travel to Libya. The only prohibited country listed was Cuba. We all knew that we would be traveling at our own risk, but none of us presumed that our government could punish such travel.

By now, Youssef had left his car and approached us. He was obviously upset by the delay.

"What's the problem, Chazzy?"

I told him that the Tunisian border guards had asked for our passports.

He stormed off toward Khaled mumbling under his breath, "This makes me crazy."

Youssef quickly became involved in the debate between his intelligence officers and the Tunisian border guards. They were out of ear shot but we knew that there was a major disagreement going on over the passports.

A few minutes later, Youssef returned to our group and explained that it would be all right to give the border guards our passports, but not to worry. When we reached the Libyan border, they would definitely not be stamped.

The only problem was that it wouldn't take a rocket scientist to ask the following question: Where did you go when you departed by land from Tunisia's eastern border, which happens to be contiguous to Libya?

We reluctantly gave our passports to Khaled, who took them into a small room in the immigration office.

There was a very long line of Libyans waiting to exit Tunisia. Libyan merchants sell their wares in Tunisia each day. For them, the trip across the border in either direction was long and tedious. We, however, quickly moved to the head of the line.

Khaled returned with and handed back our stamped passports.

I never thought that that exit stamp would cause me such so much inconvenience. Every time I entered a foreign country after this, the immigration officers would eye me with suspicion and ask me a number of questions.

With passports in hand, we were waved through the Tunisian border crossing at Ra's Ajdir and then we stopped a few hundred yards down the road at the Libyan border crossing. All of a sudden three Libyan police cars with flashing blue lights positioned themselves in front of our motorcade and three more took up positions at our rear. The police officers had obviously been waiting for us with engines running. No time was lost as our squealing tires reached 160 kph (100 mph) from a standing start in a matter of seconds.

The fact that I was actually in Libya registered very quickly. My heart rate increased. Bovenkamp and I simultaneously looked at each other without a word. My first thought was that it was too late to turn back now.

I felt some comfort knowing that I had been in similar situations like this in El Salvador, Nicaragua, and elsewhere around the world and had always made it through before. One particular trip stood out.

I went to El Salvador in the spring of 1982 to sign a contract to represent the Salvadoran Freedom Foundation (SFF) as its registered foreign agent in Washington. The foundation was a right-wing group composed of wealthy Salvadoran landowners. Some members were descendants of the original thirteen families who at one time owned the entire country. All of that changed when the government introduced new land reforms in the early 1980's. Later, the SFF was accused of operating "death squads" in El Salvador, since many of the SFF were also members of the right-wing Republican National Alliance Party (ARENA). One of my employees, Alvaro Rizo, former Nicaraguan ambassador to the United States, accompanied me on this trip.

As was customary in that war-torn country, the SFF provided us with an armored car and a contingent of heavily armed bodyguards, who remained close at hand during the day and stationed outside of our hotel rooms at night. Our first meeting with the SFF was held over lunch on the veranda of a magnificent plantation owned by a handsome young Salvadoran by the name of Orlando de Sola. What I remember most about the plantation was the iron gate, barbed wire security fences, farmers working the fields with automatic weapons over their shoulders and large, colorful Spanish pots filled with hand grenades stationed strategically around the veranda.

Each of the six SFF members joining us for lunch that day claimed to have been wounded at least once during the country's struggle against communism. The kidnapping of rich Salvadorans for ransom was in vogue at the time, and each lunch guest had come in an armored car with a small army of bodyguards. The three days we were in Salvador were marked by torrential rains leaving over 300 people dead from landslides and floods. The bodyguards who surrounded the main house in the pouring rain and fog made for an eerie sight.

In spite of the rains and the precarious political situation in El Salvador, I was able to see a little of the country. I even had time to buy my daughter, Katie, a little Salvadoran red and white jumper. Although she was just a baby, I figured that by the time it fit her, it would be a rather unique conversation piece.

After lunch, our personal security team was reinforced by a second team of six bodyguards for the drive to the airport. The ride was considered especially dangerous at the time. Not only had the rains washed out many of the main roads, but three Catholic nuns and a laywoman had been raped and murdered on the same road two years earlier.

The rain fell so hard that our driver had a most difficult time following the road. This was exacerbated by the condensation that built up inside the car due to the double thickness of bulletproof windows. We were following closely behind a Salvadoran military six-by-six truck used to carry troops. The rain and the truck's canvas cover prevented us from seeing if soldiers were actually riding inside. Both Ambassador Rizo and I were extremely nervous. It seemed like we would never reach the airport.

As we approached the exact spot where the Catholic nuns had been ambushed and killed, our car was hit hard by something. The roof above me was crushed in, just missing my head by inches. Our driver slammed on his brakes and our car came to a sliding stop. I was thrown to the opposite side of the back seat, landing with my head on Rizo's lap. As I brought my head up, our driver and the bodyguard in the right front seat jumped from the car with guns drawn. As Rizo shouted, "We are going to die!" I could see the canvas on the back of the truck in front of us had been swept away, and out jumped a dozen armed soldiers.

The little dress I had purchased for Katie was lying underneath me on the seat. My first thought was that she would never wear the dress and I would never see my wife and daughter again.

After a great deal of shouting and commotion, the guards opened our doors. As we stood in the downpour, we realized what had happened. The rains had washed out the road, and the rushing water coming down the hillside above us had uprooted a telephone pole which had fallen, full force, on our vehicle. The Salvadoran soldiers in the truck had seen the pole fall and jumped from the truck to rescue us. Luckily, the roof of the armored car had been reinforced with steel.

Now, here I was again in an armored car, surrounded by armed security police. I had exchanged the rainforest of El Salvador for the desert of Libya.

The sirens began to howl from the lead police cars. The noise was deafening. As we approached the first major intersection in the town of Zumarah, two of the lead police cars moved into position to block the progress of cars approaching from our right and left. We sped through the intersection without slowing down. Almost like clockwork, two of the police cars from our rear sped past with sirens blaring and switched positions with the cars that had stopped in the intersection. I wondered how fast those cars would have to go to be able to catch up to our motorcade. This process was repeated at every intersection on our three-hour ride to Tripoli.

The two-way highway ran parallel with the Mediterranean Sea. Cars that happened to be in our path were nudged off the road by our advance men. Our crack security detail forced one poor fellow meandering down the highway in a tiny little Fiat off the road and through a small fence that penned in goats, sheep and chickens. It was almost comical to see the dust, feathers, and fence posts upended as we sped by at the treacherous speed of 100 mph. The reason we were traveling by land was because travel by air was forbidden.

United Nations Security Council Resolution 748 had come into effect on April 15, 1992, which imposed a series of sanctions on Libya for its refusal to hand over the two Libyans accused of planting the bomb that blew up Pan Am 103. An air embargo was the key in trying to bring Qadhafi to his knees. The resolution stated that all UN member states:

> . . . deny permission to any aircraft to take off from, land in or overfly their territory if it is destined to land in or has taken off from the territory of Libya, unless the particular flight has been approved on grounds of significant humanitarian need . . .

Libya told the UN Security Council that because of the international aircraft boycott, heavy road traffic had led to 10,200 accidents since April 15, 1992—resulting in the deaths of 1,622 people, serious injury and permanent disability to 4,220 others, minor injuries to 3,124 people, and the destruction of more than 9,200 motor vehicles. I prayed that our Mercedes wouldn't be number 9,201!

The radio in our car started crackling and I heard the familiar voice of Youssef shouting instructions in Arabic. Khaled responded briefly and turned to tell us that it was all right to open our black window curtains and enjoy the view.

Libya is in northern Africa on the coast of the Mediterranean. The country is bordered by Egypt and Sudan on the east, Chad and Niger on the south, and Algeria and Tunisia on the west. Tripoli, our destination, is Libya's capital and largest city. We could see the Mediterranean to the left and the vast Sahara, which covers most of Libya, to our right. We passed little villages named Zuwarah and az-Zawiyah.

Libya has about five million people. Approximately 80 percent of them live along the Mediterranean coast or in the upland regions just south of the coast. Approximately 70 percent of Libya's people live in urban areas. About 30 percent live in small villages or desert oases like the ones we were passing at great speed. Some nomads move with their sheep, goats and camels in search of pasture. We noticed many single-family dwellings in the rural areas, with most people living in stone or mud-brick houses. Khaled told us that often families have a single room for all activities.

Most of the men we saw were wearing a loose cotton shirt and trousers covered by an outer robe. They wore flat, brimless, tight-fitting caps. Women were wearing traditional full-length gowns, many with head coverings. Khaled told us that some people in Libya's cities wore these garments to indicate their regard for Islamic values and practices, but that most city dwellers wore Western-style clothing.

Every now and then we could see sheep grazing on a desert oasis near large sand dunes. People were riding camels, and shepherds were moving their goats or sheep down the sides of the road. After almost two hours of deafening sirens, I heard Youssef's voice on the radio. Our motorcade slowed down as we entered the small village of Sabratah. Khaled said we were going to take a break here for water.

We stopped in front of a small store. Men, wearing traditional garb, were sitting at small tables in front of a makeshift café, smoking hookah pipes and drinking what appeared to be goat's milk. They looked at us with great curiosity, as we all got out of our cars to stretch our legs. Some of our guards and most of our drivers went into the store. My driver couldn't wait to have a cigarette. He had been forbidden to light up for two hours, because of my contempt for smoking.

What happened next was surreal. Hubbard was circulating among the tables in the little outdoor cafe, handing out his business cards with the official gold seal of the United States Congress embossed on them. He shook hands and said, "Hi! I'm Congressman Carroll Hubbard from Kentucky." It was as if he was working the crowd back home. It was an example of his extremely poor judgment. The mostly elderly Libyans looked with bewilderment, as they viewed the official looking cards and the fat man in the Western business suit handing them out.

Hubbard was well known on Capitol Hill for giving business cards to people, no matter how many times he saw them during the day. There were times when I would find three of his cards as I emptied my pockets after returning home from a rough day in the halls of Congress.

He also loved to have his picture taken on the Capitol steps with a constituent or friend. The House photographers were sure to have plenty of film in their cameras when Hubbard was in town. A few days later the guest or friend would find a large brown envelope in the mail with the franked congressional signature of Carroll Hubbard, inscribed, "To my good friend, Joe Blow, from Carroll Hubbard, MC, (member of Congress), Kentucky." There were many Christmases when I would receive five or more congressional calendars in the mail from "Your good friend, Carroll Hubbard, MC, Kentucky."

The drivers and guards returned with grocery bags of bottled water under their arms. We climbed back into our caravan, sirens wailing again, as we peeled out of the little village, leaving behind a confused group of hookah smokers.

As we entered Tripoli, we saw large billboards with pictures of "The Leader," Col. Muammar al-Qadhafi, every few blocks. Tripoli looked like most North American and Western European cities. High-rise concrete office and apartment buildings filled the downtown areas. Suburban areas seemed to have more spacious, single-family dwellings than those we had passed en route to Tripoli. Expensive European automobiles were abundant. There were no visible signs of poverty.

The lack of poverty was no surprise. Petroleum serves as the basis of the economy of Libya. It accounts for about half of the value of Libya's total economic production and for almost all the country's export earnings.

Youssef had told us earlier in the day in Geneva that Col. Qadhafi planned to distribute half of the country's oil revenue in cash grants to the Libyan people. Under his plan, each family would be given $7,000 to $10,000 beginning early in 1993.

He also told us that Libya was in the midst of a severe economic crisis, due to the UN sanctions over the Lockerbie impasse. I assumed the grants were intended to ease the pain of the economic embargo, and Qadhafi actually announced his grants scheme a week later on November 19th.

It was 8 PM and approaching dusk as we pulled into the entrance of the El Mahari Hotel in Tripoli, directly across the street from one of the most beautiful harbors I'd ever seen. I could see a large ferry boat making its way into the harbor.

When we arrived, the El Mahari bellboys rushed to our cars, surprised not to find luggage in the trunks. They were, as we were, even more surprised to see the arsenal of machine guns, rocket launchers, and various other heavy weapons neatly arranged in the trunks. As we made our grand entrance, hotel guests in the lobby were also caught off guard.

The lobby was modern. It looked like most Western hotels. We were escorted past the reception desk to the bank of elevators at the far end of the lobby. Several of our security guards picked up keys from the reception desk and joined us on the elevator. Then, we were all taken into my suite and given a briefing on the hotel and the special features of each suite.

In addition to the usual bedroom and living room, each suite had its own office, dining room, full kitchen and three baths. There were fresh flowers in all of the rooms and a large tray with fruit, cookies and cheeses neatly placed on the living room table. Being a Muslim country there was no mini bar, but the refrigerator was well stocked with juices and soft drinks.

Khaled told us that we would have about fifteen minutes to freshen up before meeting in the lobby. We would then be driven to Youssef's home for dinner.

Punctually, we left the hotel and arrived at the Debri home ten minutes later. It appeared to be a wealthy neighborhood. His house was distinguishable by the large security force stationed outside the front entry courtyard. Armed guards in uniform seemed ubiquitous, and the addition of our own security guards made for quite an armed camp in this quiet neighborhood.

As we were escorted through a courtyard containing a swimming pool, I was amazed to see pieces of Roman ruins neatly situated around the yard and up the long path leading to the main entrance of the house. We were told by our escorts that the Romans conquered much of this region in 74 B.C., and ruled it as a province. To the Romans, the Mediterranean was *Mare Nostrum* (Our Sea) and, on the southern shore, Roman Tripolitania developed over two centuries until the collapse of the Roman Empire.

Khaled told us that Leptis Magna, an hour's drive from Tripoli, surpassed any set of monuments in the Roman Empire, including Rome itself. Libya had been the empire's breadbasket, and Khaled pointed out to us that Libya's ancestors had provided many of its best artists and craftsmen. Khaled said that he would take us to Leptis Magna if we had time on our way back to Djerba.

Youssef warmly greeted us at the door. He was eager for us to meet his family. He introduced his wife, who was much lighter skinned than her husband. She was dressed in a Western skirt and blouse, and greeted us warmly. His two daughters looked very much like their mother and were dressed up in their finest clothes for our visit. They made every attempt to make us feel welcome. Youssef said that it had been many years since they had entertained Americans in their home and that they were delighted to do so. He thanked me with great warmth and enthusiasm for making this evening possible.

Almost all Libyans are Muslims and belong to the Sunni branch of Islam. As a matter of fact, the country's 1977 constitution required that all legislation conform to Islamic Law. Nevertheless, the Muslim prohibition against the consumption of alcoholic beverages went unnoticed that evening. Youssef had a bar equal to any home in New York, Los Angeles or Washington.

As the evening wore on, we became more relaxed with each other. It was probably alcohol assisted. The house was well decorated and had all of the modern conveniences I had in my own home.

As we sat and made small talk, we were joined by one of Youssef's closest Libyan friends, Salah el-Fituri. He was president of Fitex, S.A., a Swiss corporation located in Geneva. I later found out that this company was used by Youssef as a mechanism to do business with the West. They were into international trade, construction, resorts and banking. El-Fituri lived in Geneva with his family. He frequently traveled back and forth between Switzerland and Libya.

He had flown from Geneva that morning using the route that most Libyans employed since the U.N. air embargo. He flew to Malta and transferred to a ferry boat which brought him to Tripoli's harbor. El-Fituri was a very pleasant man who spoke excellent English with hardly an accent.

It was already after 10 PM and I was famished. Mrs. Debri finally told us that dinner would be ready about midnight, their usual hour for dining. The Hubbards and I, though starving by now, exercised great forbearance in hiding our extreme hunger from our hosts.

Youssef's daughter left the room and returned with a photo of herself and her horse. She told me that her father had mentioned my daughter's love for horses. We talked for quite a while about equestrian matters. She was a lovely young woman. I promised that I would bring my daughter to Tripoli with me someday so they could ride together. Unfortunately, the older daughter was very busy helping her mother in the kitchen and I didn't spend much time with her.

Mrs. Debri brought their young son in to meet us before he went to bed. He spoke very little English and was quite shy. Youssef told us of his son's reaction to the 1986 U.S. air raid—known as Operation El Dorado Canyon—against Libya.[4] Some of the bombs landed fairly close to the Debri home. As a result, his son had had recurring nightmares. He would wake up and cry out, "Reagan is going to kill me. Reagan is going to kill me."

All Libyan children from ages six to fifteen are required to attend school. Education is free for six years of primary school and for three years of preparatory school or high school.

About ten percent of the college-aged population attend one of Libya's five universities or attend school in another country. Youssef told us his older daughter would be attending Libya's largest university, Al-Fatah, in Tripoli

When dinner arrived at last, it was well worth the wait. Mrs. Debri was very happy to see us enjoy the fruits of her labor.

The status of women in Libya had changed dramatically since the late 1900's. Women once received little or no education and were largely confined to the home. Today, they have the legal right to participate fully in Libyan society. Libyan women make up only about 10 percent of the workforce, but this percentage is quickly growing as more women become educated. Youssef's wife was obviously well educated and had traveled extensively, with the exception, of course, of the USA.

After dinner, we arrived back at the El Mahari at 2:30 AM.

Apparently, it is customary for wealthy Libyans to eat late and sleep late. Youssef told us to sleep in and be ready to meet with the country's foreign minister, Dr. Omar Muntassir, at ten o'clock the next morning. He would have his people pick us up a few minutes before.

TEN

Libya's Foreign Minister

The El Mahari Hotel lobby was deserted when we returned from the Debri home. I wanted desperately to call my wife, Virginia, in California, but I didn't want any phone records of my visit to Libya. In all my years of traveling the world, this was the first night that I had been away from her that we didn't communicate either by telephone or fax.

I knew she would be worried. She wasn't overjoyed about my involvement with this terrorist-linked country, but she felt that I might be useful in opening a dialogue between the U.S. and Libya. I knew she would be awake most of the night, checking the fax machine and voicemail. I hoped that she wouldn't try to call me at the Noga Hilton and find out that I hadn't been in my room all night. I was sure the National Security Agency

(NSA) intercepted all communications between Libya and the U.S. I simply couldn't take the chance.

I went directly to bed and had difficulty getting to sleep. The last time I checked my watch, it was 3:30 AM. Moments later, I was startled awake by the sound of morning prayers from a mosque's loudspeaker nearby my balcony window. It was barely light outside. I jumped out of bed to see if what I was hearing was real or the result of too much food and drink a few hours earlier. It was real. My chances of going back to sleep were gone.

I lay there trying to collect my thoughts. I reviewed what I knew about Lockerbie and the circumstances that led to the indictment of the two Libyans. Could it be that they really were being framed?

If Libya was really guilty, why would they go to all this trouble to try to open a new dialogue with the West? Could it be a ploy? I decided to focus on what I knew so that I could pose intelligent questions when we met with the Libyan Committee to Resolve the Lockerbie Dispute in a few hours.

All of the reading I had done about the circumstances leading up to the Lockerbie disaster seemed to lead investigators closer and closer to the indictment of Syrian and Iranian agents. Some of the earliest articles about Lockerbie didn't even mention Libya as a suspect. It wasn't until November 14, 1991, that U.S. and Scottish prosecutors released a twenty-nine-page indictment, charging two Libyan men with carrying out the attack. This was almost three years after the Boeing 747 was blown out of the sky.

Named in the indictment were thirty-nine-year-old Lamen Khalifa Fhimah—whom prosecutors said had used his job as an airline employee to store Semtex explosives at the Malta airport—and a second man, Abdelbasset Ali Mohammed al-Megrahi, who was fifty-five at the time. A shopkeeper in Malta had identified him as the man who had bought an assortment of clothing, found at the crash scene. The indictment stated that both men were agents of the Libyan intelligence service, which Youssef el-Debri headed up. Furthermore, prosecutors charged that the Libyan government had provided them with Semtex and detonators.

It was late in 1990 when reports began to surface implicating Libya in the Pan Am 103 attack. Many of those with a special interest in the case viewed this turn of events with skepticism. Most feared the investigation was being forced in a direction that better suited the needs of the Bush Administration. Details implicating Libya seemed to coincidentally emerge at a time when the president was building a coalition against Iraq, prior to the war in the Persian Gulf.

There were also reports that U.S. and British authorities overlooked the possible Syrian and Iranian connection to the bombing in return for the 1991 release of Britain's Terry Waite[5] and America's Thomas Sutherland[6] who had been held hostage by pro-Iranian forces. Waite was released soon after Foreign Secretary Douglas Herd announced in the House of Commons that Syria was not involved in the Lockerbie bombing. Sutherland and Waite were released on the same day.

I called the front desk of the El Mahari and requested shaving gear and a toothbrush, which they quickly provided. I dressed in my day-old clothes and went down to the lobby for breakfast and a quick walk around Tripoli Harbor. The lobby was full of Germans who had entered Libya illegally, against UN sanctions, to make what I suspected were some major oil deals. Youssef had told me that there were as many as 5,000 Americans also living in Libya illegally. They were working on the oil rigs left behind by American companies when they were forced to leave the country.

At breakfast, I listened while two Americans sitting nearby engaged a Libyan in a business discussion. I was also very aware of two Libyan men sitting several tables away. They seemed to have taken a special interest in me.

The friendly hotel staff went out of their way to greet me as I passed through the hotel lobby and out the front door. I noticed that the two aforementioned Libyan men left the hotel just after I did. The day was beautiful and the water in the harbor was a sparkling blue-green color. The temperature was in the 70's. The air was clean and fresh, in spite of the cars racing past me on the harbor-side drive. The two men following me immediately split up after leaving the hotel. One fell in step about 50 yards behind me and the other about 100 yards behind me, but on the opposite side of the street. When I stopped, they stopped, either looking in a store window, lighting a cigarette, or propping a leg up on the seawall to view the large ferryboat just passing through the breakwater leading into the harbor.

I hoped that they were Youssef's guys and not the CIA. I wondered if their purpose in following me was to gather intelligence or to safeguard me in their country. Later, Youssef told me that none of his agents were assigned to follow me that morning.

I returned to the hotel with the two agents close on my heels, just as the Hubbards were getting off the lobby elevator. They were on their way to breakfast and asked me to join them for coffee. We began to discuss what the day held for us. We talked quite openly until one of the men tailing me sat at the next table. I could see his partner on a lobby telephone just outside the restaurant entrance. We decided to talk later.

Youssef was at the wheel of his personal Mercedes as he drove up in front of the hotel. He asked me to ride with him. The Hubbards and Bovenkamp rode in the black Mercedes limo behind his car. The usual contingent of JSO personnel were close at hand: three separate unmarked police cars, one in front of our car and two behind the limo. The annoying sirens that accompanied us the night before were now silent, as we made our way to our meeting with the Libyan foreign minister.

As Youssef drove me to the Foreign Ministry, I was quite surprised when he announced that he was arranging for me to meet the two Libyan suspects indicted for the 1988 bombing of Pan Am 103. He asked me not to discuss this with the Hubbards, Bovenkamp, or anyone else.

The two suspects, Abdelbasset Ali Mohammed al Megrahi and Lamen Khalifa Fhimah, were in Tripoli under house arrest and under heavy guard. Youssef said that they had not been interviewed about Lockerbie, except by their Libyan and Western lawyers.

"I want you to get to know them personally," he said. "I want you to look them in the eyes and ask them if they did it."

I felt a surge of mixed emotions of excitement and alarm at the prospect of meeting these two terrorists, allegedly responsible for murdering 270 innocent people.

As we pulled into the driveway of the Foreign Ministry, there were small groups of people staring at us from the windows of what appeared to be an office building directly adjacent to the ministry building. I was quite uncomfortable with their watching our arrival and wondered how they knew we were coming. I asked that we be driven up as close to the front door as possible so that we could exit discreetly. Youssef obliged, and I made a quick exit from the car and entered the building. I waited anxiously, hoping Hubbard would follow my lead.

Instead, Congressman Carroll Hubbard of Mayfield, Kentucky, slowly opened the back door of his limo, deliberately turned to face the office building and began waving to the crowd in the windows above. He must have thought he was a head of state arriving at the U. S. Capitol. How would his buffoonery play out on the hidden CIA cameras probably recording all comings and going at this strategic government facility?

I couldn't hide my anger as he joined me in the entrance lobby of the ministry. I reminded him that we had agreed to eschew visibility during our stay in Libya. He laughed and said surreally, "You never know when you might run into a voter from the 1st District of Kentucky. Ha-ha!"

Before I could respond, we were being graciously escorted to the offices of Libya's foreign minister, Omar Mustafa al-Muntassir. His small office reeked of cigar smoke. Muntassir sat behind a large, disorganized, government-issue brown desk, piled high with papers and reports. He was a serious looking man, who appeared to be in his fifties. He was rather round and wore large horned-rimmed glasses. He stood to greet us with a fat, unlighted cigar protruding from his mouth.

A conference table extended away from the desk at a right angle so that he could remain seated behind it while participating in a group discussion with those at the table. There were just enough chairs to seat the Hubbards, Bovenkamp, Debri, the Libyan ambassador to Tunisia, and myself. There was also a chair for a thin middle-aged gentleman I assumed to be Dr. Muntassir's personal assistant.

After a warm welcome, Muntassir lit his cigar and eased back in his swivel chair. "To begin," he said in perfect English, "I want to thank you for your bravery in coming to Libya. Looking directly at Hubbard, he said, "You are the first American government official to visit here in many years and the first since the Lockerbie indictments. I know that you have all come at great personal risk, and I want to express my thanks and the thanks of our leader, Col. Qadhafi."

I could see that Mrs. Hubbard was a bit uncomfortable with Muntassir's reference to personal risk.

He looked directly at me and said, "I have heard a great deal about you, Mr. Chasey. Col. Debri has gotten to know you and has checked you out carefully." (I wasn't sure I liked the "checking out" part.) "We have a lot in common," he continued. "We both come from academic backgrounds. I studied at the University of Michigan."

He went on to say how much he loved America and that he hoped to be in New York in a week or so, if he could obtain a visa.

"I understand that you can make things happen in Washington. You know the right people. The fact that you brought a sitting congressman to Libya is very impressive. I trust good things will occur from our meeting here today," said Muntassir.

He took several puffs from his cigar, flicked off a large ash into the ashtray and continued.

"Our leader, Col. Qadhafi, established The Committee to Resolve the Lockerbie Dispute. I am its chairman. Col. Debri and our ambassador to Tunisia are members. We are anxious to discuss the Lockerbie incident with you in hopes that you will be able to help us open a dialogue with the United States Congress and your President-elect Bill Clinton. We look forward to the new Clinton administration with great optimism. The Libyan people are very happy with your president-elect. We watched with great interest the results of your elections. We think that there is an opportunity for us to reestablish normal relations with your new president."

He reached over and picked up a sheet of paper that looked, from where I sat, to be a photocopy of a news clipping. He read a few lines of the paper to us. "On September 17, 1992, Clinton said, if elected he would make sure that all questions regarding

Syrian and Iranian involvement in the Pan Am 103 tragedy are addressed and fully answered." I hope that you, Mr. Hubbard, and you, Mr. Chasey, can be of help in making this happen.

I thanked Muntassir for his hospitality and told him that we were looking forward to our discussions concerning U.S.-Libyan relations. And I thanked him for his kind comments about me.

Congressman Hubbard expressed his interest in doing what he could to help in the U.S.-Libyan stalemate. He apologized that he wasn't a member of the Foreign Affairs or the Intelligence Committees, which had jurisdiction over the Libyan situation, but noted that "Congressman Lee Hamilton, the new chairman of the House Foreign Affairs Committee is my very good friend, and I will be happy to relate our discussions to him when I return to Washington. Lee is from Indiana, and I am from Kentucky, but our districts adjoin each other. We fly back and forth to Washington together a lot. If you want me to give him a letter or something like that, you can count on me. We are here to help."

Our discussion quickly turned to a historical discussion of U.S.-Libyan political relations. They were far more conversant on the subject. The Libyans knew times, dates, and places for events that, in some cases, I had not heard of.

Muntassir provided us with a large, green magazine-size publication entitled, *The Hostile and Terrorist Actions Carried Out by the U.S. Administration Against the Arab People of Libya.* This large, four-page publication listed forty-seven hostile acts by the United States against Libya between 1972 and 1991.

At that point, the conversation could have digressed into a nasty debate. But, the Libyans presented their case effectively and we weren't prepared to rebut their assertions. We mostly listened to Muntassir. It was as if he had all these facts pent up inside him for years, just waiting for the right opportunity to let them out.

I began to reflect on how the United States could find itself in this standoff with Libya. The most powerful nation on earth was at loggerheads with this tiny North African state of five million people.

Was there a real likelihood of a Lockerbie cover-up? I didn't believe all I was hearing from Muntassir, but I wanted to be open minded. It's possible there could be some truth in what he was asserting. Because I care so much about the truth and the facts, I don't necessarily believe everything my country tells me. It wouldn't be the first time that U.S. officials had misled us. In many cases, they were part of what I call "the unelected second tier."

ELEVEN

The Real Decision Makers

Virginia and I had made a carefully considered and difficult decision eleven years earlier not to make Washington, D.C., our permanent home. (That's why I was commuting weekly between California and D.C.) As I mentioned before, we decided to raise our daughter, Katie, in the world outside of the Washington Beltway. We didn't like the transient lifestyle that made the nation's capital a stopover duty station for people on their way to bigger and better things. There was no accountability when you served for two or three years in a particular position and then moved on. We really disliked that friendships in Washington were fleeting and often insincere. President Harry Truman once said, "If you want a friend in Washington, buy a dog."

More importantly, Washington had become a city of overload

and redundancy. The government had grown all out of proportion to what the framers of the Constitution had in mind. Washington had usurped more and more of the responsibilities and authority reserved for the states. In the process, the federal government had grown and so had the workload of the employees. Under a deluge of mounting regulations and paperwork, elected officials had not only lost control of their own lives, but the lives of the thousands of staff hired to relieve some of the ever-mounting burdens.

Unfortunately, over the years I had worked in Washington, I observed firsthand the emergence of a new power structure in our nation's capitol, which I call the unelected second tier. It would come as no surprise if a cover-up of the Lockerbie situation had gotten its start with a small lie told by one of these second-tier officials, which then quickly grew into an international cause célèbre, the ever expanding tale being passed on to one, two or more of the official's successors.

To believe that this could happen, one just needed to recall the elaborate cover-up engineered by Marine Lt. Colonel Oliver North in the Iran-Contra fiasco.[7] If this had happened with Iran, why not Lockerbie and Libya?

The American people have gotten a small taste of what this "second-tier" can do from the painful revelations emanating from some well-known scandals like the Gulf of Tonkin Resolution and Watergate. There just isn't enough time in the day for elected first-tier people like the president of the United States and members of Congress to wield appropriate oversight over their second-tier staff appointees. These, for the most part, seek and secure government jobs with grandiose titles and prestige just to have their professional resume "tickets" punched by serving a couple of years in lofty positions. An all-too-frequent scenario is that an unelected official makes a mistake and, rather than face up to his error, will cover up his actions knowing that he will shortly be leaving government.

Many of the second-tier appointees of the Reagan and Bush administrations were less than honest with the American people when it came to foreign policy matters. Some were exposed and disgraced and/or imprisoned. I have no doubt that there were just as many, or more, guilty of similar crimes and blunders that were never discovered. Many of the Reagan and Bush appointees were in positions of authority and deeply involved in other conspiracies and cover-ups when, in 1986, the United States bombed Libya. Some of the same people were in power when, in 1991, the blame for Lockerbie was shifted from Syria and Iran to Libya.

Was it possible that they had orchestrated a very successful U.S. disinformation program aimed at Libya? Was it beyond them or others like them in the White House to lie to the world about Lockerbie? I had no proof, but I had to wonder.

In addition, the day of the citizen legislator of the nineteenth century had disappeared. Members of Congress, no matter how much talk there was about term limits, had become full-time, professional legislators, with enormous support staffs of bright young people, constantly looking for ways to better serve their masters.

As knowledge doubled every two years, so did the workload of elected Washington politicians. Since information was power, staff members with the information had become increasingly more powerful in the corridors of Congress. The unelected staff had become a major political force because elected officials just didn't have the time nor the energy to devote to the voluminous data required to function in Washington.

Over the twenty years of my lobbying Capitol Hill, more than 200,000 bills had been introduced in the House—more than 20,000 bills in each two-year term! Only slightly more than ten percent were reported from the twenty-two standing committees to the House floor. The average number that became law per Congress was less than five percent.

Each bill introduced, whether passed or not, had a sponsor, a constituency, and a special-interest group that lobbied lawmakers on its behalf. It is obvious that the elected members cannot deal with each bill, each issue, and each person who calls or writes during the course of a day. The responsibility for dealing with this crushing work load falls on the shoulders of the 35,000 Capitol Hill staff, referred to as "staffers" or "Hillies."

Because of this immense work overload, staff often found themselves making major decisions. I had spent most of my waking hours positioned outside the doors of either the House or Senate chambers. I had seen it all. When you were as visible as I was in the U.S. Capitol, members and staffers regarded you as part of their team. They often spoke and acted openly in my presence, with a total disregard for discretion.

I couldn't count the number of times I had watched a staffer, not much more than twenty-five years old, brief a senior senator on the merits of a floor speech or an upcoming vote as they rode together on the underground subway to the Senate chamber, or the number of times I had heard a staffer yell, "Vote aye. You are for this!" as the senator rushed from the "Senators Only" elevator to the Senate floor to record his vote within the fifteen-minute time limit permitted under Senate rules.

TWELVE

Operation El Dorado Canyon

My head was spinning as I listened to Muntassir and tried to digest what he was saying, compared to what I remembered reading.

Fortunately, we were saved by the bell. It was time for lunch.

Muntassir suggested to Youssef that he take us to visit the Bab Azizia Barracks after lunch. He felt that we could learn a great deal about what actually happened in the early morning hours of April 15, 1986, when 13 F-111 American fighter bombers, based in Britain, and three radar-jamming aircraft launched from carriers in the Mediterranean, attacked Tripoli and Benghazi. Bombs and missiles hit the airport, the Bab Azizia Barracks—where Qadhafi and his family had been sleeping—and various other civilian targets.

After a quick lunch at the El Mahari Hotel, we decided to visit the barracks on our way back to the Djerba airport. We needed to arrive at the Geneva airport before it closed at 11 PM. Our plan was to spend the night in Geneva and return to the States early the next morning.

The barracks were located in the center of Tripoli, only ten minutes from the hotel. Youssef warned us that what we were about to see would come as a shock. As we approached the barracks, he pointed out various housing complexes and the French Embassy, which had been hit by the F-111 bombs. Qadhafi had ordered the barracks closed to visitors and had left the facility exactly as it was after the 1986 bombing. Few people had seen the remains of Qadhafi's home. Youssef said that we would be the first Americans to visit the complex since it was briefly opened to the press just after the attack.

Pilots who participated in the raid later suggested that damage to the French Embassy in Tripoli and other civilian sites was caused by errant anti-aircraft fire. However, Western journalists in Libya at that time reported that the damage appeared to be too extensive to support that explanation.

U.S. intercepted messages suggested that the Libyan military response was weak and befuddled. Commanders at the Libyan airbase near Surt, for example, ignored an order to launch their airplanes to repel the attack and suggested instead that the airbase at Benghazi should respond.

At the same time, eight Navy A6 Intruders had dropped 500 and 750-pound anti-personnel/anti-material bombs on the Benina Airfield at Benghazi. These cluster bombs scattered about 100 bomblets. They were designed to injure or kill people and damage airplanes.

U.S. bombers did encounter heavy antiaircraft fire, but their jamming and electronic misdirection equipment repelled most of it. In addition, Navy planes circling off the coast fired almost fifty missiles into Libyan radar stations. The F-111's took advantage of surprise and darkness to evade the defenders as the planes roared in at nearly 500 mph. Furthermore, the F-111's variable "swing wings" and its all-weather-target designator enabled it to hug the terrain to screen itself from radar detection. Designed for surprise attack and quick escape, the F-111's did just that over Libya.

Taking off from bases in Great Britain, the F-111 pilots faced an exhausting, fourteen-hour flight of 2,700 miles each way. Their legs went numb from sitting in one position for so long. Some returned so stiff they had to be lifted out of the cockpit.

During the long flight to Libya and back, the F-111's flew on automatic pilot. But, during several mid-air refuelings, the pilots had to maneuver their aircraft to an exact place in the sky to meet a hose nozzle suspended from an Air Force tanker.

Their Navy A6 counterparts had been taken so close to Libya on aircraft carriers that they did not have to refuel. But after their bombing runs, the pilots had to find their aircraft carriers in the dark, never an easy task, and land on their decks—at 135 mph.

Air Force tankers took off first, forming a string of refueling stations along the circuitous F-111 route over the Atlantic and Mediterranean. The Air Force and Navy bombers were under orders to coordinate their takeoffs and flight plans so they would rendezvous above Libya simultaneously in order to swoop in and out before most of the Libyan Air Force and anti-aircraft gunners could respond.

Before takeoff, crews of both types of bombers had studied maps and photos of targets around Tripoli and Benghazi. They marked check points along the route in hopes of flying a precise course, although the computerized wizardry of their planes' black boxes would do most of the navigation and bombing.

The heart of the A6 "smart" bombing system is in its big nose and a white basketball-like device hanging under it. The nose houses radar that can see a target more than 100 miles away. The heat-seeking and laser gear in the "basketball" does not come into play until the A6 is about 25 miles from the target.

F-111 and A6 radar see such big objects as buildings clearly in the dark and sketch their profiles on cockpit scopes. The radar cannot produce clear images of small targets, such as antiaircraft guns and fighter planes on the ground. If everything is working, the computerized bombing systems in each type of plane can hit a building with a single bomb but not destroy those near it. Secretary of Defense Caspar W. Weinberger said this was one reason that large buildings were chosen as targets in Libya, reducing the risk of "collateral damage," a euphemism for hitting something else, usually civilians.

The F-111 and A6 air crews were trained to follow elaborate procedures before dropping the so-called smart bombs. Those methods required the A6, for example, to match the radar profile of his target displayed from 100 miles away with the one the pilot had studied before takeoff. As the bomber, thundering at almost 500 mph, moved within 25 miles of the target shown on the radar scope, the A6 would start "mixing paint." This consisted of activating the basketball's heat-receiving gear, which displays heat from the targeted building as a black-and-white profile on a separate cockpit screen.

The bombardier would maneuver buttons and knobs to fine-tune the radar and heat sensor, the latter called forward-looking infrared. If the target matched the two sets of images programmed into the computer, the pilot would shoot a laser beam from the basketball when the plane came within five miles of the building. The building was now "painted."

With luck, the heat image would be so distinct that the bombardier could focus in his scope's crosshairs on a chosen window of the building. If the crosshairs slipped off the window as the plane maneuvered, he could move them back into position by jiggling a "joy stick." With the building "designated" by the laser beam, the pilot would punch buttons instructing the computer to take command of the bomb drop.

After the pilot and bombardier confirmed the target, the computer, calculating the plane's speed and drift, would release bombs at the precise moment required for a direct hit. A seeking device in the nose of a 500, 1,000 or 2,000-pound bomb would find the laser beam and ride it through the building window before the bomb exploded.

If, in reading his radar and scopes, the bombardier mistook an embassy or a house for his target, the smart bomb would destroy the wrong target, causing the collateral damage that President Reagan said the attackers sought to avoid. Bombs struck buildings in Libya not on the target list, including the French Embassy, but whether the smart bombs went awry or these buildings were damaged by stray Libyan fire remains at issue.

There were charges that the raid could have been conducted more simply and at less risk with only Navy aircraft, rather than the mix of Navy and Air Force warplanes. Indeed, the French had opposed the attack and did not permit the planes to fly through French airspace. And, of course, the irony was lost on no one that of all the diplomatic missions an errant bomb could have hit, it turned out to be the French Embassy. Some observers, especially those in France, wondered if it was an accident, especially with all the high-tech gadgetry that could precisely identify targeted buildings.

It was reported in *The Washington Post* on April 16, 1986, that some Pentagon officials suggested that the Air Force planes based in Britain were included only to give that service a piece of the action or to demonstrate that at least one ally, Britain, supported the mission.

The official Pentagon line was that there was a military need to use both the Air Force and the Navy planes to carry out a coordinated and simultaneous strike. Although the carriers USS Coral Sea and USS America together carry about 170 war planes, each had only a dozen planes equipped for nighttime, low-level attacks. The A6 Intruder squadrons could not have bombed all five targets simultaneously.

One of the F-111's had to turn back. Another that went missing never reached its target. A third F-111 completed its bombing mission but had mechanical troubles on the way back and had to make an emergency landing in Spain.

A fleet of twenty large KC10 refueling planes and twenty-two KC135 tankers, some of which apparently took off from other allied bases in the region, kept the F-111's flying, with four refuelings each on their way to Libya. Their flying time, six hours down and eight hours back, was lengthened by the refusal of the French to permit the planes to fly over their country.

Eight A6's carrying both unguided 500-pound bombs and 750-pound cluster bombs, attacked the Benina Military Airfield. They met no opposition and damaged five to twelve MiG23 fighters and several spare-parts hangars. Six other A6's, encountering heavy antiaircraft fire, bombed the Al Jamahiriyah Barracks, described as a Libyan alternate command post, with 500-pound bombs. The Pentagon provided no damage assessment.

As the F-111's reached their targets around Tripoli, a fleet of fourteen A6 Intruders were approaching targets in the east.

Meanwhile, other carrier-based anti-radar missiles and F/A18 Hornets were firing three dozen high-speed Anti-Radiation Missiles into Libyan radars. E2C Hawkeye command planes were scanning the skies for hostile aircraft, but none appeared.

Five F-111's, each carrying a dozen 500-pound bombs, attacked the military side of the Tripoli Airport, destroying three to five IL76 Soviet-built cargo planes. Eight F-111's, each carrying four 2,000-pound laser-guided bombs, attacked the Bab Azizia Barracks. The U.S. called these barracks the center of Libyan terrorism planning. The barracks were structurally damaged, and the intelligence services headquarters, said to be located in the barracks, was virtually destroyed. Three F-111's, also equipped with four laser-guided bombs each, attacked the Sidi Bilal Port west of Tripoli.

All attacks ended by 2:12 AM Libyan time, but the Libyans continued firing for some time thereafter. Radar at the SA5 site at Surt, which was not attacked, was turned on only after the U.S. planes had departed.

U.S. officials said the targets were chosen to hamper Libya's terrorist operations overseas while minimizing risk to U.S. pilots and possible harm to Libyan civilians. Attacks against inland oil facilities were considered and rejected, both because they would expose pilots to more antiaircraft fire and because Washington did not want to hit general economic targets.

Officials disingenuously stressed in early briefings to members of Congress that attacks on the Bab Azizia Barracks where Qadhafi lived were not intended to kill him.

"We were trying to send him a very clear message," one administration official said. "We were trying to make it clear that we would carry this directly to him and that we were prepared to impose the cost on him and his support operation, and thereby expose his ultimate vulnerability . . . "

Targets also were chosen in an effort to damage military units loyal to Qadhafi without inflicting as much harm on regular military troops. Some administration officials hoped that the attack would encourage military leaders, some of whom were already disenchanted with Qadhafi, to challenge him or his policies.

Officials also said that the missing F-111, even if downed in the Gulf of Sidra, might not have been the victim of hostile fire. One of its bombs could have exploded onboard, or it could have crashed for other reasons. No other planes were hit and there were no other U.S. casualties. Vice Admiral Frank B. Kelso, Sixth Fleet commander aboard the USS America, said he was surprised that no Libyan planes challenged the U.S. force.

THIRTEEN

Qadhafi's Home

The Bab Azizia Barracks are in the very center of a residential section of Tripoli. It was hard to imagine that civilians wouldn't have been killed in the raid. We careened through a few back alleys and came to a stop in a small parking lot. Two uniformed police guards greeted our caravan and waved us through a security gate. We had to use great care as we got out of our cars because rubble from the bombs dropped in this place six years before was strewn about the parking lot. Mrs. Hubbard had the only camera in the group. She took many pictures, including one of our party posing in front of Qadhafi's destroyed residence.

I had trouble understanding why they called the Bab Azizia a barracks at all. It appeared to be just another large cement home in a residential neighborhood. Everything was just as it was six years before. The guards opened the front door. Carefully stepping over scattered rubble, furnishings, and personal items, we entered the house. Youssef escorted us from room to room and gave us a play-by-play description of the events of that terrifying night.

First, we entered a large reception hall. Despite the disarray, one could see immediately that it had been a magnificent structure, well suited to receive presidents, prime ministers, kings and other heads of state.

I was awestruck at what I saw next. Situated almost in the direct center of the room were the remains of the fuselage of the U.S. F-111 warplane allegedly shot down by Libyan antiaircraft guns during the 1986 bombing.

Even more alarming was the sight of two flight suits and helmets inscribed with the names of the two pilots lost in the raid, Capt. Ribas-Dominicci and Capt. Lorence. It was shocking, but also puzzling. We Americans had been led to believe the U.S. account of the downing of the plane—the swept-winged, two-seat, fighter-bomber built by General Dynamics—had been hit over Libya, but crashed into the Mediterranean Sea, never to be found again.

The Washington Post reported the Defense Department version the day after the attack on April 16, 1986:

> An F-111 bomber and its two-man crew was lost at sea in the massive 12-minute raid on Libya, which officials otherwise characterized as a successful and complex mission involving 30 bombers and about 100 support planes. Libyan fighter jets, cargo planes, airport hangars and military barracks were damaged in the raid on five military targets in the port cities of Tripoli and Benghazi. But cloud cover over the areas bombed in

> Operation El Dorado Canyon interfered with U.S. photo reconnaissance missions and the Pentagon could provide no assessment of eyewitness reports that U.S. bombs also damaged embassies and residences and injured civilians.
>
> While Pentagon authorities and U.S. servicemen involved in the Libyan raid expressed pride in carrying out the complicated and dangerous raid ordered by President Reagan, officials acknowledged that it could be days before a more complete account of the damage is pieced together, and that the fate of the missing F-111 may never be known.

Well, now the fate of the F-111 and the two-man crew appeared to be known to me and the other members of our party. I reached into my memory to put the various parts of the story together. I wished that I could remember more about the details of the incident six years before.

Were these really the flight suits and helmets the two men had worn, or was it just another outlandish publicity stunt Qadhafi was so inclined to pull? I was skeptical. How was it possible for this warplane, traveling at nearly 500 mph, to have crashed right into Qadhafi's home? How could the journalists, who had been allowed to visit this site right after the raid, not have seen it?

Some of the pilots on the raid had reported seeing a fireball in the Tripoli area just before the bomber reached its target, although there was no official speculation on whether the plane had been shot down by Libyan antiaircraft fire.

Reportedly, U.S. search-and-rescue aircraft and vessels, including submarines, had searched the Mediterranean north of Tripoli late into the night. The searchers did not detect the electronic beeps that an F-111 automatically emits if its crew is able to eject before a crash.

The Air Force identified the missing crew members as pilot Capt. Fernando L. Ribas-Dominicci, thirty-three, a native of Puerto Rico, and bombardier-navigator Capt. Paul F. Lorence, thirty-one, a San Francisco native. Their plane flew from the Royal Air Force base at Lakenheath, England, where they were assigned to the Air Force's 48th Tactical Fighter Wing. These were the very names on the helmets and jumpsuits I was staring at.

Years later, in April 2006, on the twentieth anniversary of the U.S. bombing of Libya, I received the following email message that resurrected what I had seen fourteen years earlier in the Bab Azizia Barracks.

> Hello Mr. Chasey,
>
> My name is Trish Bullman and I am writing on behalf of Jeff Kruger, stepbrother to fallen USAF Captain Paul Lorence.
>
> We tried to reach you a few months back via this same email address with no response. I am hoping you will take the time to reply as Mr. Kruger has initiated intense efforts to discover what really happened to the remains of his stepbrother, Capt. Lorence.
>
> Although he has made substantial progress in his quest, he is now at a critical point in his investigation and feels strongly that you may hold answers to key questions. Of particular interest is the mention of the airmen's flight suits in your book, Pan AM 103, The Lockerbie Cover-up.
>
> Mr. Kruger's story is gaining much media attention; however it is imperative that he have as much accurate information as possible if any hope of bringing peace and closure to his family is to continue.

I sincerely hope you will grant him the opportunity to ask of you a few questions that may assist him in his quest.

Sincerely,
Trish Bullman[8]

The ground floor of the barracks looked like a Hollywood set. Although the walls were still standing, there was very little left of the interior. Amazingly, there were no signs of a post-bombing fire, but every window in the house was broken and had since been boarded up with plywood. Everything was covered with six years' accumulation of dirt and dust. We walked from room to room, imagining the terror of that early morning raid. We climbed a shaky spiral staircase to the second floor, wondering if it would support our weight.

Youssef opened the door to a second-floor room. It was the bedroom of Muammar Qadhafi. Prominent in the large space was a round bed almost completely covered with debris from the ceiling above. In place of a headboard, the bed had a wraparound stereo system, something one might have expected to find in the Honeymoon Motel in the Pocono Mountains of Pennsylvania, or the Chicken Ranch Brothel in Texas, but not in the "Leader's" bedroom. It was also quite eerie as the room was still full of personal items including pictures of his children, an electric razor, perfumes, combs, brushes and closets filled with Qadhafi's and his wife Safia's clothing.

According to Libya, Qadhafi's three children were all victims of the attack. Two of them were hospitalized in intensive care for many days, suffering from pressure shock from the 2,000-pound bomb that made a direct hit on their home. Hannah, Qadhafi's adopted daughter, allegedly died a few hours later.

We went from bedroom to bedroom and saw where Qadhafi's two sons, Saif al-Islam and Khamis, had been sleeping when the bombs fell. Khamis was allegedly rendered unconscious by the explosion and didn't regain consciousness for five days.

The most moving part of the tour was visiting one of the smaller bedrooms, which had belonged to Hannah, Qadhafi's adopted sixteen-month-old daughter. The Libyans reported that she had been killed in the raid.[9]

Hannah's bedroom was not much different from those of American toddlers her age. Her toys were scattered about the room just as she had left them. Now, they were covered with dust, cobwebs and ceiling plaster. As a father, I couldn't help but feel great sadness for this innocent little girl.

Photos of Qadhafi with Hannah were scattered, in broken picture frames, on the floor where they had fallen. One in particular stands out in my mind. Qadhafi—sitting on a large throne-type chair, with Hannah on his lap—held a small, pale-blue teddy bear in his left hand, in front of her face, as he tried to make her smile for the camera. It was quite moving, especially when, not more than five feet away, I saw the same little blue teddy bear lying with some of her other toys in the remains of her pink toy box. Again, I reminded myself that this could have been staged.

Two newer pictures were hanging on the wall above Hannah's bed. One was of her lying on a hospital bed after the bombing. She was already dead when the photo was taken. Wearing only a diaper, her body displayed the open wounds she suffered. The second picture seemed entirely out of place. It was a photograph of what appeared to be a young Western girl in her early twenties.

As I stared at it, Youssef volunteered that she was Flora Swire, one of the victims of the Pan Am 103 bombing. In December

1991, her father, Dr. James Swire, spent five days in Tripoli and met with Qadhafi. Among other topics, the two men discussed their daughters, both of whom had been indiscriminately killed. Dr. Swire, spokesman for the British Lockerbie relatives, offered—and Qadhafi accepted—a photograph of Flora. Qadhafi, touched by the gesture, hung the picture in Hannah's room as a symbol of the great personal loss both men shared.

We stood in the large reception room of the barracks once again and continued to ask questions of Youssef. He told us how the raid had affected his leader. Qadhafi became a changed man. He wanted to be a part of the world community again.

"That is why this Lockerbie thing makes him crazy," Youssef explained.

Khaled responded to a crackling call on his hand-held radio. It was obvious that this was a very important call. Khaled abruptly handed the radio to Youssef, who began a long, loud, and animated discussion in Arabic, while continuously looking at his watch, as if pressed for time.

I too was starting to get concerned about the time. It was imperative that we leave soon in order to reach Djerba before dark or else we would end up spending the night in Tunisia instead of Geneva. I really wanted to catch my flight back to Washington the next day.

Youssef finally handed the radio back to Khaled with a few instructions in Arabic. Khaled turned on his heels and hurried away.

Meanwhile, Youssef slowly turned around to us and in a very serious tone stated, "My leader wants to meet with you today before you leave."

It had been Qadhafi's personal assistant on the radio. He had been instructed to do whatever possible to arrange a meeting between us and Qadhafi.

We walked out of the barracks and continued our discussion in the parking lot, debating the pros and cons of extending our stay in Libya. On the one hand, it would be very exciting to actually meet the "most feared man in the world," undoubtedly a chance of a lifetime. On the other hand, the time available to make Djerba was running out. My plans to return to Washington the next day looked increasingly doubtful. Of course, looming over our heads was the knowledge that for all intents and purposes, no one knew where we were and that no doubt Virginia was getting extremely worried, because she hadn't heard from me.

Youssef proposed a plan. By the expression on his face, I could tell this was going to be another, "it will only take a few hours" idea. He suggested that we take a walk through downtown Tripoli and wait for his leader to call for us. We could meet with Qadhafi for an hour or so, return to the El Mahari for a few hours of rest, and then leave for Djerba at midnight. If we departed Djerba at 3 AM we would arrive at the Geneva airport when it opened at 6 AM, which would allow us to catch our flight to Washington. He would arrange for the pilots to be ready for our arrival at the Djerba Airport. And with a sly smile, he actually said, "It will only take a few hours."

By this time we were out of options. Even if we had left immediately, we would have missed the arrival window in Geneva and ended up spending the night in the Djerba airport. We decided to agree to Youssef's plan and prepare for this unique and rather daunting meeting with Qadhafi.

FOURTEEN

Clandestine Meeting

After an hour wandering around the outdoor marketplace, we returned to the El Mahari Hotel to rest and wait for the call from Qadhafi. We had the same rooms we had occupied the previous night and as before, the rooms had been catered with trays of fruits, cheese and pastries. All in all, it had been a pleasant afternoon and a rare opportunity to taste a bit of normal Libyan life.

I desperately wanted to call Virginia, knowing that by now she had tried unsuccessfully to contact me at the Noga Hilton in Geneva. I knew it would still be too much of a risk to have a record of my telephone call from Libya to America picked up by some NSA spy satellite. If my friendly CIA agent Mr. "DuPont" from Delaware didn't know where I was by now, a call to the States would pinpoint my room in the El Mahari Hotel.

I had just stretched out on my bed, when there was a soft knock on the door. It was Khaled. He asked that I go with him right away. I said that I wanted to clean up a bit first, but he insisted that we move quickly so that the others in my party wouldn't know that I was leaving the hotel. He was very firm in his manner and tone.

He explained that Youssef had promised me a special meeting before I left Tripoli and everything had now been arranged. He was very careful not to mention where we were going or with whom we would be meeting. My instincts told me that perhaps I was about to meet the two men accused of committing the most heinous crime ever against Western civilians, a crime which launched the greatest international counterterrorist investigation ever conducted, spanning four continents and nearly forty countries. My adrenaline began to surge again.

Grabbing my coat, I quickly followed Khaled to a service elevator located at the far end of the hall. As we approached the elevator, I recalled that horrible, December afternoon in Vail, when I first heard the news of the Lockerbie disaster on CNN. And now, four years later here I was about to meet the two alleged mass murderers.

The elevator door was held open by two JOS agents. Youssef and two more agents were already in the elevator. Youssef greeted me with a very stern face. As the elevator door closed, I was instructed not to talk until we were safely in the cars at the back door of the hotel. The lighthearted tone of an hour ago in the marketplace had abruptly changed.

We exited the elevator into a hall just behind the kitchen. It was a strange scene. The hall was devoid of hotel employees. Well-dressed JOS agents were posted at every entrance to the hallway—obviously cleared so that no one would see me leaving the hotel.

"I hope you don't mind if my men search you before we leave," Youssef said matter-of-factly. I was caught off guard, but calmly granted his request.

I was asked to stand with my arms extended away from my sides as a JOS agent gave me a thorough pat-down. As the search continued, I realized they were not looking for weapons, but for recording devices or cameras concealed on my person. One agent carefully inspected every little seam and pocket of my coat for hidden wires or bugs. My watch and glasses were given special attention, as were my belt and shoes which they asked me to remove. My Mont Blanc mechanical pencil was inspected with great care and then confiscated by one of the agents who handed it to Youssef. When I raised my eyebrows at this, he assured me the pencil would be returned later and that he would explain the need for these precautions when we got in the car.

Agents began to scurry about. Handheld radios were alive with static in Arabic as we approached the hotel's plain, windowless steel back door. We hesitated just long enough for one agent to help me slide into an ugly, long, tan trench coat and a wide-brimmed, 1940's-style fedora hat—better suited for Humphrey Bogart than me. The hat's huge brim easily covered my face. Youssef roughly pulled the coat's collar up so it touched the back of the hat brim. Under any other circumstances, I would have felt utterly foolish. He gave the front brim of the hat one final tug down and I was ready to leave the hotel.

"Please wait here for a moment while we make a final check outside," Youssef said.

A few of his men went ahead and quickly signaled us to follow. As we left the hotel, I could see that the streets surrounding the hotel were blocked with barricades. Except for the JOS agents, no one else was visible. I was hurried into the back seat of the black Mercedes parked at curbside. Inside, the window curtains were tightly shut. I really hoped that my instincts were correct and we were on a "friendly mission."

Youssef and one agent got into the back seat with me, and we sped away from the hotel with sirens blaring. The black curtain separating us from the driver had also been closed and, although I couldn't see him, I recognized Khaled's voice coming from the front passenger seat. I couldn't see out of the windows and no one could see us inside. Judging from the noise of the sirens, there was one police car in front and at least two behind.

I removed my Bogart hat and unbuttoned the front of the trench coat while Youssef began his explanation.

"We are going to meet with the two guys I promised this morning, Chazzy. We will meet in a special place, but I can't let you know where it is or how we get there. We don't want anybody knowing that we took you there, understand? This information would be very useful to your government, and some people would pay big money to know their whereabouts. We had to be sure that you weren't wearing a wire. After all, I have only known you a short while and you could be a CIA agent. I like you a lot, but I can't be too careful with the lives of these men."

He further explained that he was responsible for the safety of these suspects. If the U. S. government knew where we were going, it might launch a black-ops raid to spirit them out of Libya or have them killed.

"Remember what President Bush did in 1989 to arrest President Manuel Noriega of Panama and move him to the United States? He didn't get congressional approval for the invasion of

Panama, which was a direct violation of your own Constitution, not to mention international law. He would do anything to get his hands on these two men. I hope you understand, Chazzy. No matter what happens, we will always deny that we brought you here and that you met with these guys. This must remain *entre nous*," he said.

I checked my watch as we came to a rather abrupt halt exactly thirteen minutes after leaving the hotel.

"We won't have much time with them," Youssef said. "I don't want your friends to find out that you are not in your room. They may call you for some reason, so I had your phone fixed to give only a busy signal. Your Congressman Hubbard may get suspicious after a while and come knocking on your door."

I was told to cover my face again with the hat as we prepared to leave the car. I could hear people milling about outside. Youssef gave specific instructions of how to proceed when I left the car. I was to keep my head down with my eyes fixed on the ground in front of me, to move as quickly as possible, and to do exactly what Khaled told me to do. I was instructed to walk between two agents, who had the responsibility of seeing that I didn't bump into anything. Once inside, I could ask whatever questions I wanted, but Youssef had kept my pencil so that I could not take notes.

Over the years I have developed an excellent memory for details. The members of Congress wouldn't talk as freely if I was taking notes during our conversations. I was going to have to rely heavily on that skill to remember enough of the meeting to make notes afterwards. (Later, I reviewed a variety of sources to refresh my memory so that I could more accurately complete a written report of this clandestine meeting.)

I was rushed out of the car into a large, single house that appeared to be situated in a quiet residential neighborhood. I could see just below the brim of my hat that there was a lot of security around the house. I was led into a large reception area and then, without stopping, into what appeared to be the dining room of the house. And just like that, I was eye to eye with Abdelbasset Ali Mohammed al-Megrahi and Lamen Khalifa Fhimah, two of the most wanted and hated mass murderers in the world!

These were truly billion-dollar men. As a result of the international sanctions imposed because of Qadhafi's refusal to turn over these men for trial, $953.1 million in Libyan assets had been frozen in banks around the world. Libya had also run out of critical medicines and medical supplies, which had taken a major toll on the Libyan people. Libya's oil industry had been impaired due to the shortage of spare parts and a lack of maintenance.

It was easy to understand the need for all this secrecy.

Fhimah and Megrahi, along with their lawyer, whose name I believe was Ibraham B. Legwell, politely stood as I entered the room. Each vigorously shook my hand. Fhimah said something in Arabic and a young female translator said, "Good afternoon, and welcome to Libya." I thanked them and took a seat at the dining table directly across from the two accused men. Youssef sat to my right and the translator sat at the head of the table. I was offered coffee or tea. A plate of small cakes and cookies was in the center of the table between us.

I very carefully studied the two men and tried my best to memorize their individual features. They were both dressed in double breasted, designer business suits and each wore colorful neckties. Fhimah was on the heavy side and had a prominent mustache. His olive-colored skin seemed soft and smooth and shone in the light of an overhead lamp. He had a most pleasant smile and seemed genuinely happy to meet me.

Megrahi was thin. He had curly jet-black hair. He wore tinted aviator- style glasses, which obscured his eyes. I felt no warmth from Megrahi. He avoided eye contact. My first impression was that he seemed to be rather shifty. He sat quietly, his eyes focused on a writing pad in from of him.

Remembering Youssef's time constraints, I went right to the heart of the matter. I asked each man directly if he had prepared the explosives and then smuggled them aboard the plane through a connecting flight from Malta, which had destroyed Pan Am 103 and the lives of 270 innocent people. In turn, each man looked me in the eye and denied any responsibility. I looked for signs that they might be lying. They both seemed very calm and matter-of-fact in their response. There was no obvious fidgeting or beads of perspiration forming on their brows.

Of course, I'm not a psychologist, trained to detect lies. And the fact is even lie detectors are inadmissible in court.

I asked each man to respond to my second question individually. Did they know who was responsible for the Lockerbie disaster?

Fhimah responded first. "Authorities in the United States and Britain know who did it. They have had the evidence since early 1989, but have failed to act on it."

Megrahi added that the answer was to be found in Syria and Iran, not in Libya.

"We have been a convenient scapegoat for the United States," he said. "The evidence against us is circumstantial and would never stand up in court, even if we could get a fair trial in some neutral country."

Fhimah suggested that I review a February 1992, eighty-page report from the Palestine Liberation Organization, which provided fresh evidence of Iranian involvement in the Lockerbie bombing. The report focused on why the Scottish police and the American FBI had changed their minds after claiming for months that the bombing was committed by members of Ahmed Jibril's group, the Popular Front for the Liberation of Palestine-General Command under the umbrella of Iran and Syria.

Fhimah said, "The report includes the most specific evidence yet of Iran's role in the bombing."

In the report, Bassam Abu Sharif, the political adviser to PLO chairman Yassir Arafat and, coincidently, my new "friend" from the olive tree luncheon in Cap Antibes, claimed that the PLO had "gathered very accurate and sensitive information related to the Lockerbie affair," and that this information "points clearly to the involvement of Middle East parties, not Libya, in this crime." The report details meetings between Ahmed Jibril, Ali Akbar Mohtashami, the former Iranian interior minister, and other Iranians to discuss the planned attack.

The PLO itself was somewhat surprised by the seeming lack of interest on the part of the Lockerbie investigators to talk to them in their new role as a mainstream political entity. Not surprisingly, the PLO pinned the blame for Lockerbie on an old enemy, Ahmed Jibril, who broke away from the PLO in 1986. The report said Jibril's group made and planted the bomb on Flight 103 and that Iran paid them $10 million for their trouble. The PLO went further, stating that the money was handed over to Jibril in Libya, which appeared to draw Qadhafi into the scenario.

But, could the PLO be trusted as a reliable source?

The Libyan lawyer for the accused terrorists gave me a copy of an editorial to read. It had appeared in London's *Sunday Times* on November 24, 1991. He said that the U.S. motivation for accusing Libya was well documented. He had underlined the following paragraph in red: (Upon my return home, I obtained a copy of this editorial just to be sure it had not been altered.)

> Maybe it has been necessary to be nice to Iran and Syria to secure the release of the remaining hostages in Beirut. It must be more than coincidence that both countries were officially cleared of any Lockerbie involvement just a few days before Terry Waite and Thomas Sutherland were at last released. Our joy at their freedom should be tempered by the shame of the cost: the relatives of the victims of the Lockerbie bomb must now come to terms with the fact that most of those behind the murder of their loved ones are going to get away with it. The cause of justice is being sacrificed on the altar of diplomatic convenience. We will live to regret it.

Fhimah explained that the West knew full well that Libya would not turn them over to the United States or Britain for trial. He pointed out that this standoff served the United States well.

"The U.S. doesn't have to account for its actions in our indictments," he said. "This could go on for years, and the U.S. has escaped the immense political pressure that was building against them before our indictments. The U.S. has no more right to extradite us to your country, than we do to extradite one of your citizens to ours."

This theme was highlighted in a lead article in the *International Herald-Tribune* on January 17, 1992, written by UN correspondent Ian Williams, in which he noted:

> One can imagine the reaction of the White House if Nicaragua had tried to extradite Oliver North for his admitted terrorist actions against the Sandinista government. It is not necessary to be an admirer of the Qadhafi regime

> to suspect that double standards are rapidly becoming the accepted reserve currency of the New World Order.

My mind was exhausted by this bombardment of conflicting information. Was I the victim of Libyan propaganda or was there some truth to what I was hearing? Could these two men be innocent, or were they just very well-trained pathological liars?

After all, the Lockerbie investigation had been conducted in forty countries. No less than 16,000 statements had been taken and more than 20,000 names had been recorded on computers. The investigation had cost an estimated $22 million. Could the investigators have been wrong? Or was there, as Fhimah suggested, an international political conspiracy to cover up important evidence so that the blame for the bombing could be shifted to Libya? That possibility seemed far-fetched with so many investigators involved, some of whom were probably ready to blow the whistle if their evidence was suddenly doctored.

FIFTEEN

Chasing Qadhafi

Just as Fhimah and Megrahi were finishing up, the phone rang in the adjoining room. Khaled summoned Youssef to the telephone. He quickly returned and announced, "The leader wants to see you now."

He shouted instructions to the JSO agents. After handshakes with Fhimah and Megrahi, I was once again veiled in my trench coat and wide-brimmed hat and escorted out of the front door and into the waiting limo.

Again, with a multitude of blaring sirens, we sped away back to the El Mahari Hotel. Youssef said his men had notified Bovenkamp and the Hubbards to be ready when we arrived. He would put them in another car so they wouldn't notice that I had been out of the hotel. We had to hurry because his leader was going to be leaving shortly, and we had some distance to travel. We pulled into the hotel driveway in exactly eight minutes. Neither Bovenkamp nor the Hubbards were anywhere in sight.

One JSO agent reported that Mrs. Hubbard was not quite ready but would be down shortly. As we waited, Youssef became agitated.

"My leader is waiting. Don't they understand?" he asked angrily. "This makes me crazy, Chazzy."

The car phones and hand-held radios were blaring the entire time we were waiting. Bovenkamp finally arrived. It was obvious that he had been awakened from a sound sleep.

He asked, "What have you been doing? Your phone has been busy for hours!"

I told him I took the phone off the hook in order to get a little uninterrupted sleep.

The Hubbards hurriedly left the hotel and apologized for their tardiness. They had also been asleep when the call came. Bovenkamp got in the car with Youssef and me. The Hubbards rode in the car behind us. Tires squealed as we sped away from the hotel. We were on our way to meet Col. Muammar al-Qadhafi, the man so hated by the Western world.

Youssef said that we would be meeting Qadhafi in his tent located just outside of town. I had heard so much about his predilection for living in a tent, but it was hard to believe that I was about to see this for myself. The trip out of town was much like the one we took into town the night before, fast, noisy, exciting and confusing.

Dusk was settling in as we left the city. From the back seat of the car, it was very difficult to see which direction we were taking. The farther from the city we drove, the faster we went, once again reaching speeds of a 100 mph on a dark highway.

The sirens were deafening, making it difficult to hear Youssef as he tried to clarify the reason for our speed. He said that Qadhafi moved his tent frequently to avoid another surprise raid by U.S. planes. The location of his tent was top secret.

He explained that Qadhafi was a Bedouin ("dwellers in the desert") who belonged to a small tribe, the Gaddafa (literally "those who spit out vomit"). Many Bedouins have retained their nomadic and pastoral way of life. Like most nomads, Qadhafi was very much accustomed to moving frequently from one place to another. He was very comfortable living and working in a tent, although he often spent time at his home in Tripoli. As a matter of fact, he was planning on leaving the tent that very night for the city. It was imperative that we got there before he moved. Thanks to Mrs. Hubbard, we were already a half-hour late.

Almost as quickly as we had started, we came to an abrupt stop on the side of the highway. All of a sudden it was very still. The sirens stopped and the headlights of the cars in our caravan were turned off. We sat quietly as we waited for the police cars to block traffic from the front and the rear. When all traffic was stopped, Youssef gave instructions on the car radio.

We made a sharp left turn across the four-lane highway and onto a dirt road. With our headlights still out, we made our way along the winding, dusty road with only the benefit of the low beams on the lead car. I couldn't imagine how our drivers were able to see where they were going. I understood the need to keep the tent's location secret, but not at the risk of our lives.

We drove down the deserted road for about five minutes, making a few fast turns along the way. There was no chance that any of us could have ever retraced our route.

We came to a halt at a large chain-linked gate, guarded by two casually dressed Libyan guards with Kalashnikov rifles. The only light came from a small lamp located in the guard shack, which had rolled concertina barbed wire on top of it

Youssef left the car and approached the guards. The news he received was not good. It was obvious from his body language that he was upset. At one point he kicked the ground as his voice got louder.

From my vantage point in the back of the car, I could see Qadhafi's tent behind the fence and a few bushes. The typical Bedouin tent is made from strips of cloth woven from goat or camel hair and vegetable fibers. It was sewn together and dyed black. Qadhafi's tent was not black but more of a brown color. It was very large and I was told that it served as both Qadhafi's office and home. He used it to entertain heads of state as well as average citizens. Khaled said that part of Qadhafi's appeal to the Libyan people was his commitment to traditional Arab values and the Muslim religion.

Approximately a million Bedouins follow the traditional lifestyle of nomadic herders in the deserts of the Middle East. Almost all of them are Muslim and speak either Berber or some dialect of Arabic. The Bedouin travel the desert seeking fresh water and vegetation for their camels, goats, and sheep. They live in tents and wear clothing made from the skin and hair of their animals. They eat mostly dairy products, dates and rice, while trading meat and dairy products with people in nearby villages for knives, pots, and other manufactured goods. They are proud and extremely independent. They live by a moral code that emphasizes courage, generosity, and tribal loyalty. Insults often lead to bloody feuds.

It became increasingly clear that Qadhafi had just left. How disappointing! My chance of meeting Qadhafi was now in doubt. Had we delayed our departure for Geneva for nothing? Finally, Youssef threw up his arms and returned to the car.

"We missed him by ten minutes," he yelled, as he got back in the car. "These people make me crazy, Chazzy. We will go back to Tripoli and meet my leader at the Al Jamahiriyah Barracks where he is staying tonight."

Once again we found ourselves speeding down the dark dirt road with lights out and radios blaring. The dust seemed to be ten times worse than before. Once we hit the paved road, the sirens started up again. Now, we followed our police escort cars that were waiting for us at the end of the dirt road, hidden from sight behind some shrubs. I instinctively gripped the handle strap hanging from the top of the door and tensed my body for the race back to Tripoli. The ride took about twelve minutes, during most of it Youssef talked heatedly in Arabic on the car radio.

Our cars finally slowed down as we entered the city, the sirens silenced. We drove into a residential neighborhood. After a few zigzags, two sharply dressed Libyan soldiers waved us through the front gates of a military establishment. Our drivers knew just where to go. We came to a sudden halt in front of a very military barrack-type building, not much different from those I remembered from my days as a Marine at Camp Lejeune. We were once again near the Bab Azizia Barracks.

As we exited our vehicles, I quickly talked with the Hubbards and Bovenkamp. They had been in the limo just behind ours on this incredible night excursion around Tripoli. I learned that their driver and bodyguards spoke no English, so they had no idea why we had driven out into the desert and why we were back at the Bab Azizia Barracks.

Hubbard said, "What the hell is going on? That was the scariest ride I have ever taken. What are we doing here?"

I explained that we were about to be granted an audience with Qadhafi. Looking a bit shocked, Mrs. Hubbard asked if I thought it would be safe to meet him. I assured her that there was nothing to fear. Nevertheless, everyone was extremely anxious.

We walked up the front steps of the barracks and were warmly greeted by a Libyan man named Ahmed. He was dressed in casual pants and a leather jacket. He said he was a graduate of the University of Michigan and that he would be serving as our interpreter during our meeting with Qadhafi. This was somewhat reassuring. He escorted us down a long hallway and into a beautiful reception room.

Moments later, two lovely Arab women—dressed to kill in the finest Western clothing with spiked heels and tight-fitting dresses—joined us. Ahmed introduced them to us as Qadhafi's bodyguards. I remembered reading that he used female bodyguards for many years, but I had not expected them to be dressed to "kill" quite like this.

We were invited to sit in the reception room. During the thirty-minute wait, Adel, one of the bodyguards, gave us a brief lesson on women's rights in Libya. Mrs. Hubbard was very interested in the topic and questioned her extensively about the role of women in Libya.

As a good feminist, Democrat Carol Hubbard liked what she was hearing, which could have been taken directly out of the 1982 Democratic platform.

Adel and her counterpart asked Mrs. Hubbard to join them at the other end of the large room, which seemed odd and a bit sexist, but what hadn't been odd that day? The ladies sat and talked together as Hubbard, Bovenkamp, and I nervously awaited the arrival of Qadhafi. Youssef had not entered the reception room with us. We passed the time by talking with Ahmed about the American elections. He was glad to get some news from the States. He thanked us for our patience and explained that Qadhafi had just arrived and that it should only be a few more minutes before we would meet him.

Finally, Youssef entered and asked us to follow him. I think all four us were extremely anxious, because we were about to meet one of the most infamous men in the world. Mrs. Hubbard and the bodyguards joined us as we walked down the long hall to Qadhafi's office.

I could see that she was extremely agitated and couldn't wait to tell us something.

She caught up with her husband and whispered, "He wants to talk to me alone after the meeting."

Congressman Hubbard looked shocked and couldn't speak.

She continued, "Adel said that Qadhafi has something to say to me in private."

I tried to ease the tension with a bit of levity. I told the Hubbards that like the ancient *droit du seigneur,* this was part of an old Libyan tradition. The first time an important guest meets the leader, he is expected to share his wife with him. My little joke did evoke an uneasy smile, but did little else to ease the high anxiety we were feeling.

"Let's wait and see what happens during our meeting before we get too upset," I suggested. "The last thing Qadhafi wants is to create an international incident over a congressman's pretty wife."

SIXTEEN

The Leader

As we approached a double door at the end of the hall, a well-dressed Libyan man in his forties greeted us and escorted us into Qadhafi's office. I expected that we would sit and wait another thirty minutes for Qadhafi to arrive, so I was taken aback when I found myself face to face with the leader, who was sitting on an ornate, cream-colored couch at the far end of the large room. He politely stood as we entered. A photographer, already in place, started snapping pictures of our arrival, which upset Congressman Hubbard.

His first words to Qadhafi were, "I prefer that no photos be taken of our visit."

Qadhafi seemed perturbed. He said a few words in Arabic to Ahmed, and the photographer quickly left the room.

I was embarrassed by Hubbard's behavior. I could understand why he didn't want a record of our meeting with Qadhafi, but there was a more diplomatic way to have handled it. I hoped that this wouldn't set a negative tone for our meeting.

Qadhafi graciously greeted each of us as we approached. Youssef, in turn, introduced us to his leader. We shook hands and exchanged pleasantries. I was the last to meet Qadhafi and deliberately delayed my handshake as I tried to make eye contact with him. He firmly shook my hand but avoided looking directly at me. I didn't like that.

He was much shorter than I had expected. Bedouins are usually somewhat shorter than normal, and I guessed him to be about five foot ten inches tall. I knew that Qadhafi spoke fluent English, but he responded to me only in Arabic through Ahmed. He extended his arm and invited me to join my colleagues already sitting on couches arranged directly in front of his.

I studied Qadhafi carefully. I looked at every detail of his person for characteristics I could recall. His puffy face and swarthy complexion seemed almost aquiline in its features. He had a black mole just below his left nostril. His dark, penetrating eyes seemed to look right through me. Only strands of his black kinky hair on the top and sides of his head were visible from under his tan, loose-fitting headscarf, called a *kaffiyeh.*

He was dressed in a full-length brown robe, tied over his left shoulder and somehow draped over his right. The robe covered an aqua Nehru-style jacket with a gold embroidered high collar and trim that ran down the front of the jacket, disappearing beneath the robe at mid-chest level. There was a plain gold wedding band on his left hand. (Good Muslims weren't supposed to wear gold jewelry.)

Seeing Qadhafi in this attire, I was again reminded of the remark attributed to President Reagan in an August 14, 1986, meeting with George Schultz, Casper Weinberger, Bill Casey, John Poindexter and Admiral William Crowe. They were celebrating their successful bombing raid on Libya, and were considering a fresh disinformation campaign against Qadhafi. Reagan quipped, "Why not invite Qadhafi to San Francisco? He likes to dress up so much!" Schultz retorted, "Why don't we give him AIDS." Everyone laughed.

The leader began by thanking each of us by name for having the courage to visit Libya. He spoke very quietly. His deliberate speaking manner was accentuated by the time delay necessary for Ahmed to translate his remarks into English. Qadhafi said that he hoped that our visit would open a new era of positive relationships between our two countries. He stared straight ahead and made no attempt to engage our eyes or to observe our reactions to his comments. I remember thinking that this arrogant guy was one "cold turkey."

As he spoke I tried to take mental photos of his office. The room was stark and completely devoid of color, paintings, or ornamentation. The deep carpet was white, as was most of his furniture. The room was rigidly conforming in its style and decoration. Qadhafi's cream couch was positioned in front of a white folding wall, opened halfway, which separated this formal reception room from the more functional working office, located just behind the wall. This kind of decoration gave me a window into the soul of this man. He was a black-and-white kind of guy, used to giving orders without the benefit of counsel.

A small, cloth-draped coffee table separated us from Qadhafi. He had a stack of papers and a small box containing a colorful array of pencils and pens in the middle of the table. A copy of Qadhafi's *Green Book,* which outlined the sociopolitical model for Libya, was prominently displayed on the table in front of him. This philosophical model was first outlined in 1973 at a symposium in Paris and further developed into three installments, now published as the *Green Book.* Part One heralded the start of the era of the Jamahiriya (state of the masses). Part Two inaugurated an international, economic revolution, which was to do away with the old economic structures of society. Part Three launched Qadhafi's social revolution.

Obviously, Qadhafi was suffering from an extreme case of grandiosity. On the back cover of his book, which I later read, he had written the following summary:

> It presents the genuine interpretation of history, the solution of man's struggle in life, and the unsolved problems of man and woman. Equally it tackles the problem of minorities and of blacks in order to lay down the sound principles of social life for all mankind. The living philosophy is inseparable from life itself and erupts from its essence.

Congressman Hubbard thanked Qadhafi for his hospitality and time. Realizing that he had been discourteous in how he had handled the photographer, he apologized profusely. Just when he seemed to be successfully making amends, he again insulted Qadhafi with a dismal attempt at humor.

"I don't want a picture of us appearing together in the *Mayfield, Kentucky,* newspaper," he snickered.

He made matters worse when he asked Qadhafi if it would be all right for Mrs. Hubbard to take some photos after our meeting.

Without responding, Qadhafi simply started talking again. He expressed delight in the election of Bill Clinton just one week before.

"The people of Libya were celebrating in the streets as the election news started arriving here," he said. "I think there is a great opportunity for us to reestablish a cooperative relationship between the United States and Libya under Mr. Clinton's administration. We suspect that Mr. Clinton will deal with us honestly, and do all in his power to get to the bottom of the Pan Am 103 disaster."

Qadhafi repeated Muntassir's story that Clinton had told Pan Am 103 families on September 17, 1992, that he would make sure that all questions regarding Syrian and Iranian involvement were fully investigated.

"This leads me to believe that the investigation will be reopened and those truly responsible for the bombing will be indicted and brought to justice," Qadhafi said.

He also said that he was looking for our help in getting the president-elect to consider a new dialogue with the people of Libya.

"I thank you, Mr. Chasey, for bringing Congressman and Mrs. Hubbard to Libya to help us get to the bottom of this case. Col. Debri and the Committee to Resolve the Lockerbie Dispute have been trying in vain to get an elected official from the United States to discuss the issue with us for over a year now. In every case our outreach has been rejected. I want you to know how much I and the people of my country appreciate all you have done."

Qadhafi then turned and said, "Congressman Hubbard, you have the opportunity to tell Mr. Clinton what you have heard and seen here during your visit. As you know, two of our countrymen have been accused by your country in the 1988 bombing of Pan AM 103. I can assure you that these two men are innocent and are ready to stand trial but only in a neutral country. We don't believe they would receive a fair trial in your country."

He repeated what we already knew. The UN Security Council had voted to impose a ban on air travel and arms sales to Libya unless he surrendered the two indicted Libyans to the United States.

"This ban on air travel has been very hurtful to my fellow countrymen. I am asking you to relate the results of our meeting to your new president, upon your return to the United States. I am also requesting that you and Dr. Chasey relate my country's foreign policy philosophy to the members of the United States Congress. This U.S. election is a time of renewal for us."

Qadhafi continued his remarks by stating that, "No nation can afford to ignore the momentous changes that have occurred in the world in recent years. The foreign policy of every country today must reflect the new realities."

(Thankfully, Youssef had returned my pencil, so I could take notes. What I missed I later filled in from some of Qadhafi's speeches.)

He went on, "My country is affected by these radical changes. It is a fact, of which little notice has been taken in the West, that Libya has quite recently inaugurated a new assembly of elected representatives of each of the tribal groups of the nation. This assembly has just met for the first time earlier in the month. It was a time of historic change. The assembly was established in order to insure a full and fair opportunity for expression to each of the identifiable interest groups of the state. It is to insure that the government is effectively representative and is an expression of the popular will of the people. In this first meeting, the assembly fully justified its purpose."

He took several sips of tea and continued. "I want you, Congressman Hubbard and Dr. Chasey, to be the first to understand our foreign policy views so that you can express them to your colleagues in the White House and in your Congress. My country's foreign policy may be said to express five fundamental principles."

First, he said that Libya had without qualification renounced terrorism as an instrument of state policy. He would not attempt to review and rebut the record of unfounded and unjustified allegations which had been leveled against his country, except to say these claims were false.

Qadhafi didn't change position as he spoke, his eyes eerily fixed on the wall at the far end of the room. Ahmed was an able translator and was never more than a few words behind. Transfixed, we continued to listen without daring to interrupt.

"The second element of our foreign policy is cooperation against proliferation of weapons of mass destruction. We are not interested in accumulating biological, nuclear, or chemical weapons, or the means to manufacture, store, and deliver them. We are, accordingly, prepared to open our facilities, on a reciprocal basis, to full appropriate international inspection, to give the world assurances that our country is not a repository of such weapons," he said.

Next, Qadhafi addressed Lockerbie. He stated emphatically that Libya did not oppose the extradition of the two Libyan men, as long as they would receive a fair trial in a neutral country, which meant anywhere but the United States and Great Britain.

After that, Qadhafi addressed the Middle East conflict, saying how much he wanted to see it resolved so the world could avoid a nuclear showdown.

"It is our view that it is now time to redouble our collective efforts toward peaceful resolution," he said. "We welcome the Middle East peace talks. We call on all parties to those talks, not least the United States, to use every effort to bring those talks to a successful conclusion as quickly as feasible, one which fully respects the just aspirations of all the affected peoples."

Fifth and finally, he stated that Libya aspires to enjoy peaceful and mutually beneficial relations with all nations.

"It is no secret that our relations with certain countries have not been happy in recent years. Indeed, we have been the subject of an armed attack resulting in the deaths of innocent men, women, and children."

He said he did not want to debate its international legality and pledged that Libya would not retaliate.

"Indeed, any fair examination of the public record will demonstrate that Libya, in recent years, has been singularly careful to avoid giving offense to any nation, most particularly the United States, in the public statements of its policies and attitudes. We have honored the rights of the many Americans who have continued to live in Libya and insured them against all harassment."

In closing, he repeated how hopeful he was that Clinton's election would bring an end to the hostilities between America and Libya.

"We assert that there are no grounds for the continued refusal to extend diplomatic recognition, to permit diplomatic interchange or to allow travel and trade exchange between our countries. Again, I say we are prepared to give proof of our commitment against terrorism, of our refusal to seek nuclear, biological, and chemical weapons, and of our willingness to open the door to the trial of the Lockerbie accused."

Hubbard was almost speechless. He stammered a bit as he expressed his appreciation for Qadhafi's remarks. He noted that what he had just heard didn't fit with the public's perception of him around the world. Hubbard offered to help repeat Qadhafi's position to the U.S. Congress when he returned to Washington, adding that "President-elect Clinton would be very interested in hearing this position."

Hubbard went on to tell Qadhafi about his close friendship with Lee Hamilton, the new chairman of the House Foreign Affairs Committee. Hubbard said he would schedule a meeting with Hamilton as soon as he returned.

Qadhafi turned his attention to the night raid on April 15, 1986, when the United States bombed his country. It was obvious to me during my stay in Libya that this event continued to resonate throughout the country. I remembered how Youssef's children had reacted and how the fear of future bombings remained.

He started by saying that the Libyan people never sleep soundly, knowing that the United States could launch another raid at any time. His people had suffered great emotional harm during the Reagan and Bush administrations, but that he felt much more secure now that Clinton was about to become president.

"Do you know what it is like sleeping with one eye open?" he asked us. "I have been the target of assassination by your country for many years. I keep moving, but I worry about my family and my children. President Reagan had planned to circumvent your Ford ban on the assassination of foreign leaders."

Finally, Qadhafi turned, looked me directly in the eye, and said in English, "Col. Debri tells me that you have a young daughter. Her name is Katie, is that right?"

I was caught completely off guard by his perfect English. I was nervous knowing that Col. Youssef el-Debri, intelligence chief and the head of Libyan National Security, had discussed my family with one of the world's most hated and feared terrorists. Meanwhile, Ahmed seemed relieved that his translation services had been lifted.

"Yes, my Katie is ten years old," I said. "She is the joy of my life."

Qadhafi's eyes filled with tears. His voice was hushed as he almost whispered, "My daughter, Hannah, would almost be eight years old, that is, if she had survived the American bombing of my home in 1986. Have you ever lost a child, Mr. Chasey?"

I shook my head.

Much to my surprise, I began to feel some compassion. His question somewhat pierced my disgust and distrust for Qadhafi. I knew how effective the American disinformation programs in general can be, and they had certainly centered on Libya in effectively molding my anti-Qadhafi biases. Were Qadhafi's tears real, or were they part of an act designed to impress his first American visitors, as well as his first U.S. government official in years?

"I understand that you and Congressman and Mrs. Hubbard went to visit the remains of my home today. You saw the results of your bombs, the results of Operation El Dorado Canyon. I left the structure just the way it was after the American bombs fell early that morning. My family was asleep when the attacks came. The entire country was asleep when the bombs fell. Who kills innocent civilians in their sleep?"

Now, he raised his voice in anger and contempt. "Who kills little children in their beds? The world will always remember this cowardly act. You saw Hannah's little bed? Her toys in her room? I left her things just as they were when she died, so they could be a reminder to the world of exactly what happened during those early morning hours. She was only sixteen months old when she died. Can you imagine the terror she must have felt when she heard the F-111's and A6's scream out of the sky and release a 2,000-lb. bomb on her home?"

Again, he turned and addressed me directly, "You were a Marine Corps officer, Mr. Chasey, an organization for which we in Libya have a history of respect. You know the sounds of an air attack; you must have felt the concussion of bombs. Some in your country have justified the killing of my Hannah by saying that she was only my adopted daughter. Can you imagine? I couldn't have loved her more if she were my natural child. My wife Safia and I wanted a daughter very badly. We have two natural sons, Saif al-Islam and Khamis, but we have no daughter. She is gone. I hope you think about Hannah and what I have told you, when you see Katie sleeping in her bed at night."

We had been talking for over two hours, and I could see that Qadhafi was getting tired. It was well into the evening and I suspected that our audience was about to come to an end. Qadhafi thanked us again for coming to Libya and appealed to us to use our political contacts to tell the Libyan story. He looked directly at Mrs. Hubbard and asked if she would remain behind for a few minutes. She nervously nodded her head.

We stood and Ahmed handed Qadhafi four copies of the *Green Book*, which he signed and gave to each of us. He also said that he wanted to give us each a Libyan carpet as his gift to us. Mrs. Hubbard pulled out her camera and began taking photos. She asked Ahmed if he would take some of Qadhafi and her, as well as some with her husband and her.

While signing my copy of the *Green Book*, he asked if I would be able to get a congressional delegation to come to Libya. He thought that it was extremely important that members of Congress saw for themselves what was happening in Libya today. He wanted them to see how the UN air embargo was affecting the people of Libya. I told him that all I could do was try.

He thanked me again and we left the room, except for Qadhafi and Mrs. Hubbard.

We waited in the hallway and discussed our meeting, but clearly Congressman Hubbard was preoccupied. Youssef and

I tried to reassure him that there was nothing to worry about.

After ten minutes, Mrs. Hubbard stepped out of Qadhafi's office with tears in her eyes. In their first display of public affection on the trip, Hubbard held his wife and tried to comfort her.

We walked down the hall away as she explained that Qadhafi had appealed to her in a most emotional way to use her feminine, motherly instincts to approach Mrs. Hillary Clinton on his behalf. He had said that only a woman could really understand what it was like to lose a child. He wanted her to know that he was a good and honest man who could be trusted. He hoped that Mrs. Clinton would have some influence on her husband and that normalized relations with the United States could resume under his administration.

As we left the barracks, Youssef once again thanked us for coming and listening. He asked again for our help back in America and bid us adieu.

Immediately, we were back in our six-car caravan en route to Djerba, Tunisia, and our flight back to Geneva.

Some fifty miles outside Tripoli, we ran into severe ground fog. Our three-hour drive turned into six. We passed the time reviewing our amazing thirty-six hours in Libya.

I hoped that the National Security Agency had a recording of our radio conversations so that someday I might be able to laugh as hard as I did that night on the highway between Tripoli and Djerba.

I called Hubbard on the radio. He was in the car behind mine. I identified myself as the editor of the *Mayfield Messenger*, the local paper of the first district of Kentucky. I was given this number to call by the Capitol operator. My readers were wondering what in the world Hubbard was doing on a lonely foggy road in the Libyan desert. We, back home in Kentucky, had sent Hubbard to Washington, not Libya. Well, Hubbard got a big kick out of it and played along with me as we passed the time. Probably out of a sense of relief, we all laughed and laughed.

At a rest stop on the highway, Hubbard asked if I saw any opportunity for him to do additional work with Libya after he left Congress. He explained that he was going to start job hunting in a few weeks and had thought about opening his own consulting/lobbying company. He said he would love to work for Libya. He admitted he knew very little about foreign affairs, or lobbying for that matter, but he was eager to give it a try.

We arrived at Djerba at 3 AM. The airport was closed. A janitor had to be persuaded to open the front door and let us in. We were airborne an hour later. The flight attendants were a bit sleepy, but that didn't stop them from preparing a delicious breakfast at 42,000 feet over the Mediterranean.

We were finally out of Libya and headed to home sweet home!

SEVENTEEN

Panic

We arrived at the Noga Hilton at 7 AM and agreed to delay our return to Washington until the next day. Instead, we would spend the day resting and shopping in Geneva. It was raining hard so I decided to forego shopping and spend the day in my room making calls and catching up on sleep.

My first call, of course, was to Virginia. She was not as upset as I had feared, because she had assumed I'd gone to "the home country" (code name for Libya) and couldn't make any calls. She was not pleased about my little adventure, but after all these years she knew that life with me meant a little risk now and again. Just in case the NSA was listening, we used great discretion. I didn't talk about the trip other than to say that I had met with "Charlie." She seemed quite impressed.

Bovenkamp decided to remain in Geneva for a few days to complete some business and make arrangements to wire a portion of the money he owed me to my corporate account. He confided that he still hadn't finalized an agreement with the government of Libya and that it would be his own money he would be sending me. Bovenkamp felt confident that after our trip he would have no problem finalizing the contract. We met and discussed the next steps on the Libyan project. For the first time, we both approached it with renewed interest.

The following morning, the Hubbards and I flew to London. Next, we boarded the Concorde and flew to New York. It didn't go unnoticed that our route took us over the small, quiet town of Lockerbie.

After arriving at JFK, we boarded another flight to the nation's capital. As we were about to land, I detected some discomfort on the part of the Hubbards.

Now that the excitement of the Concorde, private jets, and fancy hotels were behind them and the Washington skyline visible in the distance, the Hubbards became quite anxious. He became concerned about how he would report the trip on his financial disclosure papers, required by all traveling members. He wanted to know who had paid for the trip and its purpose. He wondered if he should mention Libya at all. Would the CIA know that he had gone? And Mrs. Hubbard repeatedly asked her husband to check on the rules governing travel to Libya.

I tried to assure them that ICM, Bovenkamp's company, had paid all expenses. Because it was a U.S. corporation and did not represent the government of Libya—although it might do so sometime in the future—there was absolutely no problem.

Both Hubbards were very concerned that they had not met Bukhres as promised. They had no paperwork from him to submit with Hubbard's travel report to Congress. He asked if

Bukhres could give him a backdated letter, requesting that the Hubbards take the trip and explaining how it was paid for. I promised to see what I could do. We went our separate ways at Washington's National Airport.

I was becoming uneasy that the Hubbards might do something stupid. I wondered what I could do to alleviate their anxiety.

Sure enough, the next morning, I received an anxious call from Congressman Hubbard. His wife and he had spent a restless night talking about the potential ramifications from the trip to Libya. He sounded frightened. I told him to relax. I'd check on the legality of traveling to Libya and would call him back within twenty-four hours. I had appointments all day in the Capitol and decided to do my checking that afternoon.

Soon thereafter, I got a second call from Hubbard. He had talked to our mutual friend, Rep. Mervyn Dymally (D-CA), who had traveled to Libya a few years ago.

Dymally had advised Hubbard to call the Justice Department to find out the legal status. And that's what he had done. Now, the cat was out of the bag! The Justice Department had referred him to the Office of Foreign Assets Control (OFAC), a part of the U.S. Department of Treasury and the agency with jurisdiction over sanctioned countries like Libya. Hubbard said the OFAC had informed him that he had violated federal law by traveling to Libya. The agency wanted to question him and threatened to take the matter before a federal grand jury.

Not surprisingly, Hubbard had panicked! He now felt that he had to protect himself. He began to spin a long, convoluted web, trying to save his own neck. He asked me for written documents that would prove he was the "victim" of some kind of setup or conspiracy.

I told him I would not participate in a fraud.

He repeatedly asked for a backdated letter from Bukhres. I told him that I was meeting with Bukhres on November 24th and would request a letter of invitation asking Hubbard to meet with Col. Debri.

On the flight home to California the next day, November 13th, I decided it would be prudent to make contact with OFAC myself. I might as well find out what the travel policy was for a registered foreign agent. There had to be an exception that allowed me to meet and represent my client's interests in the United States and other countries. How else could I do my job?

I called OFAC on Tuesday, November 17, 1992, and identified myself. I then requested information on travel to Libya. Charles Bishop, the agent who answered the phone, asked if I would hold for a moment while he got my file. My file? He came back on the line and telephonically introduced me to special agent Hal Harmon, who was working on my case.

"Working on my case?" I asked. "What case? What was this all about?"

Harmon explained that I was in serious trouble with the U.S. Treasury for unauthorized travel to Libya, a sanctioned country. He did acknowledge that I was registered with Justice on behalf of ICM and its client, the government of Libya, and he just happened to have my file from the Criminal Division of the Justice Department in front of him.

"Criminal Division? This is ridiculous!" I said, my throat tightening.

Harmon said that I had violated Libyan Sanctions Regulations, under the International Emergency Economic Powers Act. The regulations prohibit virtually all financial transactions by U.S. persons in which the government of Libya has an interest, unless authorized by a general or specific license, issued by the Office of Foreign Assets Control.

"These regulations also prohibit all unauthorized travel by U.S. persons to Libya," he added.

In an official-sounding voice, Harmon warned me that these actions were punishable by civil or criminal penalties or both.

Harmon gave me an oral cease-and-desist order that he said would be followed by a written order. He made it clear that I should perform no further lobbying for ICM and its client, the government of Libya.

I quickly pointed out that I had filed my Justice Department registration on October 8, 1992, and that as far as I knew Libya was not a client of ICM. Now, some six weeks later, he was forbidding me to represent my client and claiming that my activities had been illegal.

We agreed that I would do nothing more on my ICM contract, until I received a letter from his office clarifying what I could and could not do. I felt that he was pleased with my cooperation and that we had actually established a rather cordial relationship. I felt reassured that once I received his official letter, this contretemps would disappear.

He also wanted to know how to contact Bovenkamp and Brendan Kelly. I told him.

I believe I had followed the letter of the law by registering with the Justice Department. And to be perfectly frank, I had never heard of this agency, OFAC, until the day before when Hubbard told me about it.

Virginia and I had a long talk about it over breakfast. Although we were concerned about OFAC and agent Harmon, we both felt, as we still do, that I had done everything I could to comply with my legal responsibilities as a registered foreign agent. To repeat, I had registered with the Justice Department the day I signed the contract with ICM. I had submitted all of the required forms, including a copy of the ICM contract and the contract addendum among Bovenkamp, Bukhres, and myself. I believed there was no more I could have done. The question of illegal travel to Libya was another matter. Maybe that had been an innocent mistake.

Since my return from Libya and my encounter with OFAC, I had done considerable research on travel to sanctioned countries. What I found was that the "law" against this kind of travel was enforced inconsistently and indiscriminately. Travel to Cuba was the best example.

Despite all of our bravado over trade sanctions, embargoes, and problems with Fidel Castro, U.S. citizens have been traveling to Cuba for over forty years. Former Sen. George McGovern travelled to Cuba for more than twenty years. He publicly acknowledged that he met with Castro in September 1994. Former Chrysler CEO Lee Iacocca jetted to Havana via Canada and Mexico on a regular basis to dine with Castro and hold investment talks with Cuban leaders.

On Tuesday, December 27, 1994, *USA Today* reported that sixty-nine American companies had signed secret letters of intent to do business in Cuba. Yet, prior to 1993, as noted on my passport, the only country to which travel was prohibited was Cuba.

And, of course, journalists, filmmakers, and musicians went to Cuba all the time. The most visible example was Ry Cooder's 1999 Oscar-nominated documentary, *Buena Vista Social Club.*

I guess the most outrageous example of travel to a sanctioned country was in July 1970, during the Vietnam War, when actress Jane Fonda went to Hanoi and was photographed sitting on an anti-aircraft battery, used to shoot down American warplanes! No charges were ever brought against her.

Soon after that, Americans were traveling to Vietnam—both

North and South—in search of missing American soldiers or to revisit war locations. And businessmen were soon traveling to the now unified Vietnam to open trade and commerce between our two countries.

(In November 1993, one year after my trip to Libya and two years after the indictments of Megrahi and Fhimah, Libya and Iraq were added to Cuba on American passports as countries to which travel was prohibited.)

I had always believed that American citizens had the right to travel the world freely without U.S. government interference. However, I knew that there were some countries in which I couldn't count on U.S. help if I got into trouble. These were countries with which America had no diplomatic relations.

In December 1994, Congressman Bill Richardson (D-NM) traveled to North Korea on his own, not part of an official delegation. Ironically, no one would have known about it if North Korea had not shot down an American helicopter, killing one pilot and capturing the other. Despite this outrageous act on the part of North Korea, one month later, with the return of the captured pilot by the North Koreans, the U.S. government removed trade sanctions against that country.

Finally, thousands of U.S. citizens live in Libya. Thousands more, like Mohammed Bukhres, travel between Libya and the United States on business and/or to visit relatives every year. Scores of American citizens can be found on the ferry boats running daily from Malta to Tripoli and back. This travel was done without the benefit of a license from the U.S. government.

As far as I could tell, none of these travelers—Bukhres, Fonda, Cooder, and Iacocca—had requested or been granted, a license from OFAC to travel to or conduct business in these sanctioned countries.

Why had I been singled out? Why was I being pressured to not do business with Libya or its representatives in the United States?

What were the shadowy, out-of-control, unelected second-tier officials so afraid of?

Or were they simply puppets in a callous shift of foreign policy?

EIGHTEEN

The Lawyers

On Tuesday, November 24, I arrived at Bukhres' suite on the fifth floor of the Park Hyatt Hotel in Washington, D.C. I could hear a few voices through the door as I waited for someone to respond. Bukhres opened the door and invited me in. As I entered, I was shocked to see a once famous Capitol Hill face, former Sen. Harrison "Pete" Williams (D-NJ). Williams had been convicted a few years before for his involvement in an FBI sting, called ABSCAM.[10] I couldn't believe that Williams was there. I felt a sinking feeling in my stomach as Bukhres introduced me to Williams. I had met the senator some twelve years before, but it was obvious he didn't remember me.

Williams was just finishing his business with Bukhres and was about to leave. Bukhres said that Williams had been employed by Libya to try to get some help from Williams' old friend and colleague, Sen. Claiborne Pell (D-RI), chairman of the Senate Foreign Relations Committee. I remember thinking that I was quite capable of dealing with Pell without the help of Williams who was *persona non grata* in the U.S. Capitol.

Bukhres gave me a copy of a letter from Sen. Pell to former Sen. Williams dated May 4, 1992. In the letter, Pell responded to Williams' suggestion of a meeting between Secretary of State James Baker and el-Debri. He also discussed Debri's inability to secure a U.S. visa. It appeared that, indeed, Williams was involved in representing Libya in some form or fashion.

I wondered if he had registered with the Justice Department or if he was licensed by the U. S. Treasury . . .

Next, I met a most cheerful gentleman by the name of Robert Flynn. Flynn was the attorney for Lamen Khalifa Fhimah, one of the two indicted Libyans. Flynn, and his partner on the case, Paul Riley, who represented the other indicted Libyan, Abdelbasset Ali al-Megrahi, had been hired by Libya to defend the two suspected bombers. They were the official U.S. lawyers of record for the two accused men. Riley was unable to attend our dinner meeting, but Flynn was very pleased to meet me and to know that I had been so successful in taking a U.S. Congressman to meet with "Charlie."

Bob Flynn impressed me with his in-depth knowledge of the Lockerbie case. He and Riley had been to Libya to meet with their clients. They had been licensed by OFAC to represent the two Libyans and to receive payments from the Libyan government for their services.

I asked Flynn and Bukhres to be my guests for dinner at the Jockey Club.

The Jockey Club is located in the Embassy Row section of Massachusetts Avenue in northwest Washington. At the time it was one of the most exclusive places to eat in the city. In fact, the Jockey Club was the only place in Washington where Ronald Reagan ever went for dinner, outside of the White House, during his presidency. He showed up one night while I was there with his old friends from California, Charlie and Mary Jane Wick. *The Washington Post* carried a story the next day on how shocked the president was to pay $25 for swordfish. It was obvious to all that he had lost touch with the average man during his confinement in the White House.

As we entered the Jockey Club, we paused long enough for me to introduce Bukhres and Bob Flynn to Sen. and Mrs. Lloyd Bentsen from Texas, and to Democratic stalwart Bob Strauss and his wife. They were frequent guests at this Washington landmark and I had seen them in the club many times before.

Bentsen's first senatorial campaign in 1970 was also my first political campaign. He ended up beating another Texan who later gained some political fame, George H.W. Bush. I had also gotten to know "Mr. Democrat," Bob Strauss during my political days as a faculty member at the University of Texas at Austin. Strauss and I met in May of 1972, the night Lt. Governor Ben Barnes lost his bid for the Democratic nomination for the Governorship of Texas. Barnes, the leading vote-getter in Texas just four years before, got caught up in an anti-incumbent mood brought on by the Sharpstown State Bank scandal and ended up not even carrying his home district, Comanche County. I worked hard on Barnes' campaign and, even though we lost, I got to know some of the leading political figures of the Texas past and future, including John Connally, former Governor of Texas, for whom I became domestic policy advisor in his 1980 bid for the Republican presidential nomination.

While Barnes lost the nomination for governor, Bentsen won the Senate seat, which he held until he gave it up in 1992 to become secretary of the Treasury under President Bill Clinton. He resigned that position on December 22, 1994, to return to private business. During the same time, Strauss served in a variety of high-visibility jobs from U. S. trade representative to American ambassador to the Soviet Union. He always managed to return to his law practice in between political appointments and amassed a small fortune brokering his powerful Washington connections into big financial deals.

The conversation between Bukhres, Bob Flynn, and me seemed to flow freely that evening. I recounted my adventures in Libya and my meeting with Qadhafi. Although Flynn had been to Libya to meet his clients, he had never met "Charlie." Bukhres said that he and "Charlie" were best of friends and that he was frequently called by the Libyan leader to give him advice on world issues. I listened with some skepticism, having learned by now that only a fraction of what came out of Bukhres' mouth was true.

Flynn gave me some free counsel about my unfortunate situation with OFAC. He believed that the OFAC was an agency without teeth and that I shouldn't worry about future problems coming from it. He expressed an interest in my helping him and Riley prepare a defense for their Libyan clients. He stressed that the indictments against the two Libyans were more political than legal. He admitted that he needed help on Capitol Hill to convince various members of Congress to pressure the administration into moving the trial to a neutral country. He felt it was the only way for the two Libyans to get a fair trial.

After dinner, I had Paul take the three of us back to the Park Hyatt. Bukhres, Bob and I talked long into the night.

Suite 506 was rather small and cluttered with stacks of new and old Arabic newspapers. Bukhres lived his entire life, both personal and professional, out of the suite. He often claimed to own a home in Washington State and a luxurious palace on Malta. He said he ran a medical supply business in Seattle, called American Medical Supply, which sold medical products to Libya.

In addition to the hotel telephones in his suite, he had at least three private telephone lines. A fax machine, continuously churning out documents, sat on a small table in the corner of the room. He would walk about the suite talking with us as he monitored these faxes. He had an uncanny skill of reading and talking at the same time. He made no comments about what he had read and almost unconsciously threw the faxes on a pile of papers reaching almost two feet high on his coffee table.

I asked Bukhres and Flynn why they had gotten involved with Sen. Harrison Williams and how they thought he could be of service to them. Bukhres told me that he had met Williams through his personal friend, Washington attorney William Rogers. I, of course, thought that he was referring to "the" William D. Rogers, secretary of state under President Carter. It was almost three months later, after being asked by Bukhres to get tickets for the Clinton inauguration for Rogers and his wife, that I discovered that it wasn't the same William Rogers. Bukhres's William Rogers did serve in the State Department, but never in any lofty positions. Bukhres often referred to his close association with Rogers and said that he was a frequent visitor at the Rogers' home. He also gave me a copy of a contract that Rogers had prepared for his law firm, Arnold and Porter, to represent the Libyan government. It was interesting that everyone seemed to be getting a piece of Libyan business.

The next order of business with Bukhres was the $200,000 he and Bovenkamp personally owed me for taking Congressman Hubbard to meet with Col. Debri and Col. Qadhafi. I was confronted with the first of Bukhres' many classic stall tactics. He said he had spoken to Bovenkamp, who would be sending me the money from Switzerland, very soon.

Bukhres said, "Not to worry. The money is a small thing in relation to the good that you are performing."

Bukhres was sure that Bovenkamp would pay me in full.

Upon my return to San Diego the next day, I received a series of calls from Bovenkamp, still in Geneva. He gave me a variety of excuses why the $200,000 had not been transferred to my corporate account. His major theme was that he was having trouble transferring the money from his home in Holland to Switzerland. He did agree to wire a partial payment of $50,000 from his personal account as a good-faith gesture.

Bovenkamp was true to his word. On October 30, 1992, $50,000 was wired to my La Jolla account from a Swiss bank. I insisted that the money come from Bovenkamp's personal account, and not from ICM's account. Although I was very displeased that Bovenkamp and Bukhres had not lived up to their side of the agreement, which called for me to be paid $200,000 within forty-eight hours of taking a member of Congress to meet with Debri, I was encouraged that he had at least kept his word on this partial payment. It's a fact that in the service business—or maybe any business—payments are always slower after the goods are delivered.

Life returned to normal as our family prepared for our upcoming traditional Christmas open-house and our annual vacation to Vail. After that, things quieted down. I spoke to Bovenkamp on the telephone every couple of days and he promised to pay me the balance of my fee. Bukhres became harder and harder to reach by telephone. Bob Flynn told me Bukhres had become quite ill and was spending a lot of time visiting various doctors in the Washington, D.C., area.

I finally reached him on December 1. We had some rather harsh words about the money he and Bovenkamp still owed me. He assured me that all was well and that the $150,000 balance was "small potatoes." Right now he wanted to talk with me about my involvement with the lawyers, Flynn and Riley. He asked if I could fly to Washington to meet with him and the lawyers the next day. Apparently, Flynn and Riley wanted to hire me for a one-year period to help them finesse their defense. They were offering to pay me a million dollars for my efforts. He said that he would pay my airfare and expenses for the trip. I agreed to go.

Virginia and I were to be the guests of hotelier and close friend, Larry Lawrence, owner of the famous Hotel Del Coronado, at a black-tie dinner the following evening, so I made arrangements to take the red-eye to Washington. I just made my 11:10 PM flight by changing from my tuxedo to my traveling clothes in the back seat of the car in the airport parking lot.

Paul drove me to the Park Hyatt the following evening. I asked him to stay close by the hotel while I met with Bukhres and the lawyers.

I had an uneasy feeling that I couldn't explain.

Yes, there was the unpleasantness with OFAC, but to make matters worse, I had received a terse call from an American man a few days before. He had said, "Stay away from Libya," and quickly hung up.

I didn't take it very seriously at the time, but I was beginning to wonder.

I told Paul that I would call him on his cell phone every half-hour. If he didn't hear from me, he was to call Bukhres' suite.

NINETEEN

A Big Offer

Both Bob Flynn and Paul Riley were with Bukhres when I arrived at the Park Hyatt the evening of December 3, 1992. I felt a bit more secure being in Bukhres's suite with the two lawyers close by. However, it was true that in the cloak-and-dagger world in which I was beginning to find myself now, you really never knew who the good guys were!

Finally, I had the opportunity of meeting Paul Riley. Paul was a retired CIA agent in his early sixties. He was very interested in my conflict with the OFAC and asked me what had transpired. He and Bob Flynn laughed heartily when I reported the details of my conversation with agent Harmon. Bukhres just sat, listened, and kept shaking his head in disbelief. I was assured by both Flynn and Riley that I had done nothing wrong in the eyes of the law, and that I shouldn't worry about the incident with the OFAC.

Bukhres suggested that we go to dinner at the Melrose Restaurant located on the ground floor of the hotel. On our way down, I slipped away long enough to call Paul to tell him that all was well.

The four of us continued our conversation over dinner. All three of my dinner partners had the opportunity to relate their personal experiences with the OFAC. Bukhres was convinced that the OFAC Director, Richard Newcomb, was a "Jew" who hated all Arabs. The truth was that Bukhres hated all Jews and repeatedly blamed them for all the ills of the world.

Bukhres said that OFAC agents had recently raided the Seattle office of his American Medical Supply Company. They reportedly searched his home and his office to no avail. Bukhres told me that his requests for export licenses for his medical supply sales to Libya had often been turned down by Newcomb for no apparent or legal reason. Bukhres wanted me to help him secure future export licenses for his company from the OFAC. Medical supplies were exempt from the UN sanctions against Libya, but a license from the OFAC was still required. It was for this purpose that Bukhres, along with Bovenkamp, had signed the $200,000 contract with me in Geneva.

Bob Flynn had also been frequently harassed by Newcomb and his agency. The OFAC agents had come to his office to give him severe warnings and threats about his continued representation of the Libyans.

He and Riley were each awarded a license to travel to Libya to meet with their clients. They had gone there three times to work with Megrahi and Fhimah. They were convinced after their trips that the case against the Libyans had been fabricated and was politically motivated. This was the reason they needed my political expertise.

After dinner we went back to Suite 605. Bob Flynn had a draft contract he wanted me to review overnight, and give him my comments the following day. The hour was late. We briefly discussed the contents of their contract. They offered me a one-year deal for $1 million, in return for my political advice and consultation.

Both attorneys advised me that I wouldn't need an individual license from the OFAC to perform the political activities they needed. I would be working directly under the auspices of their law firm, which was already licensed. Additionally, they explained that as the lawyers of record, they could hire anyone they needed to help in the defense of their clients. Flynn and Riley intended to hire forensic experts, detectives, and other professionals in their defense preparations. I said I would study the contract and meet with them the following day for lunch.

After reviewing circumstances related to the OFAC, it seemed the best way for me to provide political services in this matter was to work directly for the law firm of Flynn and Riley. I felt that this association with them would take me out of any conflict with the OFAC.

Later that night as I was lying in bed reading Flynn's proposed contract, I was startled by the phone ringing. It was well past midnight and I became concerned that something was wrong at home in California. The man on the phone didn't identify himself, but in a very thick Arab accent, he warned me not to pursue the Libyan case further. That is, if I wanted to "stay healthy."

Just prior to hanging up, the man said in a threatening voice, "There are a lot of people who don't want this case reopened. If you want to stay alive, stay away from Libya."

I hung up the phone in total disbelief and shock. My thoughts ran from fear to outrage to humor. This was the second menacing phone call. Was it for real, or was I casting myself into a James Bond movie? I spent a restless night pondering how seriously I should take these threats. Mostly, I was glad that my Georgetown condo telephone hadn't been forwarded to California as is normally the case. Virginia could have answered it and heard the same death threat that I had. This would have been especially disturbing, since the OFAC had faxed to Virginia that very same day, an Order to Cease and Desist and Requirement to Furnish Information. She didn't need another shock.

Was it a hoax, or was it a real threat? How much of a coincidence could it have been that the meeting with Flynn and Riley, and the threat and the fax from the OFAC, occurred the same day? I had no idea who wanted me out of the Libyan case more, the Arabs or the United States government. From here on, I needed to use special care in dealing with both.

After spending the following morning, December 4th, on Capitol Hill, I met Bukhres and Bob Flynn at the Park Hyatt for lunch. We discussed the proposed contract, and the death threat I received the previous night. Both Flynn and Bukhres didn't seem to express any particular concern over my late-night phone call. They both felt that my telephones were probably bugged by the CIA, FBI, or the OFAC. If the call didn't come from one of these agencies, the U.S. government was at least now aware of the death threat. They also warned me to be aware of anyone following me or any suspicious characters lurking in the dark—as if I had to be reminded!

I thought about my personal safety. I recalled a few years back trying to get Paul a permit to carry a concealed weapon in the District of Columbia. It was a futile task. In order to legally carry a concealed weapon in Washington, D.C., it would have been necessary for Paul to become a Deputy U.S. Marshall. It seemed only the bad guys were allowed to have guns in this crazy town. I realized that there was little value in trying this security approach again.

I wanted to have a second opinion on the legality of the Flynn and Riley contract. I understood from the two lawyers that the license they held would afford me protection from the Libyan Sanctions Act and the OFAC. If they were correct, I wouldn't need my own separate license to give them political advice. If they were wrong, I would be in deep trouble with the OFAC again.

The deal they offered me sounded attractive and logical. But, I had dealt much too long with the federal establishment to take anything for granted. I needed to get a second opinion to be absolutely sure. If necessary, I would apply for my own license from the OFAC.

My schedule called for me to leave for Switzerland on December 7th on some personal business. I told Flynn that I would work on the license situation and our pending contract when I returned five days later. Bukhres said that he was going to be at the Noga Hilton in Geneva on December 10th and suggested that we meet in Geneva. He said that being in Switzerland would make it easier for him to pay me the balance due on my account.

On December 7, 1992, I flew to Zurich. After completing my business, I took the train to Geneva on December 10. As agreed, I tried to contact Bukhres at the Noga Hilton. Bukhres had not checked into the hotel, and there were no messages for me. I personally went to the Noga Hilton that night to see if Bukhres was there.

Once again, Bukhres had disappeared

TWENTY

A Christmas Surprise

It was great to be back home in San Diego, especially with the Christmas holidays quickly approaching. We were scheduled to leave for Vail on December 19th, just two days away. I was spending the day catching up on some final paperwork in preparation for our upcoming ski trip.

On that morning, Virginia was in La Jolla doing a few last minute errands and giving Santa a helping hand with his upcoming visit to Katie in Colorado.

She planned to stop at the bank and pick up enough cash for the trip, pay some bills, and return home to complete our last-minute packing. We always looked forward to our traditional Christmas trip. But this year, I especially needed the break. For ten glorious days I would be free of the OFAC, Libya, Bukhres,

Congressman Carroll Hubbard, and that haunting threat on my life.

It was a morning I will never forget. Virginia called from the bank in a panic.

"They froze our bank account," she said. "The United States Treasury has frozen all of our money. They won't give me a penny at the bank. The bankers can't tell me any more except that they were sorry. Apparently, the Treasury has the right to freeze bank accounts without notice and without giving a reason. How can they do that? What will we do for Christmas and for money?"

I tried as best I could to calm her down. I asked her to come home right away. While waiting for her to return, I immediately called the Office of Foreign Assets Control and asked for Agent Hal Harmon. He took my phone call.

I asked directly, "Did you freeze my bank account?"

"Yes, we decided that the $50,000 paid to you was dirty Libyan money, and the U.S. Treasury had every right to freeze your account."

I wondered how many companies could survive the loss of their business bank account without any notice. I wondered how we would survive . . .

With great anger, I said the money paid to me came from Bovenkamp's personal bank account. It didn't come from ICM or the government of Libya. Even if it had, it didn't matter because ICM is a U.S. corporation and currently had no relationship with the government of Libya. OFAC had no right to do what it did. I tried in vain to tell Harmon that the U.S. Treasury had no evidence that the money came from Libya. In fact, I had plenty of evidence that it didn't. In addition, the money in my company account came from a number of my clients, not just from Bovenkamp. Why freeze the entire account?

Nothing I said was going to change Harmon's mind.

He had deceived me. We had already agreed that I would be open and forthcoming in his investigation, and that I would cease and desist all of the activities contained in my foreign agent registration. I had agreed to cooperate in all matters related to Libya. Now, without the benefit of a trial, hearing, administrative review, or even a warning, this faceless government bureaucrat took it upon himself to freeze my account just days before Christmas. Merry Christmas Mr. Harmon!

None of this seemed real—first the death threat, now the frozen account.

After a lengthy discussion, Virginia and I decided to go forward with the ski trip. We would attempt to enjoy our vacation for the sake of our daughter and family members who had already made plans to stay with us in Vail. We would decide what action to take upon our return to La Jolla. In the meantime, we would use our credit cards for our vacation.

No matter how hard I tried to put it out of my mind, the death threat and the unconscionable action taken by Harmon were constant companions as I slalomed down the slopes of Vail.

TWENTY-ONE

Bureaucratic Maze

I continued my discussions with Bob Flynn and Paul Riley over the next few weeks. I was convinced that they were honest and committed to providing their clients with quality representation in the United States. Although both lawyers felt that I could work for them without my own separate license from the OFAC, I decided to file an application just to be sure I was not violating the Libyan Sanctions Act.

In addition, I sought a second opinion from Washington lawyer Chris Myers, of Dunnells, Duvall & Porter. He also advised me that I didn't need to file for a separate license. However, he said to be safe, I might want to apply anyway and that he would help me.

Myers prepared my application to OFAC to engage in extra-judicial consulting and assistance on behalf of my clients,

Riley and Flynn. Myers worked closely with them in preparing the application. It was finally filed with the OFAC on February 23, 1993.

There was little doubt among all three attorneys involved that the OFAC would comply with my request for a specific license. What else could they do?

The U.S. Constitution guarantees that every defendant, no matter how heinous the crime, is considered innocent until proven guilty. The Constitution also provides that every defendant is guaranteed the right to full and complete legal representation. An attorney must use all of the legal resources available to provide his client a quality defense. This representation very often includes private detectives, expert witnesses, forensic experts, legal scholars, and political consultants.

> February 23, 1993
> Mr. R. Richard Newcomb
> Director, Office of Foreign Assets Control
> Re: [William Chasey]
>
> Dear Mr. Newcomb:
>
> Pursuant to 31 C.P.R. §550.BQl<b), our client, [Chasey] submits the following application for a specific license to engage in extra-judicial consulting and assistance on behalf of its clients, attorneys Paul J. Riley and Robert J. Flynn.
>
> Messrs. Riley and Flynn represent Libyan nationals Abdelbasset Ali Al-Megrahi and Lamen Khalifa Fhimah, respectively with regard to their indictments related to the 1988 aviation incident over Lockerbie, Scotland. In connection with this representation, Messrs. Riley and Flynn have informed us that they are authorized by the office of Foreign Assets Control to engage in transactions in connection with the provision of legal services to their

clients pursuant to License Numbers L-OQ723a and L-00722a. In furtherance of their representation of their clients, Messrs. Riley and Flynn would like to retain the services of [Chasey] to assist them in resolving the current impasse between their clients and the United States government regarding resolution of the indictments.

Based on our reading of the relevant Executive Order and regulations, we are of the opinion that [Chasey] may be able to conduct this activity without obtaining prior approval from the Department of the Treasury. First, as more fully described below, [Chasey] has been asked to undertake this assignment by attorneys Riley and Flynn as part of their provision of legal services to their clients. The Office of Foreign Assets Control has already issued a license authorizing transactions related to those legal services. Since [Chasey]'s activities will be under the direction of Riley and Flynn, and all compensation will be made through them, we believe that your office has already given sufficient approval to this activity, and [Chasey] need not submit a complete application for a license of its own. Instead, [Chasey] need only be identified as an "interested party" operating under the license which has already been granted to Riley and Flynn.

Second, while not specifically referenced in the regulations concerning trade activities with Libya and Libyan entities, we note that the Office of Foreign Assets control has taken the position that a license is not needed to engage in the provision of certain legal services including "the provision of legal advice and counseling on the requirements with U.S. law," and the "defense of [Libyans] when named as a defendant in domestic U.S. litigation or administrative proceedings . . . " We believe this exception should apply to [Chasey's] proposed activity, since it would be directly related to the provision of legal advice.

Although we are of the opinion that [Chasey] could engage in this activity without specific approval from the

Department of Treasury without violating [any regulations], [Chasey] has decided to seek approval from the Office of Foreign Assets prior to accepting this assignment in order to avoid a situation similar to the misunderstanding surrounding [Chasey's] activities this past fall . . .

In the proposed representation, [Chasey] would perform [his] services as a subcontractor to Riley and Flynn [who] represent Abdelbasset Ali Al-Megrahi and Lamen Khalifa Fhimah, the indicted Libyan nationals.

As described above, Riley and Flynn seek [Chasey]'s services to provide extra-judicial assistance and consulting with respect to their efforts to accomplish a political solution to the current stalemate between their clients and the United States government.

It is expected that Mr. Chasey will be called upon to assist in contacts and negotiations with relevant congressional committees and their members, executive branch officials and international political bodies. All of the work will be directly related to Riley and Flynn's representation of their clients.

As noted in the attached copy of Rule 2.1 of the District of Columbia Rules of Professional Conduct, in rendering legal advice a lawyer may need to "refer not only to law but to other considerations such as moral, economic, social and political factors, which may be relevant to the client's situation." In the situation in which Messrs. Riley and Flynn's clients find themselves, expert consultation with respect to political factors may be as, or more important than their courtroom representation of their clients, just as there is no doubt that as part of their criminal representation of their clients, Riley and Flynn would be entitled, and perhaps obligated to retain the services of a forensic expert, the circumstances of the case make it necessary to retain a political consultant like Mr. Chasey.

In conclusion, we hope that this submission provides the information that the Office of Foreign Assets Control needs in order to issue a specific license forthwith. However, if you need any additional or clarifying information, please feel free to contact me directly, and we will respond to your needs as quickly as possible.

In advance, thank you for your prompt attention to this matter.

Christopher A. Myers

In a brief, one-page, three-paragraph response to the above request, dated March 22, 1993, OFAC Director Richard Newcomb, denied my request:

> . . . my [providing] political consulting and advisory services to the Attorneys constitutes an indirect export of services from the United States to Libya and the beneficiaries of such services would be the Defendants who are presumed to be currently located in Libya.

Given the clarity and substance of Myers' legal arguments, I was outraged by Newcomb's response. Flynn, Riley, and Myers were amazed at the blatant disregard for the law cited in my application. We all wondered how Flynn and Riley would be able to fully represent their clients without my political advice and expertise.

The denial didn't respond to the legal points contained in my request. Newcomb did what most federal bureaucrats do. He copied a few boiler-plated lines from a federal regulation and disregarded all questions or points of law. In between the lines, Newcomb was saying that if I didn't like his decision and had enough money to take on the federal government, I should file a lawsuit.

Realistically, the decision said that Megrahi and Fhimah couldn't receive a fair trial in the United States. I, of course, had heard this said directly by Qadhafi, Youssef el-Debri, and others, but now for the first time I had confirmation.

Was it true that the U.S. system of justice didn't apply to major international crimes? I realized that if the defendants were tried in the United States, their lawyers would be engaged in a political courtroom battle without the benefit of political advice and expertise. They wouldn't have their full complement of arrows in their quiver.

I was confronted with a major decision. Should I spend the time and money required to appeal the OFAC decision? The answer came after a great deal of prayer and consultation with Virginia. I decided not to appeal the decision.

I never saw any of the key players in this drama again. It was over for me; it was time to get back to my normal life, or so I thought . . . [11]

TWENTY-TWO

Hubbard Stings Me

My priority was to continue to make a living as a Washington lobbyist. I tried putting the Libya intrigues behind me. I had never been paid the remaining $150,000 that Bukhres and Bovenkamp still owed me. The payment of $50,000, which I never received, was chump change for arranging for a sitting congressman to meet with Libya's foreign minister and Qadhafi. Sometimes you get stiffed, but I had no inkling how bad the stiffing was going to get.

Virginia, Katie, and I had visited Hungary in 1987 and Poland in 1989. Virginia—a direct descendant of the famous Polish poet and statesman, Adam Mickiewicz—always had a keen interest in Poland. Her enthusiasm quickly spread to me. The fall of the Berlin Wall and the new transformations taking place in the Eastern Block presented me with new business opportunities. I began establishing U.S./Polish joint business ventures in Poland.

On September 8, 1993, six months after the OFAC denied my application, I was having lunch in the House members' dining room with a client, David Otten, president of Celsat Corporation of Los Angeles, when Carroll Hubbard unexpectedly walked up to our table and engaged us in lighthearted conversation. He accepted my invitation to join us.

Now out of Congress, Hubbard was anxious to pump some blood into his new legal and lobbying business in Washington. He claimed that he had tried to reach me for some inside lobbying tips, although I had no record of any such calls. I agreed to give him whatever advice I could. He suggested that we get together for dinner sometime soon, so he could "pick my brain."

A month later, Hubbard called me at my La Jolla home and invited me to be his guest at dinner the following week at Duke Zieberts, one of Washington's "in" restaurants. After agreeing on a time, Carroll reflected on how much he enjoyed the time he had spent in our La Jolla home, and how much he appreciated having Virginia, Katie, and me as friends.

I met Hubbard at the restaurant at 7 PM on October 12th. The man I met that night was a new Carroll Hubbard, full of life and vigor. He enjoyed being recognized by the maitre d', who greeted us at the door with a "Welcome back Congressman Hubbard." He had money in his pockets for the first time that I could remember and suggested that I order anything I liked from the menu, because the meal was on him. He was actually going to pick up a check! I liked Hubbard's new doppelganger.

Most of our conversation focused on his attempts to become a business consultant and lobbyist. He mentioned all of the business people back home in his former district who were anxious to have him represent them in Washington. He liked what he was doing domestically, but thought he would prefer working in the international world like me.

This brought us to the topic of Libya. He was curious about my work on the Lockerbie disaster. He wanted to know how he could get involved with Qadhafi and make some "big bucks." He asked if I had had any more contact with the Libyans, and if I still had a good relationship with Youssef and Muntassir. I told him I had had no contact with the "home country." Hubbard asked if I could use my Libyan contacts to help some of his clients back home, who would love to tap into some of that Libyan oil money.

I explained the ramifications of doing business in Libya, especially as far as the OFAC was concerned. I outlined the government's policy.

I said, "In a word, it can't be done."

We had a few glasses of wine and reminisced about our Libyan adventure, including the laughs we shared during the trip. He wanted to know more about my clients and how I was so successful in having so much access to the members of Congress. Carroll always had a way of probing deeper and deeper into an issue, so his interest in my business activities didn't seem unusual. He asked if I would be willing to work with him in representing some of his new clients, but admitted that he needed me to show him the ropes, especially in the international marketplace.

Hubbard went into detail about one of his new prospects, a man who was interested in developing a foreign operation out of his home base in northern Virginia. He suggested a meeting with this person in a week or so, if I was interested. I agreed to a meeting. With the exception of a few of his annoying questions, the evening was rather enjoyable.

Hubbard phoned me sometime during the week of October 18th and asked me to join him and his client at the same restaurant, on October 26th, for dinner. I accepted.

I had arrived early and was sipping a glass of wine when Hubbard and a man in his early forties were escorted to my table. Hubbard introduced me to his client, Robert Vieta, president of Crystal Trading Ventures of Falls Church, Virginia. He said that Vieta and I had a lot in common, as former Marine Corps officers.

After telling a few Marine Corps war stories, we got down to some serious business discussions. Then Hubbard shocked me by handing me an envelope containing photos of me with Qadhafi, which his wife had snapped during our trip. Hubbard had previously refused to give them to me, because he felt they might be used against him in some future political campaign. It was all I could do not to burst out laughing when I looked at them. He had carefully cut himself out of all the pictures! It seemed strange that he would still be concerned about exposing his photo with Qadhafi, since it was clear that the OFAC knew about his trip and our meeting with the Libyan leader. It also seemed odd that Hubbard didn't mind that Vieta saw the photos and heard all about our Libyan trip.

Vieta said that he was a former Marine helicopter pilot and had served a tour of duty in Vietnam. He'd launched Crystal Trading Company when he left the Corps. His company manufactured and marketed medical supplies throughout the United States. Now that his business was doing well, he was interested in expanding into the international marketplace. Hubbard suggested that I was the best person in Washington to ask about getting a business going internationally.

Vieta used the photos to direct our conversation to the sale of medical supplies to Libya. He asked if it were possible to sell them to a sanctioned country. Could my Libyan contacts help him work a deal?

I replied that he really didn't need me or my contacts to sell his products to Libya. Medical supplies were exempt from the Libyan Sanctions Regulations. All he needed was to apply to the OFAC for a license. As I found out later, they were disappointed in my response.

I quickly changed the topic to business opportunities in Eastern Europe, where I was now more focused. Vieta seemed to lose interest.

The dinner concluded with a promise that Vieta and I would talk again about doing business internationally. It was a strange evening. I was left with the impression that Hubbard and Vieta had had a hidden agenda.

Still feeling uncomfortable about the dinner meeting, I called Vieta's telephone number in Virginia the next morning to see if his business was real or a front of some kind. A female secretary promised Vieta would return my call. When he did, I determined that he really had no interest in doing international business with or without my help. He said he would get back to me if he decided to get involved in Eastern Europe.

My unease about my two dinners with Hubbard and the one with Vieta persisted. For some reason, I sensed that Vieta could not be trusted.

I put the entire episode in the back of my mind until December 11, 1993, when I opened *The Washington Post.* There on the front page was Hubbard's photo.

The article's headline read: "Ex-Representative Reveals FBI Duty." It claimed that Hubbard had turned FBI informer, because he feared prosecution resulting from serious campaign-finance violations. My heart began to pound as I kept reading. For six months back in 1993, Hubbard had worn a wire, taping conversations and phone calls.

> Carroll Hubbard, whose nine terms in Congress ended after his loss in a Democratic primary last year, said he was an informer from April to October. Justice Department spokesman Carl Stern confirmed that Hubbard had worked as an informer for the FBI this year but would not elaborate.

When Hubbard learned he was the subject of an FBI probe into campaign-finance violations, he agreed to cooperate with the FBI and go undercover. My heart stopped beating as I read:

> Hubbard said he recorded two conversations with a lobbyist for Libya.

Dear Lord, that was me!

> In September, Hubbard said he refused to sign a plea agreement, fearing he might eventually be asked to investigate his former colleagues on the Hill.

In other words, he wouldn't rat out his Hill colleagues, but he felt no compunction about entrapping his good friend, Bill Chasey.

Since Hubbard had rejected the plea deal, he risked prosecution on charges of theft, mail and wire fraud, obstruction of justice, and federal election-law violations. Apparently, he was being investigated for improperly using his congressional aides in his wife's unsuccessful race in another Kentucky congressional district. In addition, Hubbard lacked documentation for extensive campaign expenses. He was facing over seven years in federal prison, twice what he had been offered in his plea deal.

> "I've been absolutely destroyed by this," said Hubbard.

He went on to deny that he had obstructed justice, conceding that he may have violated federal elections laws, and if so, they had simply been honest mistakes.

The next day, *The New York Times* carried a similar story; "Ex-House Member Aided FBI Inquiry." Most of it repeated *The Post* story of the previous day, with a few notable exceptions.

Dennis L. Null, a former law partner of Hubbard's, who represented him in dealing with the government, said:

> The congressman was attempting to cooperate with the government to the fullest extent, even at the risk of his own life. He was willing to risk everything in helping the U.S. government . . . Mr. Hubbard traveled to Libya, and met with the Libyan leader, Col. Muammar al-Qadhafi, in the course of his work as an informer.

What a fabrication! Carroll Hubbard was working for the FBI when I took him to Libya? How ridiculous! It seemed obvious that Null was trying to put a positive spin on Hubbard's trip to Tripoli and save his neck. Or was it possible that when I innocently asked Hubbard to come to Libya, it just so happened that he was coincidentally working as an FBI informer?

The nature of Mr. Hubbard's work for the FBI is unclear. But it is common for the Bureau to use suspects as informers to help uncover crimes. In such cases, the government typically promises that if a suspect is convicted, federal prosecutors will recommend a reduced sentence in return for the suspect's cooperation with law-enforcement authorities.

The purpose behind my dinners with Hubbard had become crystal clear. The FBI was trying to entrap me. Robert Vieta was simply an undercover FBI agent. My instinctive apprehension had been justified.

But why? Why would the FBI go to such great lengths to entrap me? Were they short of major criminal cases, or were they really afraid of what I knew, or what they thought I might uncover about Pan Am 103? Could it be they didn't want me to "spill the beans" to my friends on Capitol Hill?

A few months later, I phoned Vieta of Crystal Trading Ventures in Falls Church, Virginia. He actually took my call. He was caught off guard when I directly asked him if he was an FBI agent. Vieta danced around my question, never giving an answer. He didn't have to.

My reaction to this absurd scenario ranged from fear and apprehension, to anger and outrage. Who did these people think they were?

TWENTY-THREE

Facing Major Fines

Several months passed by. I went about my business, but I was holding my breath, waiting for the next shoe to drop.

It finally did on May 19, 1994.

OFAC served me with a Pre-Penalty Notice, alerting me that they were going to fine me $50,000. The notice charged me with five violations of the Libyan Sanctions Regulations and stated their intent to fine me the maximum amount permitted by law, which was $10,000 for each violation.

I was never afforded the benefit, or even courtesy, of a personal meeting, an interview, a hearing, a trial, or any similar form of due process guaranteed by the Constitution. Other than my written response to their inquiries, I wasn't provided an opportunity to defend myself against the government's charges and/or fines. I was left at the mercy of a small, faceless merry band of Washington bureaucrats, whom I had never met. They sat in judgment, found me guilty, and fined me for the following five egregious violations:

> Violation I
>
> On October 8, 1992, Chasey entered into a written contract with ICM to lobby members of Congress to assist in the development of normalized relations between the United States government and the government of Libya, in return for remuneration of $120,000. Fine: $10,000.

I was being fined $10,000 for signing a business contract with a U.S. corporation, even though I hadn't done—and never did—anything to fulfill that contract. And what had I done immediately after signing the contract? I had filed my foreign agent registration papers, along with a copy of my contract, with the Criminal Division of the Department of Justice, which accepted my registration without comment and assigned me foreign agent registration 4221 on behalf of ICM and its client the government of Libya. By the way, I never received a penny of the $120,000.

> Violation II
>
> On or about October 29,1992, Chasey entered into a contract as memorialized by a written confirmation dated October 29, 1992, with Gerrit P. Van de Bovenkamp, a principal of ICM, and Mohammed Bukhres, to arrange for a U.S. Senator to meet with the government of Libya officials Youssef el-Debri, head of government of Libya (GOL) National Security, and Omar Muntassir, GOL secretary of Planning and Economics, to discuss the normalization of relations between the United States government and the GOL, in return for remuneration of $150,000, and to pro-

> cure medical export licenses, in return for remuneration of $50,000. Fine: $10,000.

Now, I was being fined for entering into a personal contract with two American citizens—Bukhres and Bovenkamp. There was no law that prohibited me from doing business with U.S. citizens. The only payment I had received was $50,000 from Bovenkamp's personal account. I deposited that sum into my corporate bank account, which contained other monies I had deposited from other clients. OFAC had subsequently frozen the entire account.

Bukhres did what was commonplace in Washington, D. C. He hired a consultant to assist in the process of securing an export license. The sale of medical supplies did not constitute a violation of the Libyan sanctions regulations, because these items fell under the category of humanitarian assistance and did not require an export license.

> Violation III
>
> On or about October 30, 1991, Chasey received $50,000 from Gerrit P. Van de Bovenkamp as payment under the Agreements. Fine: $10,000.

The $50,000 in question had been wired to me by my client, Bovenkamp from his personal account. I was paid in U.S. dollars by a U.S. citizen for services I had performed. There was never any evidence presented by the OFAC that the money I received was anything but clean U.S. money. There was no evidence that I was paid from frozen or unfrozen, blocked or unblocked Libyan accounts. And to repeat, OFAC had already frozen my account containing the money.[12]

Violation IV

Between November 8-9, 1992, Chasey traveled to Tripoli with (now former) Representative and Mrs. Carroll Hubbard, Jr. and Mr. Bovenkamp in performance of the Agreements. Fine: $10,000.

The Justice Department had been aware of my activities related to my representation of ICM. They had never registered an objection concerning any of my actions. Further, there were no restrictions on travel to Libya in my passport. Only travel to Cuba was prohibited.

Violation V

On November 27, 1992, Chasey entered into a written contract with Flynn to provide assistance and direction in the preparation of extra-judicial effort directed toward lobbying the U.S. Senate and House of Representatives in connection with international efforts related to the indictment of Lamen Fhimah and Abdelbasset Al-Megrahi, Libyans charged in the bombing of Pan Am Flight # 103. Fine: $10,000.

This violation really took the cake. Once again, I was being fined for entering into a written contract, whose approval I sought from OFAC itself before I performed any duties or received any money! And when OFAC denied my application, I accepted the decision and I immediately voided the contract. To repeat, I never did anything for Flynn and Riley, and they never paid me a single penny. I couldn't believe OFAC's audacity in fining me for requesting a license from them, a license that three lawyers had advised me did not fall under the purview of OFAC.

One didn't need to be a legal eagle to realize that not a single violation was valid or would have been upheld in a court of law.

Perhaps this sounded farfetched, but I believed that OFAC had been directed to silence me about what I knew or might discover about Lockerbie, and prevent me from sharing my views—which went against the grain of government policy—with my congressional friends. OFAC would silence me by employing fear and intimidation.

These tactics also seemed designed to keep me out of Libya and away from top Libyan officials. There seemed to be some in my government who even feared my advising the American lawyers representing the two indicted Libyans. They tried to strap me financially with frozen bank accounts and fines. And they had unsuccessfully tried to entrap me into an illegal business deal, which would have conveniently put me behind bars and out of their hair forever.

I don't want to sound grandiose, but I was beginning to suspect that there were a plethora of former and current government officials, from three administrations, who were apprehensive about what I would say to Congress. My disclosures could very well lead to a full congressional investigation of a possible Lockerbie cover-up that would make Watergate pale by comparison.

I was indignant and angry. I wanted to share and reveal what I knew and suspected.

I decided to write a book.

TWENTY-FOUR

It Gets Worse

The mounting pressure began to take a toll on our emotional and financial well-being. We had to prepare for the worst. I needed to develop business outside of Washington, D.C., just in case the government decided to shut me down completely. I also felt a great sense of urgency to finish writing and publishing my book.

Finally, early in 1993, it became obvious that we could no longer afford to pay the mortgage on our La Jolla house. Our "dream home" went up for sale, and that summer we moved twelve miles away to a rented home in Rancho Santa Fe. It was hard on all of us. We really missed our incredible white-water ocean views, family walks around the La Jolla Cove, friends, La Jolla Presbyterian Church, the La Jolla Beach & Tennis Club, and of course the beach lifestyle we had so enjoyed over the past eleven years.

This was the home in which we had raised our daughter and had so many festive family times, from our Christmas brunches to the birthday parties for Katie. Our home was always open to friends and family. It was also the home where we had hosted many political events on behalf of governors and federal lawmakers, corporate CEOs, and Hollywood types. It was with great sadness and a sense of surrealism that we closed the door on our home, but not on its wonderful memories.

However, as always, with a strong spiritual faith and resiliency, we moved forward. As Christians, we firmly believe that God never gives us burdens that we can't bear, as long as we trust in Him. It gave us great strength. On a lighter note, our favorite jingle was "pick yourself up, dust yourself off, and start all over again."

We soon adapted to the laid-back, "ranchy" environment of our newly rented Rancho Santa Fe home. It wasn't La Jolla, but we had a lot of amenities—from our own horse corral, a black-bottom pool with a waterfall, my grand, sunlit study where I loved to write, four fireplaces, six bedrooms and 16,000 square feet of luxurious appointments. All this abundance was for far less than our mortgage payments in La Jolla. Virginia helped out by substituting full time as a Spanish teacher at Katie's new school, Santa Fe Christian, where Katie was now in seventh grade. The two of them enjoyed and gained great sustenance from being a part of this wonderful, God-filled school.

Our first priority was to keep life as normal as possible for Katie by financially supporting her education and special talents. She had been riding horses and competing since she was seven years old and was showing great potential. She had become quite a rider on the children's circuit in California on her pitch black, Dutch Warmblood mare "Private Party." We moved the horse to the prestigious Rancho Santa Fe Riding Club where she progressed quickly under the expert tutelage of one of the top rider/trainers in the world, Hap Hansen. It seemed she was competing every weekend. And for six weeks every spring, we literally moved to Indio, California, for the national competitions. She was winning big shows and eventually earned the right to represent the West Coast in the finals of the National Children's Medal Competition in Washington, D.C., in the spring of 1997.

She loved her school, and horseback riding was her passion. No matter what the government did to me, I was determined that Katie's life would not change as long as I could sustain it. At least for now, she could enjoy life and was shielded from the black clouds that were beginning to form on the horizon.

Virginia and I even got into the riding scene, acquiring two trail horses that we kept in our home corral. We became a riding family, trotting together along the beautiful trails surrounding Rancho Santa Fe. It was one of the few ways we could escape the tremendous pressure we were beginning to feel from the government—and very soon, even from our friends.

While I was trying to keep my family somewhat sheltered in Rancho Santa Fe, the U. S. government continued to relentlessly put pressure on my business. Clients were dropping like flies. Finances were getting tight.

To stop the bleeding, in the summer of 1994, we decided to sell our Georgetown condominium in Washington, D.C. Unfortunately, the country was in the midst of a severe recession. There were no buyers. I couldn't keep making the mortgage payments, so the bank foreclosed.

My weekly commutes to Washington, D.C., and my lobbying business continued to slow down. I decided to focus on the development of a new line of environmentally responsible Swiss cleaning products I had created called BCD (biodegradable-cleaner-degreaser). Long before the current "green revolution," I had come up with this concept and had the BCD formula developed by a chemist friend of mine in Switzerland. In addition, we created a unique biodegradable package for the product. The packaging was so unique that we received three National Packaging Awards from the National Hardware Association.

It was at this time that I also brought in Arlan Boyd, a longtime friend and former lobbying client of mine, into the BCD deal as my financial partner. I regarded BCD as my potential "safety net," free from government interference. But, once again, I was sorely mistaken.

TWENTY-FIVE

Friends Jump Ship

I didn't think there was anyone I could trust more than Arlan Boyd. Our families had been friends for a long time. We looked after each other as only close friends do. We vacationed twice together at their home in Maui, Hawaii, and in return we hosted the Boyds in Washington, D.C., numerous times. Boyd and his wife, Myra, were our special guests at the second inauguration of President Reagan in 1985. We introduced the Boyds to Vice President George Bush and a whole array of political luminaries and Hollywood stars during the inaugural festivities. The Boyds loved it! They especially enjoyed "mugging" with the politicians and stars for the cameras of the Washington social press corps.

I was elected chairman of the board of a large senior living center and retirement community project that Boyd had developed in Virginia. It offered a continuum of independent- and assisted-living homes for its residents, as well as health-care services and a full-service hospital. The center also had a dementia-care unit available for each resident as the need arose. We had well over 200 full-time employees under the supervision of my board.

I served without pay and watched over Boyd's financial interests on the board. I covered his back when a municipal bond company, J.C. Bradford, filed a $1 million lawsuit against the center's board of directors over the defeasance of a series of B bonds owned by Boyd.

Virginia and I attended the funeral of Myra's eldest son from a prior marriage in Los Angeles in mid 1984. I was honored to serve as chairman of a charitable foundation the Boyds had established to honor her son's memory. The foundation provided summer-camp experiences for needy children from the Los Angeles area. I served as its chairman for ten years without pay. It was my pleasure to do it.

Given all this, it never occurred to me that Boyd would ever turn on me.

Boyd was very much aware of the difficulties I was having with the Treasury and Justice Departments over my involvement with Libya. He often said that he wanted to keep our business ventures completely discrete from my personal political problems.

We manufactured BCD in Switzerland and shipped it to Boyd's office in Carlsbad, California, for distribution to our newly organized team of BCD marketing representatives throughout the country.

Throughout 1994, I worked day and night out of Boyd's offices and split my time between California and Switzerland where we began selling BCD in a number of Swiss retail outlets.

I received no pay for my services, but rather waited impatiently for the day when my 50 percent of the BCD stock would eventually pay off. I had a lot of faith in the business and felt sure that our family would soon be on the road to emotional and economic security.

In the meantime, our savings were being depleted and my Washington lobbying business was suffering. I still had a few clients, but there was apprehension and uncertainty in the air.

To supplement our income, Virginia went to work as a temp at a low hourly wage.

Before we had even met, she had earned her master's degree and was an "all-but-dissertation" doctoral candidate at the State University of New York at Albany. She had been a teacher, director of libraries, a high school vice principal, and was selected as a National Level Doctoral Fellow working for a year in Washington, D.C., with the National Association of State Directors of Special Education on the implementation of the newly enacted Education for All Handicapped Children Act.

This woman, whom I loved so much, was now doing this menial work to help keep us afloat. She had moved about California's and Washington's social circles with such ease. It was only months before that she had enjoyed a truly bi-coastal lifestyle replete with the trappings of wealth and prestige. She had chaired the California Ballet Company and was chairwoman of the San Diego Symphony Ball. In Washington, she was a committee member of the highly respected CARE International Foundation.

She was president of our own charity, the Third World Prosthetic Foundation, responsible for putting 1,000 prosthetic devices on young children who were the innocent victims of land mines in El Salvador. She had chaired the La Jolla and Rancho Santa Fe Republican Women's groups, and only a short time before, had received a presidential appointment from President Reagan to serve on the United States Selective Service Commission. And now, here she was, working as a temp to help us make ends meet.

How could all of this have happened in such a short period of time? Could things get any worse?

Unfortunately they could. They could get much, much worse.

It was in the spring of 1995, when the FBI and IRS began subtly turning the screws on me. When Boyd began feeling the squeeze, he became more and more nervous about my legal situation. At one point he told me that he didn't need federal investigators snooping about his Carlsbad offices and business activities.

Boyd began spending less time with me over the next few weeks. I knew something was wrong. I was told by his secretary that the FBI had arranged an appointment with him the following week concerning "his relationship with Bill Chasey."

A week later, my face went ashen when I opened a certified letter delivered to my home, from Boyd. All of my worst nightmares had come true.

My good friend and business partner was pulling the plug on our BCD business relationship. Boyd claimed that he had spent enough money on the project and that he was confiscating my shares of the stock. I could, however, purchase the shares I already owned from him at a price he knew was far beyond my means. I was no longer welcome in his Carlsbad offices and our relationship was summarily terminated.

I was devastated! I had taken BCD so far in two years, and now I was being financially strangled by my best friend. Boyd knew that he could steamroll me financially and that I could not put up much of a fight. He also must have known that his actions would put not only my future, but my family's well being, in jeopardy. He didn't care. He had unlimited wealth and his own full-time lawyers. He knew no *pro bono* lawyer would take my case in a civil suit because it could drag on for years. My BCD dream was extinguished, and with it any hope of a financial recovery from the business that I, not Boyd, had created.

I never heard from him again.

BCD and an important friendship became two more victims of the Lockerbie disaster.

In the end, sweet justice was served. Boyd, with all of his money, couldn't make BCD successful without me. In short order, the company failed and Boyd lost a great deal of money in the process. However, at that point, he was the least of my worries.

Our finances were in a state of ruin.

One of our most embarrassing moments occurred one Saturday morning when the three of us returned from a trail ride on our horses. Our black Mercedes was missing from the parking lot of the Rancho Santa Fe Riding Club. It had been repossessed! I remember Virginia, trying to save our daughter the shame, making up some story about forgetting to let us know about having the car serviced that day. Well, we couldn't afford to get the car out of hock and had no credit left to purchase a new one, so we resorted to using monthly rentals from Avis. In fact, we were never able to own or lease a car in the U.S. again.

Now, in the spring of 1995, with my lobbying business fading fast and the BCD business gone, we had no choice but to scale down even further. The FBI was doing a very thorough job of tightening the noose.

It wasn't long before we could no longer afford to make the rental payments on our Rancho Santa Fe residence. In the summer of 1995, we held three garage sales and sold all the contents of our 16,000-square-foot home. One of the hardest things for Virginia was selling her baby grand piano, which I had bought her for our La Jolla home. She loved playing it, and it always was the center of our parties. Rather than sell it to just anyone however, she made sure it went to a deserving family who could never have afforded it under other circumstances.

We finished packing up what was left of our belongings and moved a few miles away to a lovely, but much less expensive, furnished home, in Olivenhain, California.

Moving the horses was another matter. That was Katie's and my job. We rode our horses over the tops of canyons, down into gullies, and across dirt roads to our new home. It took several hours and was much more difficult than we had anticipated. It would prove to be one of our fondest memories together, taking the sting out of an otherwise painful situation.

How had we gotten to this place in our lives? What lay ahead? And most importantly, why was the government so unremitting in its pursuit of me and my family?

It took me a while to figure it out.

TWENTY-SIX

My Controversial Book

Despite all these troubles, I was more determined than ever to finish my book. I had spent a lot of time in the fall and winter of 1994 in my study, researching and writing. I can still picture our horses grazing lazily in the corral outside my window, the morning sun filling the study with warm light, and flames dancing in the fireplace. It was my refuge. Little did I know the FBI was enjoying the same sights and sounds in the "privacy" of my own home.

The book—*Foreign Agent 4221: The Lockerbie Cover-up*—was published by ProMotion Publishing of San Diego in April, 1995.[13] We had a champagne celebratory book party at our home. No matter what happened next, at least my children and grandchildren would know my side of the story, not just the government's version.

Next, we introduced the book to the public at a very well-attended press conference held at the United Nations, in New York City, on April 18, 1995. The United Nations Press Bureau and my publisher had arranged it. Reporters from major media outlets covered the release. In addition to the press, I was both surprised and delighted to see that two families of Lockerbie victims were in attendance. They took part in the question-and-answer session that followed my formal presentation. My side of the Lockerbie story was now public knowledge.

There was no turning back.

The fanfare was short lived. On the very next day, April 19, 1995, the Alfred P. Murrah federal building in downtown Oklahoma City was bombed. It erased my Lockerbie story from the front pages of many newspapers. Although early reports claimed the attack was carried out by three Arab-looking men, it was actually committed by Timothy McVeigh, an American militia movement sympathizer, who detonated an explosive-filled truck parked in front of the building.

McVeigh's co-conspirator, Terry Nichols, had assisted in the bomb's preparation. It would be the most destructive terrorist act on American soil until the 9/11 attacks. The Oklahoma blast claimed 168 lives, including 19 children under the age of 6, and injured more than 680 people. The blast destroyed or damaged 324 buildings within a 16-block radius, destroyed or burned 86 cars, and shattered glass in 258 nearby buildings. The bomb caused at least $652 million worth of damage.

It seemed rather ironic and bad timing that my book on the Lockerbie tragedy was released one day prior to such another horrific act of terrorism.

Nonetheless, at some point in this process I had a revelation. I finally figured out why the government was after me. I knew I was a good and honorable man. I was a good and charitable Christian. I had done an excellent job as a lobbyist, friend, father and husband. I had always been an honest businessman.

But what I had done to bring the wrath of the government down on me was to take an unpopular position on who was culpable for the Lockerbie bombing. It was so convenient to pin it on the much-hated Qadhafi. There was no love lost for this bizarre and self-righteous monster. But the 270 innocent people who died didn't want a scapegoat. They wanted the actual perpetrators brought to justice. In my opinion, Syria and Iran were behind the bombing. It was wrong—no matter how vile Qadhafi was—to blame it on someone who was not at fault.

Obviously, the government did not want this viewpoint and my research to reach the eyes and ears of Congress or the public. The government was trying to silence me by sullying my good name and reputation.

TWENTY-SEVEN

The FBI Follows Up

Rather than return immediately to California from New York, I stopped in Washington, D.C., to spend the night and visit some friends.

The following morning, I arrived at Washington National Airport for my flight back to San Diego. Much to my surprise, I was greeted at the security checkpoint by FBI special agent Robert Core. He presented his credentials and asked if I remembered meeting him in the House dining room almost two years before.

Of course. How could I forget him?

It was me, who not only met him, but bought breakfast for him and his FBI associate Chuck Anderson in the House dining room that day. At the time they were investigating the now infamous House Bank scandal.

He asked if we could find a quiet place "to talk." I suggested the American Airlines Admiral's Club located just inside the security check-point area of the main passenger terminal.

Not wasting any time, Core served me with a federal subpoena, demanding copies of all of our financial records, tax returns, canceled checks, contracts, and other written records for the past five years.

Core then asked what I knew about the Oklahoma City bombing the day before. Had I heard anything about it from my "Libyan friends?"

Although Timothy McVeigh had been arrested right after the bombing, the feds—not necessarily the brightest bulbs on the Christmas tree—were still searching for three Arab-looking men.

Core sternly warned me that I would be prosecuted if I didn't tell him everything I knew or had heard about the Oklahoma City bombing then or in the future. Of course, I didn't know anything about it and hadn't been in contact with anyone in Libya for years, which Core already knew. This intimidation was nothing more than something with which to garnish the subpoena.

Core's visit came as quite a shock. I remember how my heart started pounding when I first noticed him across the airport reception area. He obviously had been tracking me during my stay in New York and Washington. He probably attended my press conference at the UN, and obviously knew of my travel plans back to California.

It became apparent that he had been working on this "surprise" visit for some time, since he had applied for and secured a federal subpoena well in advance.

What lies could Core have told a federal judge to persuade

him to sign this subpoena? None of this happened by accident. It was all planned and well-orchestrated.

I felt caught up in a situation I had only watched in documentaries or films about WWII when people were "fingered" as "enemies of the state," or during the McCarthy hearings, accused of being "anti-American."

What had happened to America? Was this really happening to me?

No, it couldn't be. I was just having a nightmare. All I had to do was to rub my eyes and I would wake up!

My hands literally shook as I paged through the demands in the subpoena on my cross-country flight. I had no idea how I was going to break this to Virginia. We were being treated as criminals and traitors. It was beyond comprehension.

Back home, I showed the subpoena to Virginia and I told her about my visit with Core. She also became visibly upset. But in her usual quiet, stoic way, she assured me that all of our papers were in order.

The very next day, we began digging out the boxes in the garage that contained all of our records. Would this be the end or just the beginning of another episode in this Kafkaesque nightmare?

It took us weeks to put our financial records in order and to mail them off in accordance with the subpoena. We had spent hours going over every tax return, every cancelled check, every contract, wondering what could possibly be wrong with any of them. Then we made copies of everything and rechecked the papers. We couldn't afford an accountant. It was just the two of us, sitting on our garage floor, day after day, surrounded by stacks of papers.

Some couples may have cracked under the pressure, but there was never a time that we weren't committed to each other and believed that I had done absolutely nothing wrong and had done nothing to deserve this outrageous treatment. We just hung in there together and prayed a lot.

We sent box upon box of material to Washington. In the end, we couldn't imagine what the FBI could possibly decipher from their contents. We had always filed our tax returns timely. We'd never had any problems with the IRS.

Nevertheless, when you receive a federal subpoena, compelling you to provide all of your records for the past five years, your mind begins to wander and play tricks on you.

What had we missed? Had we somehow inadvertently broken the law? The tension was enormous . . .

TWENTY-EIGHT

Business Declines

I tried my best to conduct business as usual with my few remaining lobbying clients. Yet, I continued to be fearful and distracted knowing that the FBI and IRS were sifting through our personal and business records. If they scrutinized anybody's tax returns, they would invariably turn up something that could be deemed improper or illegal.

One day, I received an unnerving call from one of my clients—a call I will never forget. It was from one of my newest clients, Dr. Ivor Royston. He was a prominent oncologist, researcher, scientist, entrepreneur and venture capitalist

Virginia and I met Royston many years before when we purchased two limited partnerships in Hybritech, one of his first biotech companies. Hybritech was quite successful in harnessing monoclonal antibodies to quickly diagnose and treat diseases. His firm provided the $300,000 startup funds, and Hybritech's first product was antibodies for the hepatitis B virus. Later, the company developed the Prostate-Specific-Antigen (PSA) test for the early diagnosis of prostate cancer, which probably saved countless lives. Hybritech went public in 1981. Five years later, pharmaceutical giant Eli Lilli acquired the company for $480 million. Our stake in Hybritech proved to be one of our most successful investments.

As a result, we became social friends with the Roystons, and our daughters became friends through their equestrian activities in Rancho Santa Fe. Recently, Royston had hired me to help him get selected for a six-year presidential appointment on the National Cancer Advisory Board (NCAB). He was aware that I had been successful in helping out two of his friends—Ellen Siegel to the NCAB and Peter Preuss to the National Institutes for Health (NIH) Advisory Council.

Although Royston was more than qualified for the NCAB position, he still needed my help in the political process of winning the appointment.

My job—any lobbyist's job—was to introduce a candidate to powerful members of Congress and to seek their support in the presidential appointment nomination process. Hopefully, this would result in the member writing a letter of support or talking directly to the president on behalf of my client.

For example, I introduced Royston to Sen. Diane Feinstein (D-CA). She was a natural, because she represented his home state of California. We met in the Senate dining room. Dr. Royston and Sen. Feinstein hit it off right away.

Later, I asked Sen. Feinstein if she would be kind enough to write him a letter of support for the Cancer Board. She agreed and I followed up with her staff to make sure the letter went out to the president in a timely fashion.

I also introduced him to three other senators and six congressmen. All wrote him letters of support.

Royston was very pleased with my efforts.

However, this was a very different Royston on the phone. His voice was very shaky. He said he had just been through something he "thought only happened in the movies." Two FBI agents had come to his office at the San Diego Regional Cancer Center and demanded to see all of his records related to William C. Chasey. They told him that they were investigating me for possible obstruction of justice, wire fraud, mail fraud, money laundering, conspiracy, federal racketeering, grand theft, and forgery! Was there anything they had left out?

The agents had donned rubber gloves and confiscated all of Royston's documents related to me and his would-be presidential appointment to the National Cancer Advisory Board. Included were copies of the letters from the senators and congressmen written on Royston's behalf to the president.

The agents had the audacity to tell him that they suspected I had "stolen" congressional stationery from various congressional offices and forged the senators' and congressmen's signatures on the letters written to the president. The reason the agents had worn rubber gloves was that they hoped to find my finger prints on the letters. Despite his trepidation, Royston knew how absurd this was, because the letters had come directly from those lawmakers' offices, not from me. Yet he was scared to death.

I didn't know whether to laugh or cry. Was this what it had come down to—accusing me of stealing stationery from members' offices? How low could the FBI stoop and how vile could they be to make a case against me?

Needless to say, this was the last time I ever heard from Dr. Ivor Royston.

Nevertheless, my efforts proved fruitful, because shortly thereafter he was appointed by President Clinton to a six-year term as a member of the National Cancer Advisory Board.

Within days, I received two very similar calls from other clients. In each case, they reported that they'd been visited by FBI agents, claiming to be investigating me for a series of heinous crimes.

In addition, some friends on the Hill told me that the FBI had also visited a number of members with whom I was close.

In less than a month, I was left without a single client. My reputation had been desecrated and my very successful twenty-one year career as a lobbyist had been destroyed.

It is astonishing what damage someone in a three-button suit with a badge, a gun, and an FBI identification card can do. There were no indictments, no trials, no verdicts—just guilt by innuendo from the "G" men.

It's hard to describe the despair Virginia and I experienced during this time, as we watched our business and life crumble, and waited to hear back from the FBI's investigation of our financial records.

BCD was gone. My lobbying days were over. And most of my friends had abandoned me.

To make matters worse, our bank account was still frozen, I had no income, and the rent was due.

TWENTY-NINE

FBI Investigation Expands

For the next few weeks, nothing happened. We were beginning to think that maybe the FBI and IRS had finally decided that they had bigger fish to fry, especially since they had so successfully managed to neuter me so completely that anything I had to say about Lockerbie no one would listen to anyway.

It was obvious I wasn't going to be doing much business in the U.S. anymore, so I began to renew my contacts in Poland. Virginia had accepted a job as development coordinator for the Santa Fe Christian Schools, which was in the middle of a fundraising campaign to build an activities center/gym. Katie was now in eighth grade at that school and we were excited about the new center she would be able to enjoy in high school.

We were sure in our hearts that we had done nothing illegal and we began to breathe a little more freely.

Then, one day, that dreaded phone call came.

It was FBI special agent Robert Core. He asked me to meet him in the FBI office in downtown Washington, D.C. He reassured me that "it was nothing to be concerned about." He just wanted to review some of my financial records with me.

I asked him if I needed an attorney. Core said it wasn't "necessary", but it was up to me. It sounded like the meeting would be rather harmless, and I felt quite relieved. Maybe he just wanted to tie up some loose ends.

Nonetheless, I asked a lawyer friend, Dan Ripley, to attend the meeting with me. He was not a criminal attorney and had a very small civil law practice in Maryland. At the very least, I wanted a witness to make sure I understood everything clearly.

Once inside the FBI headquarters, we were escorted to a rather non-descript room with one small window and a large conference table. Core and IRS special agent Kevin Kelcours stood to greet us as we entered.

As I gazed around, I saw row after row of wooden shelves, packed with books, tapes, films, and scores of documents neatly organized with little tabs and file separators. Little did I know that this room was "the Chasey criminal investigation documents room!" These were my books, tapes, recordings, videos, tax returns, and various business documents related to my activities and movements over the past five years!

Core, pointing to the shelves, proceeded to give me a brief orientation of the materials the FBI had collected. It was then that I learned that I had been followed; our phones and cars had been tapped; and electronic bugging devices had been planted in our homes in California and in Washington, D.C, since 1992.

(I will never forget the shock on Virginia's face when I told her that the FBI had been listening to and recording our conversations and monitoring our activities—even in the privacy of our own bedrooms—over the past several years!)

I especially remember Core's sneer as he opened a rather large, flat box containing the "bugged" voice recordings secured by Congressman Hubbard and FBI agent Vieta during my dinner meetings with them at the restaurant in 1993. They had tried to lure me into doing an illegal deal with Libya. What was he sneering about? I hadn't fallen for it.

Core had a number of questions about our personal finances, business contracts, and tax returns. Once again, the focus seemed to be on the fact that I had signed contracts with a rather large number of people who wanted my help in securing presidential appointments, ambassadorships, agency positions, and memberships on prestigious federal commissions and boards.

I remember wondering, "What does all of this have to do with Libya? Or taxes?"

If this was what all this investigation was about, then for sure I had done absolutely nothing wrong. I was proud of the fact that over the years I had been very successful in developing support for my clients with key Members of Congress. Royston was an excellent example.

In almost every case, my clients had achieved their goals and were very satisfied with my assistance. However, they couldn't have done so if they hadn't possessed the education and specific credentials for the positions they had sought and won. Nor would I have taken them on as clients unless they were open and straightforward with me. They had to be totally transparent about their records and resumes. The majority of them ended up making valuable contributions to the organizations and institutes that they served on.

No one is perfect, including me. There had been one client who snookered me and a lot of other people, including the president of the United States. The memory haunts me to this day.

His name was Larry Lawrence—a very wealthy real-estate developer, and hotelier. In 1991, Forbes named Lawrence among the 400 richest Americans and estimated his fortune at $315 million. Over his lifetime, Lawrence contributed at least $10 million to Democrats and to Democratic causes, although Lawrence had a propensity for supporting the wrong presidential candidates. He went all out to raise funds for Sen. Eugene McCarthy (D-MN), Sen. Frank Church (D-ID), Vice President Walter F. Mondale, Sen. Gary Hart (D-CO), Sen. John Glenn D-OH), and Sen. John Kerry (D-MA) in their unsuccessful bids for the presidency. He had used his business, personal influence, and resources to attract his friends and colleagues to support these candidates, only to be greatly disappointed.

Lawrence had a major political resource that proved most helpful in his efforts to support political candidates for various offices. He owned the exclusive Hotel Del Coronado on Coronado Island in San Diego. With its iconic red turrets, the "Del" radiates over the Pacific with a gracious Victorian splendor that is without equal.

Virginia and I were good friends of Lawrence and his previous wife Jeanie, as well as his last wife, Shelia.

Over the years, he and I had hosted a series of fundraisers at the "Del," including one for Al Gore's 1988 presidential campaign. Once again, Lawrence rode the wrong horse, and Michael Dukakis, not Gore, ended up as the 1988 Democratic nominee for president.

That all changed in 1992, when Lawrence became the new best friend of Gov. Bill Clinton of Arkansas. He had served on Clinton's national finance board, while his wife, Shelia, headed up the Clinton-Gore campaign in Southern California. Lawrence suddenly became a major "player" during the Clinton campaign and early presidency. Lawrence even bought a luxurious home in Georgetown just to be close to their new best friend and neighbor, President Clinton.

In 1993, Clinton nominated Lawrence as U.S. ambassador to Switzerland, an appointment that required Senate approval. Unfortunately, the confirmation ran into trouble right away. It came out of the Foreign Relations Committee without a recommendation, after which a senator placed the nomination on "hold" for two months. (A single senator, whose identity usually remains secret, can block a vote on any presidential nomination. However, a cloture vote—sixty senators or more—can unfreeze that block.) In the meantime, the Republicans and the 11,000-member American Foreign Service Association questioned Lawrence's credentials, maintaining that he had been chosen only because he was a major contributor to the Democratic Party. This was a fair point.

Lawrence asked me to help him shake his confirmation free from the Senate hold. A few days later, I bumped into my friend Sen. Larry Pressler. I asked him if he would mind finding out who had placed the hold on the Lawrence nomination. It didn't take him very long.

"I did," he said.

Laughing, I asked if he would mind removing the hold. He did so forthwith.

On February 8, 1994, the Senate voted 70 to 16 in favor of Lawrence's appointment. And in March 1994, he was sworn in as the U. S. ambassador to Switzerland. His wife Shelia was appointed as special envoy to the World Conservation Union in Geneva, Switzerland. And President Clinton spent his first vacation in office at the Lawrence mansion just down the street from the Hotel Del Coronado.

As a surprise gift, I secured the original tally sheet on Lawrence's nomination with the 79-16 recorded vote from the Senate Recording Clerk. Virginia had it professionally framed, and we presented the happy document at an elaborate farewell party for the Lawrences at the "Del," just before their departure for Switzerland.

My major disappointment and embarrassment came about a year after Lawrence died of natural causes in Switzerland on January 10, 1996, at age sixty-nine. Because of his military service in the Merchant Marines, he was buried at Arlington National Cemetery, and President Bill Clinton delivered the eulogy.

In 1997, I was shocked to learn that Lawrence's body was being disinterred and taken to California after congressional investigators had searched military records and found no evidence that he had ever been a Merchant Marine.

Lawrence had falsely claimed that he had served and been injured on the S.S. Horace Bushnell during World War II. In fact, at that time Lawrence had been attending Wilbur Wright College in Chicago. I'm not sure how much personal credibility I lost in having supported Lawrence on Capitol Hill.

To my relief and surprise, special agent Core didn't bring up Larry Lawrence. Instead, he seemed to imply that my "influence peddling" was somehow illegal and that it needed to be investigated further. I really felt as if he was grasping at straws. What I did was what every lobbyist did. It was obvious the wiretaps and whatever else they had been investigating hadn't panned out.

My lawyer and I spent about two hours with Core and Kelcours. I protested the fact that the FBI had destroyed my lobbying business with little or no proof of any wrongdoing on my part. I told Core that I was entering the hotel business in Poland and that I wanted him to promise that he would not contact my new partners. He smiled that FBI smile again and promised they would not interfere.

He concluded by saying that the FBI and the Justice Department had a lot more work to do on my case, and that I should expect to hear from them in the next few days or weeks.

Of course, I continued to be worried. I was also concerned that special agent Core was trying to concoct that something illegal had been done in my having helped my clients secure federal appointments. I knew there was nothing illegal about hiring an advocate, lawyer, or lobbyist to help secure a presidential appointment. It had been common practice in the United States from the beginning of time.

However, I needed to satisfy my own curiosity about it.

THIRTY

Presidential Appointments

I started with the White House Office of Presidential Personnel (OPP). Its director oversees a staff of forty to sort through the more than 350,000 resumes that arrive at the White House every year to fill just 3,000 jobs. In other words, the OPP rejects 1,000 people for every one it hires.

Two former OPP directors were friends of mine—Fred Fielding, three-time White House counsel under Republican presidents; and John Harrington, Reagan's deputy assistant for Presidential Personnel from 1983 until 1985, before serving as secretary of energy from 1985 to 1989. I felt no hesitation in dropping them a note, especially to Harrington, who had participated in a weekly Bible study with me in the White House during the first two years of the Reagan presidency.

In their written replies, both expressed surprise that I would ask such rudimentary questions. They both said that lobbying for presidential appointments was a very well recognized and acceptable practice that had been a part of how business was done in the nation's capital since the early days of the republic. They both pointed out they had worked with countless lobbyists seeking appointments for their clients.

I also sent a note to Fred McClure, an associate deputy attorney general under Reagan. He wrote back, concurring with Fielding and Harrington.

I sent these three letters to Special Agent Core, just in case he foolishly decided to continue making an issue of this matter.

THIRTY-ONE

Serious Charges

About two weeks after my meeting at FBI headquarters, I received an upsetting phone call from my lawyer, Dan Ripley. Earlier that morning, he had been summoned by and had spent most of the day with Core and Kelcours reviewing my "case."

I'll never forget the sullen tone of Ripley's voice when he said, "It doesn't look good, Bill."

He had spent hours listening to the FBI outline twenty-one potential felony charges against me, and much to my horror, against my wife, Virginia!

Ripley had just returned home. He said he needed some time to collect his thoughts and study his handwritten notes. He promised to fax me the list of the felony charges, along with a detailed summary of his notes and reflections later that evening.

Several hours later, Virginia's eyes welled up and tears started to flow as every new criminal charge rolled off our fax machine. I've never been so terrified in my life, especially with what my lawyer stated on the first page: "The Justice Department is committed to prosecuting you and Virginia for each charge, and you could each be facing up to thirty years in prison!"

What in heaven's name was going on? We were dumbfounded. This was a huge leap from being accused of stealing congressional stationery to a litany of federal indictments that could put me behind bars essentially for the rest of my life!

Virginia and I spent most of the night studying and discussing the charges and trying to understand how the federal prosecutors could have misconstrued so many things. Up to that point, it was the most difficult night of our lives.

Most of all, our primary concern was the welfare of our now fourteen-year-old daughter, Katie. What would become of her if federal prosecutors could make any ONE of these charges stick?

There were so many charges it's hard to know where to begin.

I was charged with wire fraud for bank transfers we had made to and received from foreign bank accounts. If you commit fraud by using "electronic communications," it adds to the severity of the penalty.

It was alleged that I had secret offshore bank accounts in Switzerland, Costa Rica and Japan.

There was a money-laundering charge related to foreign exchanges and payments we made and received outside of the United States. Of course, I had represented a large corporate client in Japan, a number of clients in Central America, Europe, South Africa and Libya during the previous five years. That was my profession. But money laundering? It was alleged that I engaged in financial transactions to conceal the identity, source, and/or destination of illegally gained money.

I wondered how I would have ever had the time, let alone the staff, to have even figured out such schemes. Besides, it was all a lie.

I was charged with tax evasion for income we allegedly failed to report. Since we both signed joint tax returns, the government was charging Virginia for tax evasion as well. Generally, tax evasion is the term for efforts to not pay taxes by *illegal* means.

I was charged with mail fraud for money we had received via the U.S. Postal Service for various business and charitable activities.

We were also being charged with conspiracy to defraud the United States government out of money. Under U.S. law, conspiracy is an evil, unlawful, treacherous, or surreptitious plan formulated in secret by two or more persons. In other words, it is an illegal "plot."

Prosecutors were also charging me for using my influence and money to illegally secure governmental positions for several of my lobbying clients.

And, most ludicrous of all, I was being charged with larceny, for stealing congressional stationery from several congressional offices, as well as forgery!

They were actually alleging that I had written letters and forged the signatures of several members of Congress on purloined congressional stationery, which I had then sent to the president of the United States in order to secure political positions for my clients!

Franz Kafka, I've got a story that should interest you. I really wondered what country, let alone what planet, I was living in!

For more than twenty years I had worked in Washington, relying on my reputation and integrity to lobby on behalf of my clients—from corporations and countries, to consortiums, as well as for important social issues, such as education for the handicapped, peace in Central America, banning smoking on airlines, among other things. I liked to think of myself as a "shoe-leather lobbyist." I was someone who walked the halls of the Capitol and worked hard at what I did because I absolutely loved it and I believed in what I was doing.

I didn't rely on spending big money, giving free trips, or throwing lavish parties—the usual tricks of the lobbying trade. I was not an industrial mogul, a former congressman or White House assistant, a Washington lawyer, or a slick PR man. I was a former academic who had found his real niche, not in the research lab, but in the political labyrinths of Congress.[14] My whole staff consisted of my wife, a driver, and a part-time secretary—all devoted to what we were doing to improve the lives of the people who needed my special skills.

I not only loved my job, I relished the access to some of the most intriguing and powerful people in the world, access I earned through trust, personal relationships, and hard work.

I had been elected by my peers as chairman of the Ethics and Conduct Committee of the American League of Lobbyists. I wrote the first draft of the league's code of ethics, under which most league lobbyists operate today. No one had ever questioned my motives or integrity.

Surely, if Core and the other agents had *really* followed me, if they had *really* interviewed, not intimidated, my clients and members of Congress, this is what they would have determined.

But instead, they chose to violate their sacred oath—to seek justice—and concoct these trumped-up charges. I was shocked, angered, humiliated and sick at what I was reading. I felt like I was the protagonist in some "Theater of the Absurd" play. But it wasn't a play and these were very serious charges. Surely, someone wanted me put out of the way. But who? And why? What had I done to deserve this? Whom had I antagonized that they wanted to rain this wrath down on me and my family?

There was no merit to any of these charges. Unfortunately, however, we had to defend ourselves and needed expert legal help. And this kind of help is very expensive. Financially, we were barely staying afloat, and we had no place and no one to turn to.

THIRTY-TWO

The Federal "Judicial" System

I called my friend Paul Riley of Flynn & Riley for advice. He suggested that I contact a Washington colleague of his by the name of Brian Shaughnessy, a former federal prosecutor. Riley thought that Shaughnessy would be able to give me superior representation at a fraction of the cost most D.C. lawyers would charge.

I remember the feeling of relief in that first meeting with Shaughnessy in his downtown office. He listened and took notes, but he gave me the impression that he really cared about me and loathed what the government was trying to do to destroy me.

After a few more meetings, he was ready to do battle with the federal prosecutors on my behalf. He and I spent the next five months discrediting and repudiating the federal government's evidence against me. Shaughnessy became increasingly confident that we could beat the charges in a court of law.

However, aware of our tenuous financial situation, he always kept me apprised of the expenses involved in pursuing this course of action—something the government was well aware of and counted on.

Shaughnessy told me that I should expect to spend at least $1 million for my defense, plus another $1 million for Virginia's. One firm could not represent both of us. Virginia would need her own, separate defense team, which would mean doubling our legal expenses. He warned that even if we won our case, we could be ruined financially for the rest of our lives, or as he put it, "innocent, but broke."

There were some other mitigating factors that needed to be weighed before we decided to go to war against the limitless resources of the U.S. government.

According to Shaughnessy, my chances of acquittal were intrinsically slim.[15] Apparently, juries assume that a defendant must be guilty if the Justice Department chooses to prosecute him or her.

But what I soon realized was that I was just another victim of prosecutorial misconduct. As I said earlier, federal prosecutors swear a solemn oath "to seek justice," but that's not what they do. Most just want to put another notch in their belt, so they can resign in a few years and set up a lucrative practice as criminal defense attorneys.

In 1994, a *USA Today* investigation found that prosecutorial abuses regularly put innocent people in prison. For decades, judges have blasted prosecutors for "flagrant" or "outrageous" misconduct. Prosecutors have been caught hiding exculpatory evidence and/or lying to judges and juries. As a result, many innocent people have been wrongly convicted and imprisoned.[16]

All this was quite daunting. We had to make a decision. Did we fight the Justice Department or not?

There was something else to consider.

Shaughnessy told us that we could expect a trial to last as long as five years. This would require our full-time attention, leaving little time or energy to make a living or have any kind of personal life. We were already broke. How could we possibly pay our legal bills, never mind our personal ones, if we couldn't work for five years?

Finally, our most important consideration was our daughter. What affect would all of this have on her?

Our heads were spinning, but faith, and our belief in our innocence, kept us steadfast and gave us strength. Nevertheless, our situation looked bleak and hopeless.

THIRTY-THREE

Business Abroad

Our waking hours were devoted to meetings or phone calls with my lawyer and negotiations with federal prosecutor David A. Frank and Kevin Kelcours of the IRS. Our sleeping hours were haunted by the prospect of going to prison. Some progress would be made on a few charges, only to lose ground on others. We were so financially strapped that we could barely breathe. The relentless stress aged us considerably.

I had to make some money, so I decided to concentrate on new business opportunities in Poland, which I had been dabbling in since 1991.

Between 1994 and 1997, I started commuting to Poland almost on a weekly basis, desperate to generate a new income stream for my family.

In 1995, I had applied for and been awarded three feasibility grants to study various industry sectors in this large emerging former-Eastern Bloc economy by the Overseas Private Investment Corporation (OPIC). I formed and led teams of experts from the United States to Poland to investigate potential business opportunities for American investors in the poultry, entertainment, and hotel industries. In the process, I picked up a few business contacts for myself.

One business client was interested in purchasing a number of Polish poultry farms; another considered opening a chain of chicken restaurants in Poland, and a third was interested in opening a chain of "extended stay" hotels in some of the country's largest cities. I was particularly attracted to the hotel business.

At our church, we had befriended Stan Harder, an American hotelier. I had established a close relationship with a savvy Polish businessman from Lodz. Together, we formed a new hotel development company in Poland. And so I became president of Genesis Suite Hotels. (Our daughter Katie actually came up with the name Genesis. She said it was "a new beginning" taken from the first book of the Old Testament.) Harder made the initial capital investment, for which he retained 60 percent of the stock. My Polish partner received 20 percent, and I had the remaining 20 percent.

I successfully arranged hotel development deals with three major Polish cities: Lodz, Poznan and Gdansk. The deals were new and creative for this part of the world, and I somehow managed to get these cities to contribute 36,000 square meters of their most valuable parcels of land to our new upstart venture. Our part of the deal was to develop the properties into shopping malls, multiplex movie theaters, office buildings, and restaurants, along with an extended-stay hotel.

After making the rounds of most Polish banks, I landed a $20 million loan from the Polish Development Bank for the construction of our first Genesis Hotel project in Lodz. I knew I was on my way to financial recovery!

Genesis Hotels started attracting potential investors from around the world, and I began to think that we would be able to develop all three city projects at the same time. I was flying high again. But most of all, I was able to temporarily free myself from the clutches of the federal prosecutors back in Washington, D.C.

At the same time, my Polish partner from Lodz and I launched our first American Kaffe restaurant. I really missed my daily routine of drinking a cup of flavored coffee and munching on a bagel every morning back in the States. I figured Lodz, a city of over one million people, could use one good coffee and bagel shop!

American Kaffe was somewhat modeled on Starbucks. The store had a warm, light, and airy design, which contrasted with the dark and dreary former Communist Poland. We sold a variety of flavored coffees, salads, baked potatoes, smoothies and sandwiches. We even found a Polish baker who could make American-style bagels. We eventually opened two additional American Kaffes in Lodz, and a fourth one in Warsaw.

I put my heart and soul into Genesis Hotels. My time was spent commuting between Southern California and Lodz, Poland. I used all of my personal and lobbying skills in the development of the three Genesis Hotel projects. I did the same, but to a lesser degree, in expanding our fledgling American Kaffe coffee shops.

Stan Harder and his wife became dear friends. The five of us made many trips to Poland together to meet with Polish politicians and businessmen, and to break ground on the hotels. Katie became the Harder's favorite babysitter for their young children.

Since I was spending more and more of my time in Poland, Virginia and I began thinking about moving there. After all, it was my only source of income, and it appeared that my future investments would come to fruition there as well. Maybe it was just the kind of change we needed and to get away from the miasma of the United States for a while.

In the spring of 1997, Harder and I agreed that my family should move to Poland, where I would continue to operate the Genesis Hotel Company as president, for the foreseeable future. My salary would remain $10,000 per month until we were able to secure outside investment capital. Occasionally, Harder expressed concern over my problems with the Justice Department, but I assured him that the FBI had promised it would not contact him or interfere with our project in any way.

Enthusiastically, we began to prepare for our move to Poland. We gave notice to our landlord and moved out of our Olivenhain house in May 1997. Sadly, we had to bid adieu to our trusty trail horses, Joey and Ketchum, and put the rest of our belongings in storage. We rented a beach-front condo from friends in Del Mar for two months, while Virginia and Katie finished the school year. I was scheduled to go to Poland in a few weeks to find an apartment and prepare for their arrival in Warsaw. Things were looking good.

Then, late one Sunday afternoon in June 1997, I received a call from Harder. He wanted me to come see him at home right away.

When I arrived, he was visibly shaking. I instantly knew that Special Agent Core had broken his promise. In a few days, the FBI and IRS agents would be visiting his offices to scrutinize all of his financial and business records related to me and the Genesis Hotels in Poland. I was outraged.

Harder, however, went ballistic. He fired me on the spot and immediately proposed a financial settlement. He would purchase my 20 percent of the company for $200,000. I could take it or leave it. He would give the money to Virginia before she left for Poland on July 15th.

I had no choice but to agree to his terms.

Discouraged, but still determined, Virginia and I decided that we would still be better off starting anew in Poland, where the FBI and the IRS would be less likely to interfere. The $200,000 Virginia would receive on July 15th would last quite a while and give me the seed money for a fresh start.

I flew to Poland on July 1st with virtually everything I owned in two suitcases. In downtown Warsaw, I rented a recently renovated, two-bedroom apartment, which was about the size of my Rancho Santa Fe study, on the fourth floor of a drab, gray, walk-up, apartment building constructed during the Communist era. It was okay though, as I was buoyed by the prospect of starting a new life.

I worked on my American Kaffe development project and eagerly waited for Virginia and Katie to join me in a couple of weeks.

However, the day before Virginia, Katie, and our dog, Ribbons, were to depart for Poland, I received an urgent call from Virginia. She and Katie had gone to Harder's office to collect the $200,000.

When they arrived, the somewhat nervous secretary told them to wait in the reception area. An hour later, they were still waiting. Finally, Virginia asked the secretary if there was a problem. Harder immediately appeared and showed them into his palatial, floor-to-ceiling windowed office, overlooking the downtown San Diego skyline. He curtly asked them to sit down.

He announced that he wasn't going to pay the money he had promised after all. Marching back and forth, he proceeded to berate me, calling me every name he could think of. He mentioned all the federal allegations against me and said I had "betrayed" the United States. (Apparently the dishonest FBI had done its job.)

Virginia sat there stunned. Despite her efforts to explain, he continued to rant.

He had decided that he would not pay the $200,000 for my stock. Instead, he would give us $50,000, but not a penny more. Stunned, Virginia called me in Poland. She put Harder on the line.

I tried to reason with him. We battled for more than an hour. He refused to budge.

Finally, Harder threatened to give Virginia nothing. If I didn't like it, I could sue him. He knew I was already stretched to the limit paying the legal fees to my lawyers in Washington. I didn't have the money or the stamina for another lawsuit. I told Virginia to take the $50,000 and come to Poland as fast as possible.[17]

The Genesis Hotels project became another victim of the Lockerbie disaster.

THIRTY-FOUR

A New Life in Poland

It was on a dark, hot, and rainy day in July 1997 when Virginia, Katie, our little dog, and I began our new life in a sixty-square-meter apartment in Warsaw. We had all of our clothing and personal effects stuffed into four suitcases, $50,000 in cash from the "sale" of my stock, and lots of love and faith that God would provide for us in our new home.

Warsaw was a far cry from the luxurious lifestyle we had recently enjoyed in Washington, D.C., and Southern California. Nevertheless, we did our best to stress the positive and see this as another adventure. We believed that God had a plan for our lives and we trusted that He was in this.

We knew the $50,000 wouldn't last long. Katie's tuition at the American School of Warsaw would quickly eat up half of the money. Fortunately, the school's director had heard about Virginia's educational background and administrative skills and offered her a job as the high school's office manager. Praise God, at least we would have some steady income!

Life was difficult during our first years in Poland. The country had just pulled out of fifty years of repressive Communist rule, and the smiles on the faces of the Polish people were few and far between. The streets were dark and dreary; the buildings as gray as the weather.

During the winter months, the sun set around 3:30 PM. We had no car, so Virginia and Katie commuted the hour to and from the American School in Wilanow by two local buses. We tried to impress upon our daughter that this was a journey and a historic experience that someday she would appreciate.

Thank goodness the American School of Warsaw was a warm and inviting community. We all made new friends with fellow expats and enjoyed sharing our stories of the new challenges we faced living in an emerging economy.

I worked on the American Kaffe project from our Warsaw apartment and spent two or three days per week working out of my Polish partner's office in Lodz, a city 120 km from Warsaw. American Kaffe in Lodz now had two locations. I focused on expanding the business.

Looming in the background was federal prosecutor David A. Frank, who was in constant discussions and negotiations with my lawyer Brian Shaughnessy in Washington, D.C. He and I would talk or email on a daily basis. It seemed the prosecution wasn't about to give up on us and was out for blood. There had to be "something" in those twenty-one charges that they could make stick, although they were now four years into the investigation and we had not seen any concrete evidence of wrongdoing.

Over and over, Frank expressed certainty that Virginia and I would be convicted on a number of charges, for which he would seek prison time. He always made sure to include Virginia in his threats, knowing that husbands will do almost anything not to see their spouses go to prison.

In January 1998, he claimed the government was about to take our case to a federal grand jury. Given prosecutors' successful indictment statistics, he knew this would intimidate anyone under investigation. Everyone knows that trite saying about how any good prosecutor can indict a "ham sandwich," after which the defendant spends millions of additional dollars on legal fees.

The prospect of prison was terrifying. With both of us incarcerated, what would become of Katie? We spent many nights talking, arguing, crying, and praying. Throughout it all, we continued to believe that God would bring us out of our despair and deliver us from this incredible and evil nightmare.

THIRTY-FIVE

A Plea Deal

Just before Christmas, Shaughnessy called to say that the government had suggested we explore a plea deal that would bring an end to the "hell" we had been enduring for the past four years. We knew we lacked the resources—financial and emotional—to take on the Justice Department, so we agreed in principle to this proposal.

During the negotiations, Shaughnessy and I quickly realized that the government's case was spurious. They had nothing they could prove against us. Their twenty-one charges bordered on fiction. Although they never admitted it, the fact that they abandoned these charges without much of a fight implied that they knew they didn't have a chance to succeed in court.

In the early spring of 1998, the government offered a recommendation of probation in return for my pleading guilty to one felony charge—"Filing a False Tax Statement." As a part of the deal, no charges would be brought against Virginia.

I was upset but also relieved. Yes, I would be a convicted felon, but there would be no prison time and Virginia was off the hook.

The Filing a False Tax Statement charge emanated from the IRS investigation and the audit of five years of our financial records. The IRS claimed that we had failed to report $30,000 in income on our 1992 federal tax returns. Virginia—an innocent spouse—had also signed the return. Hence, she too was liable.

There was never any intention on our part to defraud the IRS. We owned and operated a number of closely held companies, both for-profit and not-for-profit. The William Chasey Organization, a California sole proprietorship owned by Virginia and myself, had loaned $30,000 to one of our non-profit entities when it was temporarily strapped for cash, but we foolishly failed to memorialize the transaction with a loan agreement. The loan was later repaid.

The IRS charged that the William Chasey Organization had received $30,000, which was the loan repayment, but didn't report it as income. Our explanation fell on deaf ears at the IRS. The fact is, it wasn't income. Indeed, it was after-tax money that we had loaned out.

Unfortunately, we had no documents to substantiate our claim.

It was obviously an innocent error on our part. Under normal circumstances, the IRS would have allowed us to amend our 1992 return, with interest and penalties. But for someone like me, someone who could be an embarrassment to the United

States, there would be no “amended return” or “late payment” allowed.

Instead, I would be charged with a felony.

Although we knew we had not knowingly done anything wrong, we also knew that the prosecutors would continue to pursue us until they could save face with some kind of conviction. After all, the government only needed one felony conviction to destroy me. As a convicted felon, my reputation and credibility, which I had worked so hard to build and maintain on Capitol Hill and elsewhere, would be ruined. No one would ever trust me again. The government wouldn’t have to worry about anything Bill Chasey had to say about who was responsible for the Pan Am 103 bombing.

I flew to Washington in March 1998, to sign the plea agreement, to be arrested and fingerprinted by the FBI. The long flight over the North Atlantic gave me much time for introspection, soul-searching and prayer.

After a two-hour meeting with Shaughnessy in his downtown office, we drove to the Justice Department office on McPherson Square to sign the agreement. After that, we drove to the FBI Northern Virginia office where I was processed by none other than . . . FBI Special Agent Robert Core!

He seemed to get special delight in fingerprinting me, taking my photo, and coldly processing documents into his computer. We barely spoke.

I don’t think I’ve ever hated anyone as much, but I kept my emotions in check.

The last thing I did was sign a document releasing myself from custody, pending sentencing on May 8, 1998.

THIRTY-SIX

Assassination Plot

Shaughnessy drove me to Washington Dulles Airport for my return trip to Poland.

Dulles employs a series of buses that ferry passengers between the main terminal and outlying concourses, where most of the arrival and departure gates are located. I boarded a bus, took a seat near the front, and began to review the day's events.

All of a sudden, I noticed someone approaching. No, it couldn't be! It was Mr. "DuPont."

He sat down next to me and smiled rather sheepishly. He shook my hand and said, "Hi, the name's DuPont." The only way he could have known that name was if he had read my Lockerbie book.

He said he was familiar with what had just transpired with the prosecutors and the FBI. DuPont then leaned in and whispered that he was authorized to make a deal that would erase the government's case against me and expunge all records of my arrest, plea bargain, and criminal conviction.

DuPont explained that his agency was impressed by my ability to establish so many personal relationships in Libya, and how Col. Qadhafi had taken an instant liking to me and almost immediately seemed to trust me.

He was also awed with the ease at which I was able to get a member of Congress into Libya to meet Qadhafi, and how I was trusted enough by the Libyan leadership to actually meet the two indicted Libyans, Megrahi and Fhimah, in their secret hideaway.

What he said next was shocking. DuPont said it would be in the best interest of the United States if Megrahi and Fhimah were taken out of the Lockerbie picture.

He asked if I would be willing to go back to Libya and reconnect with Megrahi and Fhimah.

With a shrug, DuPont admitted that the CIA had been unsuccessful in pinpointing the two Libyans' location. He then tried to play on my patriotism—which had been sorely tested over the past four years—by telling me that I would be providing a "great service" to my country by leading them to the Pan Am 103 suspects.

"You are trusted by Qadhafi, and it shouldn't be a problem for you to ask to see Megrahi and Fhimah again," he said. "This time, we will ask you to lead us to their hiding place in Tripoli, and we will do the rest."

I asked what he meant by "the rest."

He said Megrahi and Fhimah had to be "silenced. You don't need to know the details, just lead us to them."

DuPont assured me that the "Company" would do its best

to get me out of Libya, but there were no guarantees. (That sounded so reassuring.) He asked if I would think about it, and he would reach out to me again in the near future.

The short ride to the mid-field terminal was over. The doors opened and the throng of passengers anxiously rushed out to catch their flights. DuPont quickly disappeared.

I sat there, wondering if I had been hallucinating. Had I read too many Robert Ludlum novels?

DuPont's words resonated in my head as I flew through the dark sky back to Warsaw. There was much to consider.

First, I couldn't believe that the CIA still murdered our country's enemies. Wasn't that illegal?

Secondly, I couldn't believe that I was considered a "critical player" in the implementation of this murder plot—for the "good of my country."

Why would the United States want Megrahi and Fhimah dead? Why had the blame for Lockerbie abruptly shifted from Syria and Iran, to Libya?

I began to grasp the logic, which would explain DuPont's mysterious visit. If Megrahi and Fhimah were assassinated, the matter would be closed. Most likely, the culpability for the Pan Am 103 bombing would go with them to their graves, and the true responsibility might never be known.

Maybe it was not a coincidence that the blame for Lockerbie shifted away from Syria and Iran in November 1991. It was the beginning of the Persian Gulf War—August 2, 1990, to February 28, 1991. A UN-authorized coalition force of thirty-four nations, led by the United States and the United Kingdom, liberated Kuwait from Iraq's clutches. One of the nations supporting the war against Iraq was Syria with its 14,500 troops. From a Machiavellian perspective, it would have been impolitic to continue linking Syria to the Pan Am 103 bombing.

And there was only one country that defied President H. W. Bush by backing Iraq. That country was Libya.

Although the chance of persuading Iran to join any coalition led by the United States was slim, President Bush implicitly sought and hoped for Iran's non-interference as he built the coalition to undo Iraq's aggression. Blaming Iran for Lockerbie would have jeopardized this.

What made Libya such an easy scapegoat? Qadhafi. Everybody hated him. He was considered the "Mad Man of the Middle East." Blame it on an international pariah and everyone would be more likely to jump on the bandwagon.

When I returned to Poland, I did not share DuPont's visit or proposal with Virginia. I wasn't sure what game the CIA was really playing with me, and there was no need to worry her over the prospect of her husband becoming "the jackal" in some far-fetched espionage scheme. For the moment, there was already enough stress in our lives, especially with my formal sentencing hearing only two months away.

Shaughnessy had told me I had nothing to worry about. In a plea deal, the judge almost always follows the prosecutor's recommendations regarding a defendant's sentence. But, of course, there were no guarantees.

THIRTY-SEVEN

Judge Ellis

I purchased a round-trip airline ticket from Warsaw to Washington, D.C., for my sentencing hearing before federal judge Thomas Selby (T. S.) Ellis of the United States District Court for the Eastern District of Virginia in Alexandria, Virginia, on Friday May 8, 1998. With the federal prosecutor's plea bargain in hand recommending probation, I felt certain I would be able to catch my return flight home the following day.

After a great deal of prayerful consideration, Virginia and I had decided that I would make this trip alone. For days, Virginia had insisted that she be with me to lend her support, even though she knew we couldn't afford two transatlantic airline tickets. We had never faced a more serious or stressful situation in our married life, and she felt strongly that she should share it with me. My argument was that I would only be gone for two days, and we both knew what the outcome would be, so there was really no need for her to come. It would be best for her to stay in Poland with Katie.

It wasn't that I didn't take the sentence of probation lightly. I was about to take responsibility for, and plead guilty to, a felony. I had never committed the "crime" but I had no choice but to plead guilty for expediency's sake. I knew that I would live with this criminal conviction for the remainder of my life, and the title "convicted felon" would always be a part of my otherwise, unblemished resume. It was gut wrenching, to say the least.

The courtroom was much more crowded than I had expected. There were other people waiting to be sentenced, and there seemed to be a rather large contingent of press in the first few rows of the courtroom.

My sister, Georgiana, and her husband, Gene, were seated a few rows behind the defense table. Very early that morning, they had driven me to the Alexandria Court House from their home in Allentown, Pennsylvania, where I had spent a very restless and prayerful night. They planned to drive me to Baltimore Washington International Airport immediately after sentencing for my return flight to Warsaw.

I took a seat in the empty last row of the courtroom and spent a few minutes with God. I felt refreshed and relaxed knowing that I was not alone, and that, in reality, He was my only judge in that courtroom that day.

I was delighted when my longtime friend Bob White, vice president of National University in San Diego, entered the courtroom. I had shared so much with White over the years during my representation of National University in Costa Rica and on Capitol Hill. He knew and loved me like a brother. At his own expense, he had flown the "red eye" from California the night before in order to make my 9 AM sentencing hearing. He wanted to help me at a time when most of my friends had abandoned me.

Shaughnessy and I had asked White to testify as a character witness, refuting two misrepresentations written by my probation officer, Mary Beth Simpson, in my pre-sentence report (PSR). White was prepared to testify and present evidence to disprove both of her "inaccuracies."

The PSR contains material that the Probation Department prepares to assist the court in sentencing a defendant after his or her conviction. Pre-sentence reports usually include prior convictions, prior arrests, employment history, education history, and family and social background.

There were two falsehoods in my PSR, which seemed to be intended to discredit me before Judge Ellis. Without White's testimony, those falsehoods would remain in my PSR and potentially could adversely affect my sentence, not to mention what little was left of my reputation.

First, Mary Beth Simpson had stated that I didn't really know Oscar Arias Sanchez, former president of Costa Rica and winner of the 1987 Nobel Peace Prize, as I had claimed. She seemed to have intentionally disregarded the documentary evidence that I had been registered as a foreign agent with the Justice Department on behalf of President Arias and the government of Costa Rica. Ms. Simpson also disregarded the evidence I had given her that I had lobbied Vice President George Bush, Sen. Richard Lugar (R-IN), and Congressman Bob Dornan (R-CA), persuading them to attend Arias' presidential inauguration in 1986. In fact, I had greeted all three of these gentlemen after Air Force II landed in San Jose, Costa Rica, for the Arias inauguration.

I felt comfortable that White would testify that Arias and I were good friends and colleagues. He would describe the friendship and mutual respect between the two of us that he had personally witnessed over the previous thirteen years. White would deliver his eyewitness testimony of the numerous senators, congressmen, and congressional delegations that I escorted through the front door of Arias' presidential office and his home in San Jose. These included Sen. Larry Pressler (R-SD), and Reps. Bill Lowery (R-CA), Mickey Edwards (R-OK), Jerry Lewis (R-CA), Donald "Buzz" Lukens (R-OH), and Julian Dixon (D-CA).

White was also in Washington with me in 1987, when I personally led President Arias and his entourage around the Capitol. I arranged meetings for him with Sens. John Kerry (D-MA), Robert Bird (D-WV), Paul Simon (D-IL), Claiborne Pell (D-RI), and Frank Lautenberg (R-NJ), as well as Reps. Bob Dornan and Jack Kemp (R-NY). Bob witnessed me briefing President Arias every step of the way.

White could also attest to my lobbying efforts on behalf of Arias' nomination for the Nobel Peace Prize. My lobbying generated letters of support from House Speaker Jim Wright (D-TX), and Sen. Chris Dodd (D-CN). He was also present when Arias personally invited Virginia and me to attend the Nobel Peace Prize award ceremony in Oslo, Norway in 1987.

To help substantiate my claims that I knew Oscar Arias, White had even brought a copy of my book, *Pan Am 103: The Lockerbie Cover-up,* to the courthouse. The book contained photos of Arias and me taken in the presidential office, along with three U. S. congressmen that I had persuaded to go to Costa Rica to meet with him in 1986.

Shaughnessy and I had decided not to introduce my book into evidence, however. I had pleaded guilty to, and was to be sentenced for, one charge of filing a false document. This had nothing to do with Lockerbie and its investigation, and shouldn't have been mentioned during my sentencing. We didn't know if Judge Ellis even knew about my involvement with Lockerbie. Shaughnessy was sure that he would rule my book and any discussion of Pan Am 103 as irrelevant.

Therefore, I relied on and believed that White's brief, but well-prepared, testimony would dispel any notion that I had fabricated my relationship with President Oscar Arias Sanchez.

Shaughnessy and I were quite puzzled how Mary Beth Simpson could have honestly ignored all the evidence we had presented to her. How could it be anything else but deliberate?

Mary Beth Simpson had also stated in my PSR that I wasn't eligible to receive the National Defense Service Medal during my time as a United States Marine Corps Officer.

This was absurd. White, who was a retired Navy Commander, would read from my Marine Corps discharge papers that *"William C. Chasey honorably served on active duty from June of 1962 to June of 1965."* Next, he would read from the Code of Federal Regulations that the "National Defense Service Medal was authorized on April 22, 1953 and amended on January 11, 1966. The medal is awarded for honorable active military service during a time of war or conflict as a member of the United States Armed Forces, between January 1, 1961, and August 14, 1974 (Vietnam War Period)."

Since I had served in the Marines during the time period specified to qualify for the medal, I obviously deserved and had received the medal! This was not rocket science.

Hence, White's testimony would contradict any notion that I wasn't eligible to receive the National Defense Service Medal. Again, Ms. Simpson's ignorance on this documentable and irrefutable matter could only have been a deliberate effort to discredit my military service, for whatever reason.

Suddenly, I heard the bailiff announce, "The United States of America versus William C. Chasey."

I got up and took my seat at the defense table next to my lawyer.

Prosecutor Frank spoke first. In a straightforward manner, he stated, "William C. Chasey has pleaded guilty to one count of Filing a False Document, a felony under federal statutes. He appears before the honorable court this morning for sentencing."

As he sat down, Judge Ellis slid forward in his chair and positioned himself in front of his microphone.

Shaughnessy stood and stated that before the court passed its sentence, "Mr. Chasey would like to present one witness, Mr. Robert White of California, who will testify concerning errors in Mr. Chasey's pre-sentencing report."

Angrily and abruptly, Judge Ellis denied the request. He stated that he had already read my PSR and saw nothing out of the ordinary that would affect his decision. He went on to say that he "already knew all he needed to know about Mr. Chasey."

Shaughnessy gave it a second try. He informed the court that there were two major misrepresentations in my PSR that should be corrected before sentencing, and he emphasized that Mr. White had traveled all night from California at his own expense to testify on my behalf.

Now even more agitated, the judge pulled the microphone closer and shouted: "Mr. Shaughnessy, I have ruled on your request. Now, sit down!"

I was utterly alarmed by the judge's tone. I took a deep breath, settled down, and focused on the positive. The prosecution had recommended a sentence of probation. That's all I cared about.

Judge Ellis was going to follow that recommendation, right?

After all, I had no previous convictions and I had never been in trouble with the law, ever. Instead I had spent my entire adult life doing good and contributing to society around the world. All of this had to count for something.

However, instead of feeling secure, I sensed an impending doom. Instinctively, my hand found its way inside my coat's left breast pocket, touching the airline ticket that would take me 6,000 miles back to Virginia and Katie, waiting nervously for me in Warsaw. I prayed on those tickets.

With a very stern expression, the judge asked, "Do you have anything to say, Mr. Chasey, before I pass sentence?"

In accordance with my plea agreement, I answered in the affirmative. In a clear voice, I stated that I accepted responsibility for my action and promised that I would be much more diligent with my tax filings in the future.

I expected the judge to scold me for not reporting the income on my tax return, and then sentence me to probation.

In the back of my mind, I couldn't help but think about what had really brought me to the lowest point in my life—the government's obsession with silencing me because of my controversial views on the Lockerbie disaster.

What was only seconds seemed like an eternity. I braced myself, as Judge Ellis brusquely adjusted his robe and noisily gathered his notes. Waving his index finger, he angrily began to assail me.

"Mr. Chasey, you have committed a very serious crime against America!"

What? My lowly tax charge was "a serious crime against America?" I started preparing myself for the worst.

"You collaborated with the terrorist state of Libya, and with one of America's staunchest enemies, Muammar Qadhafi. Isn't that true, Mr. Chasey?"

"No, your honor, it is not true," I responded firmly.

I said that I had pled guilty to a single charge of filing a false document, and that his assertions about Libya and Qadhafi were not only mistaken, but were irrelevant to my sentencing.

Ellis then launched into a tirade. He accused me of being rude, impudent, and disrespectful to the court.

My jaw dropped open. My stomach reeled.

He said that I deserved to be treated harshly for my "un-American" activities!

Shaughnessy quickly leapt to his feet and tried valiantly to object to the court's emotional outburst, but the judge abruptly shut him down.

Ellis shoved his notes aside and glared at me over the microphone.

"Isn't it true that you were paid $50,000 by the government of Libya to promote Qadhafi's position on Pan Am 103 on Capitol Hill?"

"Absolutely not," I said, raising my voice. "I have never taken a single penny from Libya or Qadhafi!"

Ellis declared that I had even written a book defending Qadhafi and that I stood to profit greatly from the deaths of so many people, including young American college students. How could I possibly deny that Pan Am 103 had not been blown up by Libya's intelligence agents, when the world knew it to be true?

"How could you help such terrorists and make money from them in the process?" he asked.

I stood my ground. I replied that I hadn't made any money from the book and how could he be so certain the two indicted Libyan agents were guilty when they hadn't even been tried?

My body tensed as Judge Ellis screamed: "ENOUGH! I am prepared to impose your sentence, Mr. Chasey."

Following this heated exchange, you could have heard that proverbial pin drop in the courtroom.

"Mr. Chasey, you will have plenty of time over the next three years to think about your actions."

What? Three years? What was he babbling about? From probation on a single tax charge to three years for being a traitor?

I knew that Judge Ellis was not the most respected jurist on the federal bench and had been overturned on appeal more often than most, but this guy was an absolute madman.

"First, I sentence you, beginning today, to supervised house arrest in the vicinity of the court to give the Bureau of Prisons time to find a place for you in a Federal Bureau of Prisons facility."

Out of the corner of my eye I could see two burly federal marshals rise from their seats and move directly behind me.

"Secondly, I sentence you to four months of confinement in a federal prison, and thirdly, I sentence you to two and a half months in a federal half-way house facility.

Federal Prison?

Halfway House?

Lastly, I sentence you to two years of supervised release under the supervision of the probation department of the United States District Court for the Eastern District of Virginia in Alexandria, Virginia."

Two years probation?

In a state of shock, I felt the marshals gruffly pull my arms behind me and handcuff my wrists together. The "click" of those cuffs will forever resonate in my soul. I thanked God that Virginia and Katie were not there to witness this travesty of justice.

Chaos erupted in the courtroom. I don't think anyone believed what had just happened.

"Your Honor, your Honor!" Shaughnessy shouted. "What about the plea bargain and the probation agreement?"

Ellis ignored him and gaveled the court to order. He gave me a sinister, triumphant sneer as I was led from the courtroom.

Just as the door closed behind me, I heard him order the bailiff to call the next case.

I was searched and signed a document that my gold wristwatch, gold glasses, belt, wallet, $21.35 in U.S. currency, and 120 Polish zloty had been taken from me. I caught myself welling up as I looked down at my possessions lying on the table. I realized that $21.35 was all of the money I had to my name.

What would I do now? How was I going to support Virginia and Katie back in Poland?

A cold chill ran down my spine.

I have never felt so empty or alone as I did at that moment. Now, I didn't know when I would see Virginia or Katie again. I had no idea what God had in store for us. Nevertheless, I closed my eyes, gave Him thanks and asked for strength.

I was confined in a holding cell with five other detainees in the basement of the courthouse for almost three hours while Shaughnessy negotiated the terms of my release.

Since I had no residence or family in the Washington, D.C., area, Judge Ellis finally agreed to release me on my own recognizance, so that I could travel to my sister's home in Allentown, Pennsylvania, where I would serve my house arrest under the supervision of the local federal probation department.

How would I break this ghastly news to Virginia? How would she react, and what would she think of me? How would she explain all of this to our sixteen-year-old daughter? What would Katie think of her "hero" father now? How would we sustain ourselves during these next nine months?

Would I be permitted to serve my two-year supervised release in Poland, or would sadistic Judge Ellis insist that I remain in the U.S.? If that were the case, what would I do here with a felony conviction and as an ex-con?

Would my sister want me serving all of my "house arrest" at her home? Because I had thought that I would be going home the next day, I had only brought enough clothes to get me through the hearing. In fact, I only had the clothes I was wearing.

The marshals returned my possessions and I was released. Thank you, Lord, for small favors. If space had been available in a federal prison, I would have spent that night in a repulsive federal prison cell, instead of the warmth and comfort of my sister's suburban Allentown home. I would have time to adjust and to strategize with Virginia how she would manage in my absence.

My anxiety diminished somewhat as I was reunited in the courthouse lobby with my sister, brother-in-law, my lawyer, and my dear friend Bob White.

It was unanimous. Judge Ellis was certifiable.

It was clear to all of us that he had sentenced me for my views on the Lockerbie investigation, not for filing a false tax return.

Shaughnessy returned to his office in Washington. We would stay in contact by phone and email from my new residence in Allentown. My sister and her husband hurried off to squeeze in a short visit with their daughter, who lived nearby.

White and I grabbed a quick lunch across the street from the courthouse. My dear friend then reached into his pocket and handed me a no-limit paid phone card. He wanted me to make sure I could stay in touch with him, and with Virginia and Katie in Poland. I was so touched by his gesture that my eyes filled with tears.

Next, he grabbed a taxi to Dulles to catch his flight back to San Diego. I never saw him again. My dear and loyal friend died a few months later. The Bureau of Prisons refused to let me go to his funeral, but I know for a fact that Bob White is with God in heaven.

While I waited for my sister to pick me up for our return trip to Allentown, I used the phone card to make that dreaded call to Virginia. I found a public phone booth a block down the street and hastily punched in the endless series of numbers inscribed on the back of the calling card. With a six-hour time difference, it meant it was early evening in Warsaw.

Virginia answered on the first ring, which meant she'd been anxiously sitting by the phone waiting for my call. Of course, she was devastated by the news. She began asking a series of rhetorical questions about the morning's events. How could the judge refuse to let Bob White testify? How could the judge even bring up the Libyan situation? How could he ignore the plea bargain? Why had he been so hostile? What kind of man could this judge be? What kind of legal system was this? Could we file an appeal? How was I coping? She couldn't contain her outrage and felt helpless in consoling me.

I felt just as helpless, trying to comfort her from 6,000 miles away. I said I would call again when I reached Allentown. She told me how much she loved me and that I had done absolutely nothing to deserve to be treated this way.

In the end, as she had repeated so often during the past five years, she said, "We will get through this, Bill."

THIRTY-EIGHT

Under House Arrest

It took the Bureau of Prisons, which falls under the aegis of the Department of Justice, five weeks to find a place for me among its 118 prisons located throughout the United States.

Shaughnessy filed a motion requesting that I be permitted to return to Poland during this time to get my personal affairs in order before I reported to prison. Judge Ellis denied the motion. Furthermore, even though I was under house arrest, Ellis refused to allow the five weeks to be credited to my sentence!

House arrest in my sister's home was not very trying, just boring. For someone who had spent his life on the go, the 2,000 square-foot house seemed to get smaller with every passing day.

I spent a good part of the time on the Internet communicating with Virginia and Katie, and doing business with my American Kaffe business partner in Lodz.

The Bureau of Prisons website was on my computer's "favorites" list so I could easily click and absorb all I could about what to expect as a federal prisoner.

I had long talks and played board games with my eighty-seven-year-old mother. My father had died the summer before, and Mom had moved into one of my sister's upstairs bedrooms. Of course, she was heartbroken over my circumstances, but remained strong—until the day a federal probation officer came to inspect the home for weapons, drugs, alcohol, and various types of contraband disallowed under "Federal House Arrest Regulations."

The residence was deemed suitable for my house arrest, but the probation officer read a list of rules that had to be observed by all residents. Finally, he handed me his business card and instructed me to report to him in his downtown office at the U.S. Courthouse in Allentown every Tuesday morning at 10 AM.

As hard as I tried to explain how all of this had happened, I'm not sure Mom fully understood.

"How could the U.S. government put my son in prison?" she would ask.

Her son had always been a "star." He had always been at the top of his class in school and in athletics. He had earned his commercial pilot's license, along with a Ph.D. and an honorary doctorate. And he had helped all those handicapped kids in the United States, and the poor people of Costa Rica and El Salvador.

She had been so proud when I'd received my second lieutenant's gold bars at my Springfield College graduation in 1962. She loved seeing me in my Marine Corps dress blue uniform and especially enjoyed watching me practice my precision drills with my officer's Mameluke sword.

She kept repeating, "How can they do this to you? All those honors and awards. How could they do this?"

I felt badly for my mom, my sister, and her husband. None of them had ever had as much as a traffic violation their entire lives. Now, their home had been inspected for weapons, drugs, and alcohol by a total stranger. Now, they were subjected to strict probation rules in the privacy of their own home. To make matters worse, they were warned to expect surprise visits, inspections, and telephone calls to check on my whereabouts at any time of day or night.

I don't know what I would have done without them. They bought me clothes and all essentials necessary to keep me going for five weeks. They gave me money and did my laundry. I had read on the BOP website that I couldn't wear expensive glasses or a wristwatch in prison, so my sister bought me new inexpensive glasses and a Wal-Mart wristwatch. We never had a cross word during my stay, and I will be forever grateful for everything they did.

I used the phone card to call Virginia and Katie frequently. Virginia was not one to complain, but I knew things were deteriorating at home. She would receive one more paycheck before her job as high school office manager ended in June. She would start her new teaching position at the American School in late August, but would not receive her first paycheck until the end of September. What were they going to do for the next three months without any money coming in?

To make matters worse, we were already a month behind on our rent and the next payment was due on July 1st. Our landlord was getting anxious. He was calling Virginia a couple of times a day asking for the rent. She adroitly held him off as we explored the limited options that were available to us.

Thank God we had paid Katie's fall semester tuition before I left Poland. If Virginia paid the past-due rent with her June paycheck, she would have nothing to live on until the end of September. If she didn't pay it, they would be evicted and homeless in a foreign country.

I felt terrible. I had no way to help them, and I had no idea how long it would be before I could return to Poland! What if Judge Ellis insisted that I spend my years of supervised probation in the United States?

For the first time since this Pan Am 103 saga began, I questioned my judgment. How I wish I had walked away when Sen. Pressler had introduced me to Gerrit Bovenkamp. Why, of all people, had I ended up taking the corrupt Congressman Hubbard and his wife to Libya? And why in the world had I written my book, challenging the conventional wisdom on Lockerbie and defending such a hated man as Qadhafi? Was this really what God had planned for my life? I had to keep my faith, no matter what.

As the end of school approached, Virginia was getting more and more concerned about Katie. At sixteen years of age, she was beginning to openly rebel and act out at her displeasure with her new life in Poland. She missed the comforts and friends of her former life in the United States and was angry about living in a dark and dreary Eastern European country.

She was forbidden to talk about my situation to anyone, because we didn't want it compromising whatever opportunities I might develop in Poland. On top of that, the American School was so small and had rather limited facilities, compared to those of the school she had previously attended in Southern California. Although she was an outstanding member of her school's volleyball team and star of the swim team, she missed her horses and riding.

Our efforts to arrange a suitable riding facility and trainer in Warsaw were not successful. One day, quite by accident, she impressed the trainer of the Polish National Equestrian Team with her riding prowess and was invited to train with the team. Unfortunately, since we couldn't buy her a show horse, she had to ride a barn horse. When the trainer finally insisted that we buy her a horse of her own, which we couldn't afford, the practice sessions came to an abrupt halt.

During her angry outbursts, she would blame me for what had happened to our family and to her life. She complained that all she had heard about for years was Libya, the FBI, the CIA, lawyers, money, and that it was time to move again. Now, her dad was going to jail and they were about to be evicted. I know she wanted to believe in my innocence, but if I was really innocent why had all of this happened?

Marie, Virginia's older sister, understood what we were going through and kindly offered to fly Katie to her home in El Paso, Texas, for the summer. We quickly agreed. This would give Katie some time to get away from it all and allow Virginia an opportunity to find suitable living arrangements for the fall.

In a sense, Katie was another victim of the Lockerbie disaster.

As Virginia watched Katie's plane lift off from the rain-soaked runway, holding our little Ribbons in her arms, she felt unbelievably empty and lonely. Her husband was going to prison, and her only daughter was angrily leaving her for the next few months. There was hardly any money in the bank, and soon she would have no place to live. She hugged our little dog and prayed that God would provide for all of us.

Virginia, too, was a victim of the Lockerbie disaster.

But, my dear enterprising wife "picked herself up and dusted herself off." She made arrangements to house-sit an apartment belonging to an American School teacher who was returning to the U.S. for the summer. She also arranged to care for her principal's cats in exchange for housing our belongings in her garage until we moved to a new home.

The most important goal was finding a place to live come September. Without a car, Virginia rode a bicycle around town and to prospective rental housing in the general vicinity of the American School.

THIRTY-NINE

Allenwood Federal Prison

On the morning of June 12, 1998, my sister and her husband drove me to the Allenwood Federal Prison in White Deer, Pennsylvania, which is about 150 miles from Washington, D. C. We hardly spoke. During that three-hour interminable ride, my mind was clouded with anxiety about life in prison and uncertainty over my future.

During house arrest, I had become a minor expert on the federal prison system.

The Federal Bureau of Prisons operates institutions at four different security levels, which are characterized by such features as the presence of external patrols, towers, security barriers, detection devices, the type of housing within the institution, internal security features, and the staff-to-inmate ratio.

At Allenwood, there are minimum-, low-, medium-, and high-security prisons. I was to report to Allenwood's minimum-security prison camp

Typically, the minimum-security facility or prison camp has dormitory-style housing, a relatively low staff-to-inmate ratio, and limited or no perimeter fencing. These institutions are work and program-oriented, and many, including Allenwood, are located adjacent to larger institutions, where prison-camp inmates help to serve the labor needs of the higher-security prisons nearby.

Built in the 1930s, the Allenwood prison camp employs about 55 staff and houses about 170 prisoners. Only later were the other three prison facilities constructed, and they are actually located quite a distance away. There are only 10 prison camps in the United States.

In the Allenwood parking lot, I said my sad goodbyes to my dear sister and husband, and I implored them not to visit me during my incarceration. I promised to stay in touch by phone. Since I could not take my phone card into the prison, I had memorized all of the numbers and codes.

Clutching my pocket-sized Bible to my heart, I was engulfed by a miraculous feeling of peace and tranquility. I knew God was there with me, as I murmured, "Yea, though I walk through the valley of the shadow of death, I will fear no evil; for You are with me; Your rod and Your staff, they comfort me . . . "

I walked into the main administration building and spent the next hour in the receiving and discharge department, filling out a stack of government forms and taking a breathalyzer test. I shed my civilian clothing and put my belongings into a small sack that would be mailed back to my sister in Allentown. I won't describe the dreadful details of my first body-cavity search, except to say it was the most humiliating experience of my life.

What came next severely tested me. They confiscated my Bible! I was instructed to put it in the mail sack. It could be mailed back to me, but it would be counted as one of the four books I would be permitted to keep in my cubicle.

The injustice of this became apparent when I soon discovered that there were no such restrictions on embroidered prayer rugs, prayer beads, and skull caps kept by the large number of black Muslim prisoners.

I couldn't help thinking that I could have annulled this unjust practice with just a few hours of lobbying on Capitol Hill.

I received three sets of standard khaki prison uniforms, complete with work boots and a long list of rules on how they must be worn. I collected my bedding, posed for my mug shots, and hung my lovely new prison ID card around my neck. I was then escorted to my new home in a tiny two-man cubicle in Dormitory B. Without fanfare, the now much-diminished fifty-eight-year-old Foreign Agent 4221 had become Federal Prisoner 42938-083.

Much to the satisfaction of the U.S. government, Bill Chasey had just become another victim of the Lockerbie disaster.

Mr. DuPont was still waiting for my answer . . . The prison dining hall began to fill and become noisy as more and more prisoners were released from their work assignments for lunch. Their presence added to the pressure I was feeling to give DuPont an answer. I could see that he was getting fidgety. He turned to his associate, the other Mr. DuPont, and whispered something under his breath. I continued to quietly stare at both of the agents as I pondered the unbelievable choice I was about to make. Either cooperate with the CIA assassination plot of Megrahi and Fhimah, or serve out my full sentence and be labeled a convicted felon for the rest of my life.

This was a very sensitive plan. I realized that there must be some very important people who thought highly of my ability to get difficult things done. To base their entire assassination plan on my persuasive skills in gaining access to Megrahi and Fhimah was "mind blowing." I understood why they thought I *could,* but I didn't understand why they thought I *would.*

Did they really think that all the temporal distress they had caused me and my family to endure would lead me to lose my moral and spiritual compass? Obviously, they didn't know me at all. And these people were asking me to count on them? I didn't think so.

I calmly pushed my tray aside, leaned intently forward, and looked squarely and angrily into DuPont's eyes. I admitted that he and those he represented had been successful in destroying my reputation, credibility, businesses, finances, homes, friends and associates and put me in federal prison all to further their political agenda.

I continued: "With all of your vast resources, the one thing you will never be able to destroy is my character."

I told DuPont that he had seen with his own eyes that Virginia and I could take everything he and the government could dish out. We were not afraid of him nor were we afraid of the only superpower on earth, because "If God is for me, who can be against me?"

I stood up, collected my tray, and resolutely stated:

"I reject your offer and I will honorably serve the remainder of my sentence. We will succeed in putting our lives back together, without your help."

I blended into the throng of inmates emptying their trays and departed the Chow Hall.

I never saw Messrs. DuPont again and, except for Virginia, I have never told this story to any other living being until now.

I quickly got acclimated to prison life. I learned the do's and don'ts, the personalities, the written and unwritten rules, and the general ebb and flow. Nights were the worst times, and sleep was elusive as prisoners boisterously roamed the main cubicle room, adjacent hallways, and TV lounge. They entertained themselves by playing cards, cooking strange smelling concoctions in the lounge's single microwave oven, and planning transgressions against the weakest inmates.

From the moment I joined the inmate population at Allenwood, I thanked God for the nine years I spent as a Marine Corps officer. The Corps had prepared me to handle anything that could possibly come my way. Within a short time, I was surprisingly known as the "Captain" among my fellow prisoners. Although my highest rank in the Marines was First Lieutenant, I still considered "Captain" as a mark of respect that most inmates held for the Marine Corps.

I was always spared the recurring violence that took place in the darkened, secluded recesses of our dormitory after lights-out. I remember well the words of a black gang leader during one such incident. On the way to the bathroom one night, I inadvertently attracted the attention of some his cohorts attacking a new inmate. He yelled to his fellow gangbangers, "Don't f . . . with the Captain; he'll kill your ass!"

There was an underground flow of information that somehow made its way throughout the prison population. For example, I was surprised to find out that my fellow prisoners knew a great deal about me before my arrival. I surmised that inmate clerks working in the administrative offices were the source.

It seemed that the real and make-believe stories that were circulated about me proved helpful in securing me a safer and more comfortable reception, and the prison library actually had the first edition of my book, *Foreign Agent 4221: The Lockerbie Cover-up*. There was already a long waiting list for the book before I even arrived. The inmates must have assumed I was a foreign spy and should be treated with due caution.

In many ways, prison was like an episode of *The Twilight Zone.* It was a strange alternative universe that mimicked reality, but was just a bit off kilter. From the start, prison life was an adjustment. The administrative structure was set up to make life as difficult and miserable as possible for its residents. We were treated with disdain and condescension. One would think a prison should focus, at least part of the time, on rehabilitation, not making people feel worse than they already felt.

There were many cases where the staff, when confronted with an inmate's problem, refused to help, but rather suggested that the inmate should use means outside the established norms, better known as problem solving by "extra-legal behavior." I often thought about the Georgia Gov. Lester Maddox's quote when asked about his prison-reform agenda. He said, "We're doing the best we can and before we do much better we have to get a better grade of prisoner."

There is the general impression that prison camps are "cushy," and that most inmates have committed white-collar crimes, and serve short, safe confinements in a "clubby" atmosphere. To help dispel this misconception, I would like to introduce my cubicle-mate, Juan from Puerto Rico, better known as "Juan, the Rock Sitter." Juan didn't speak one word to me and never made eye contact with me during the four months we shared a cubicle. He would spend his entire work day staring into space while seated on a large granite rock outside of our dormitory.

As was the case with all hardened prisoners from the medium- and high-security prisons on the Allenwood campus, Juan was required to serve time in the prison camp to help him slowly readjust to the outside world before his release from prison. He had recently come from the high-security penitentiary after serving twenty-six years for murdering his stepfather with an ax handle. In my dormitory building, there were twenty-three inmates who had committed violent crimes.

The important thing was to keep as busy as possible. All inmates had one kind of job or another, most of them menial or janitorial. I lobbied to get a job as an electrician in the electrical department. I knew nothing about electricity, but it provided me the chance to spend time in air-conditioned buildings during the summer heat. I quickly became an expert smoke-detector inspector. However, it wasn't my job to see if the smoke detectors were operating properly. My job was to see if the smoke detectors were still there. Creative inmates had figured out all kinds of illegal things to make with a smoke detector's parts. They were much sought after among prison tattoo artists and others.

My twelve-cents-per-hour pay was automatically deposited into my commissary account each week. There was nothing to send home to Virginia and I hardly had enough to buy toothpaste. My sister supplemented my account by mailing in various amounts of money for the personal-care items I needed. Of course, I quickly went through my meager income on postage stamps for letters to Poland.

I made sure that my smoke-alarm inspections landed me among the stacks of law books in the prison library every afternoon about 2 PM. There, I would focus my attention on how I might persuade Judge Ellis to allow me to spend my supervised probation in Poland. However, it was safe to assume that he would be pre-disposed against me.

I could find no legal precedence in which a federal prisoner was granted permission to serve his supervised release outside of the United States. What would I do if I couldn't go back to Poland for two more years?

Virginia was offered a great teaching job at the American School of Warsaw in the fall, and we couldn't think of a better school for Katie to attend. But what would become of my fledgling American Kaffe restaurant chain that had now expanded to three locations?

Virginia and I talked by phone daily, and she wrote to me almost as often. There were days when I received two or three letters from her on the same day. I was the envy of Dormitory B inmates at each evening mail call.

Some good news arrived in early August. Virginia's older brother—Hank Borys and his wife, Dolores—had arrived in Warsaw from their home in Seattle, Washington, to give Virginia some assistance. They helped her find just the right apartment near the American School where Virginia would be teaching and where Katie attended. They also paid the security deposit and the first month's rent. Virginia and Katie would now be able to begin the new school year in a home of their own and with a renewed feeling of optimism. What would we have done without the Borys' help?

I got into the routine of speed walking five miles twice a day on the prison's outdoor track and down the two-mile road that connected the main camp to the camp chapel. I enjoyed visiting the chapel twice a week to check on the frequently missing smoke detectors. Rarely was there anyone there, which meant I could enjoy two hours of solitude with the Lord. I would pray, read, and catch up on much needed sleep. I'm sorry to say that I found the chapel the least used facility at Allenwood. I saw few signs of organized church services, and no signs of any of the national prison ministries that I had heard so much about in the media.

I had lots of time to ponder the injustice I had suffered at the hands of my government. I had been sentenced to federal prison for a felony because of an inadvertent error on one of the forty federal tax returns I had filed over my lifetime, during which I had paid hundreds of thousands of dollars in taxes.

It was ironic that I was a convicted felon, while the inmate in the cubicle next to mine was serving a thirty-day sentence because he was a tax protester, which is a misdemeanor. He had never filed a tax return and had never paid a penny of income tax in his forty-five years as an adult. But, unlike me, he would never have the title of convicted felon. What kind of system was this?

I never thought it would happen, but I found myself saying goodbye to inmate "friends" as they transferred to other prisons, halfway houses, or headed home after many years of confinement. My "skid bit" (short sentence) was only four months. Most had much longer sentences. I was surprised to find myself missing those hardened faces, especially those who had helped me adjust to life in prison. Society calls them—calls me, for that matter—criminals. We are marked forever. Many deserved it; some did not.

I spent the final weeks of my stay preparing for the next phase of my sentence—a two-and-a-half month confinement in a residential re-entry center, known as a halfway house. The alleged purpose of a halfway house, or "recovery house," is to allow prisoners to begin the process of reintegration into society, while being monitored and supported. This is believed to reduce the risk of recidivism.

In my case, the halfway house was nothing more than additional punishment. I didn't need special assistance in "reintegrating" into society after a four-month prison term. Judge Ellis knew exactly what he was doing. He added these seventy-five days to my sentence as pure retribution, because I had gone against the grain on Lockerbie.

I was warned that the halfway house could be much worse than prison. In addition to federal prisoners, most halfway houses serve state and county inmates as well. This wasn't good. Some of the most dangerous prisoners end up in state and county prisons, and in their cases the halfway house was the step-down from serving hard time prior to their release back into society.

Some halfway houses are notorious for being threatening and dangerous. Before leaving Allenwood, I requested an assignment to one near my sister's home. She was the closest family I had in the United States, and I knew the Bureau of Prisons tried to accommodate such requests. The Bucks County Work Release Halfway House in nearby Doylestown, Pennsylvania, had the reputation for being safe and well managed. It seemed like the appropriate place for me.

However, a week before my release, I was notified that I would be reporting to a notoriously dangerous and mismanaged facility—the Shaw Residence II in northwest Washington, D.C.

My time at Allenwood had dragged by slowly, but when it finally ended there was frost on the prison campus, giving it the appearance of a small Swiss village. I had only been there for four months, but I felt like an old-timer. Well, I was! At fifty-eight years of age I was the oldest inmate in my dormitory, if not the entire camp.

Some new inmates arrived the day before I was released with that deer-in-the-headlights look. I wondered if I had looked like that when I arrived an eternity ago, back in mid June. I knew that it's a look that only time could reshape, and time was the one thing we had in abundance.

I never became comfortable in prison. I simply adjusted, adapted, and endured. I went through the motions, did what was expected, and prayed I would never have to go through this kind of ordeal again.

FORTY

Residential Re-entry Facility

The Shaw Residence II Halfway House was located in the Mount Pleasant neighborhood in northwest Washington, D.C. The neighborhood is bounded by Rock Creek Park to the north and west; the Adams Morgan neighborhood to the south; and 16th Street and the Columbia Heights neighborhood to the east. There are some affluent and middle-class residents, but it is predominantly poor.

I was given five hours to travel from the Allenwood prison and report to my halfway house, about 150 miles away, which gave my sister, brother-in-law, and me barely enough time for a brief lunch en route.

Otherwise, I would have made the journey in handcuffs and

in the back seat of one of those plain, gray, banal government sedans, compliments of the U.S. Marshal Service.

My sister became quite concerned about my personal well-being as we drove into the neighborhood where I would be residing for the next seventy-five days. She made sure our doors were locked and advised me to be vigilant as I moved about this part of Washington.

Except for a substantial fire escape located on the left side of the four-story building, Shaw Residence II looked just like all of the houses on the street. They were all old, large Queen-Anne-style homes, prevalent in the Mount Pleasant and Adams Morgan neighborhoods. Most of the homes seemed to have fallen into disrepair.

I climbed the wooden steps onto the large front porch of 1740 Park Road with mixed emotions. I certainly didn't want to be there, but I knew that this would be the final test in what seemed to be a never-ending challenge. I paused and prayed for strength and guidance as I entered this new unknown in the next chapter of my ordeal.

I carried a small canvas bag containing my belongings that my sister had packed for me that morning. It contained my sentencing suit, shirt, tie, shoes, my Bible, personal-care items, as well as the gray workout shorts, shirt, and running shoes that I had purchased during my incarceration.

I rang the doorbell and was buzzed into what would be my new home for the next ten weeks. From what I could see from the entryway, the building looked empty. It was mid-afternoon and I was told that most of the residents wouldn't return from work until dinner time. A few people were lounging in the living room. I learned that they were new arrivals like me and couldn't leave the facility during their first week at the halfway house. After that, they were expected to find a full-time job and begin paying room and board while residing there. Each resident was given two weeks to find a job or else they would be returned to prison.

The resident manager on duty had been expecting me and unceremoniously handed me a stack of government forms to fill out and sign. He also presented me with a list of house rules and regulations and then escorted me up four flights to a drab room in the rear, which I would share with another resident for the rest of my stay.

Very early, on my first morning, I used the lobby pay phone to call my best friend in the world, Dick Schubert.

He was my hero and one of the most remarkable human beings anyone could ever meet. We had been friends from our Sunday school days in the Nazarene Church across the street from my boyhood home in Trenton, New Jersey. As a matter of fact, Schubert's mother was my first Sunday school teacher—the one who introduced me to the Lord at the ripe old age of five.

If I needed a job in Washington, Dick Schubert was the man to call. However, considering my present circumstances, I was a bit hesitant and embarrassed about calling him at all. What would I say? As far as I could tell, he knew nothing about my current predicament, and I didn't know if he had even read my book. I wondered how he would react. As I listened to his phone ring, I imagined him saying, "You knucklehead, what did you get yourself into this time?"

There was plenty of reason for Richard F. Schubert to be my hero. He was the chairman and founding board member of the Peter Drucker Foundation in Washington, D.C, and he served as chairman emeritus of the International Youth Foundation and the Josephson Institute of Ethics.

I had always admired Schubert's accomplishments in law,

business, government, and the non-profit sector. A Yale Law School graduate, he had served as a solicitor for the U.S. Department of Labor, and under secretary of labor under President Nixon. He served as president and as vice chairman of Bethlehem Steel Corporation when he was in his thirties. He honorably served as president of the American Red Cross for six years. Later, he was appointed by President George H. W. Bush to serve as president and CEO of The Points of Light Foundation. He had five honorary doctorates and served on the board of the National Alliance of Business (NAB), and too many others to mention.

Once we got past the "You knucklehead" response, Schubert insisted that he visit me in the halfway house on Sunday afternoon. I really wanted to see him in the worst way, but I didn't want him driving into this dangerous neighborhood or seeing me in this godforsaken place. Nevertheless, we agreed that he would come that Sunday afternoon.

Soon after my arrival, something extraordinary happened. It could have been a scene in a cheap reality TV show.

Along with most of the other twenty residents, I was in the dining room finishing my evening meal. It happened to be payday for most of them, and there was a bit of laughing and kibitzing going on.

Suddenly, two Halloween-masked gunmen, brandishing 9 mm automatic pistols, entered the room. We were instructed to empty our pockets and place all valuables on the dining-room table. Most of the residents, who had just been paid in cash, reluctantly placed their pay envelopes on the table. As a new resident, I wasn't permitted to bring any money into the halfway house, and I had given my Wal-Mart wristwatch to a new inmate when I had left Allenwood. I had nothing to offer the thieves. When they asked for my money, a young resident I had just met came to my defense, telling them that I was a new arrival and wasn't allowed to have any money.

After that, they ordered us to stand and face the wall. The gunmen quickly collected the money and valuables, and fled.

One of the residents who had been in his room, heard the commotion, fled down the fire escape and summoned the police. Police cars, sirens blaring, had arrived just a few minutes after the two intruders had made their escape.

The police, who questioned us most of the night, were convinced that the assailants were former residents. They seemed to know the layout of the residence, the daily routine, and the fact that it was payday.

It became clear that my halfway-house stay would be far more dangerous than prison. Again, I thanked Judge Ellis for his malevolence.

My orientation week went very slowly, and I couldn't wait until I would be able to leave the confines of 1740 Park Road. In pursuit of a full-time job, I called a few Christian friends of mine that week for help.

Virginia and I had been spiritual and financial supporters of Campus Crusade for Christ International (CCCI) for many years, and I had served on the board of directors of Here's Life Washington, an inner-city ministry of CCCI, directed by a young pastor by the name of Crawford Loritts. Ironically, as I thought about it, just a few years earlier, Virginia and I had personally funded a two week "Here's Life Summer Outreach Program" for thirty poor inner-city youth in Washington, D.C. As I recalled, the program had been conducted in a church facility not far from where I was currently a resident.

Surely, these Christian friends would be able to help me find a ten-week full-time job. Nope, I never heard a word from them.

I also called someone I thought was my very special friend,

Frank Hogan. When I first met him, he had lost his job and had fallen on hard times. He was about to lose his Rockville, Maryland, home and had lost confidence in himself. Not knowing which way to turn, he spent his days, weeks, and months sitting in an old green chair in his living room, staring into space, and waiting for the phone to ring with a job offer.

I felt sorry for Hogan, so I intervened on his behalf and landed him a high-paying, prestigious job as legal counsel to the newly organized Merit Systems Protection Board, an independent, quasi-judicial federal agency. He held the job until he was eligible to retire. Hogan was able to keep his home, his family, his pride, and dignity; and he retired to Florida with a full federal pension.

Surely, Hogan would be willing and able to help me find a job for a few weeks. Nope, I never heard from him either.

Of course, the following Sunday afternoon, I was embarrassed to welcome Schubert to my halfway house. I stood by helplessly as the residence manager patted him down, searched his belongings, and made him sign the daily register. Schubert's warm and penetrating smile, however, immediately put me at ease, and we spent the next couple of hours talking, praying, and getting caught up.

Schubert could hardly believe my story of woe, but was more than willing to help me find a job and do whatever else he could do. He told me that he was on the board of the National Alliance of Business in downtown Washington, D.C., and that he was also chairman emeritus of the International Youth Foundation (IYF) in Baltimore, Maryland.

"These would be two good places to begin the job search" he said. "Let me make a couple of calls." And that's just what he did!

Thanks to Dick Schubert's telephone calls, I had two remarkable jobs waiting for me the very next week. First, I was employed as a business consultant for the NAB, a national labor trade association with a membership consisting of several hundred prestigious American corporations. Praise God, I was back in my element!

Bob Jones, president of NAB, was a most gracious and understanding gentleman in his fifties who treated me like a true professional and colleague. Schubert, of course, had briefed him on my bizarre situation and it was agreed that no one at NAB, other than Jones, would know that I was leading a double life—business consultant during the day and halfway-house resident at night.

During our first meeting, Jones and I spent almost two hours discussing our many mutual friends in Washington, two of whom, Mack Lovell and Bill Kolberg, actually served on the NAB board, along with Dick Schubert. Like Schubert, both were former high-level U.S. Labor Department officials who transitioned into Washington businessmen at the end of their government service. Lovell and Kolberg, along with their wives, had attended our wedding in 1980, and Lovell was a Georgetown neighbor of ours during our first two years of marriage.

I was a bit worried about the next part of my employment process, but Jones actually got a laugh out of some of the awkward requirements of the halfway house. For secrecy's sake, he decided not to involve his huge human-resource department. Instead, he dealt directly with the halfway-house representatives himself.

Jones had some "hoops" to jump through before I was permitted to take the NAB position. He had to confirm by telephone and by letter that he knew I was a resident of a federal halfway house and a convict. He then had to attest that I would be employed by NAB for two-and-a-half months and describe what my responsibilities would be. The halfway-house representative needed to know when and how much I would be earning, I had to be paid in cash, and Jones had to agree to permit halfway-house representatives to call and/or drop by my work place during working hours to make sure I was really there.

My second job was concocted for me. I would be employed as an international consultant to the esteemed International Youth Foundation (IYF). I had to take three buses and a train every Wednesday to work all day at the IYF headquarters in Baltimore.

The IYF President and CEO, William Reese, welcomed me with enthusiasm. He knew of my passion to help needy children in general, and Schubert had briefed him on our Third World Prosthetic Foundation.

The IYF Human Resource Department made all the administrative arrangements with the halfway house, and that very day, I began working on a research study that involved Israeli children. I was so fortunate to be working with the IYF staff for the next two and a half months.

Every morning, after cleaning one resident's bathroom and one staff bathroom, I would don my sentencing suit, sign out, and walk or take the bus the four miles to my job at the NAB.

I was assigned an executive office just down the hall from the president's office, where I was well positioned to make a lot of new friends on the NAB executive team. I felt very comfortable when I was called into Jones' office to give my professional advice on some up-and-coming piece of labor legislation on Capitol Hill.

My main problem was a chronic lack of sleep. The noise in the halfway house kept me awake almost all night, every night. During business hours at NAB, I made it a practice to close my office door and take a nap on the floor, with my head uncomfortably propped up on two books of the Washington Yellow Pages.

I worked on a variety of labor projects and helped organize the NAB annual CEO dinner that was going to be held at the Capital Hilton Hotel at the end of October. This created a problem for me.

I had to be back to the halfway house every evening by 6 PM. If I didn't show up on time, the staff would alert the U.S. Marshal Service to find me and escort me back to Allenwood Prison. What to do about the NAB dinner, which didn't start until 7 PM?

I submitted a written request to stay out until 9 PM for the dinner and was so relieved when it was granted. Going to these functions had been a big part of my lobbying life, and here I was asking permission to go to this one. It was demeaning, but I needed to be there as much for my own self-worth as my obligation to NAB.

I had a delightful time talking with my old friends, Mack Lovell and Bill Kolberg. They, like all the other CEOs I met that evening, had no idea I was a resident of a federal halfway house. Like Cinderella, my mandatory departure time was drawing near, so I hurried from the Hilton with great speed and waited for a bus on Columbia Road. After a few minutes, I started running up 16th Street. I ran the entire four miles without a single Metrobus passing me. Sweating and breathing hard, I was buzzed through the front door and signed in exactly at 9 PM. I was still breathing hard as I did the urinalysis and took the breathalyzer test, which were mandatory every time I came "home."

From time to time, I would leave NAB early in the afternoon to visit my lawyer, Brian Shaughnessy. We were preparing a motion asking that I be permitted to return to Poland after my halfway-house sentence was completed. I didn't look forward to standing before Judge Ellis again, and I especially didn't like the idea of asking him for special treatment. As far as we knew, no federal convict had ever served supervised probation outside of the United States.

At Shaughnessy's suggestion, Virginia and Katie wrote heartfelt letters to Judge Ellis in support of my motion. We pondered various alternatives for my release to Poland. Since everyone we knew in Poland thought that I was in the States on business, Virginia took an FBI agent assigned to the U.S. Embassy in Warsaw into her confidence. He had a son in Katie's American School class and sympathetically agreed to serve as my probation officer, if the court requested. Unfortunately, he backed out when pressed further on the subject by my lawyer.

We finally proposed in our motion that I would return to the United States as often as the judge ordered and report to a court-appointed probation officer in the Eastern District of Virginia.

Other than the armed robbery, the rest of my time at the halfway house was uneventful. There wasn't much to distinguish me from the other residents, except that I was the oldest, the only white, the only Christian, the only one with a high-school diploma, and the only one who hadn't been imprisoned for committing a violent crime. Thank you again, Judge Ellis.

Be that as it may, I got along well with most of my housemates and knew enough to avoid some of the others. I spent as little time as I legally could in the halfway house. I was permitted to take weekend runs through the National Zoo, located just a few blocks away, and I was authorized to go to church on Sunday mornings.

In fact, I attended the Georgetown Presbyterian Church—

the very same church in which Virginia and I were married, and the one we would attend whenever we were in town. It is the oldest church of any denomination with an unbroken ministry in the District of Columbia, and it was wonderful to see our pastor and friend, Rev. Campbell Gillon, each week. He knew nothing of my plight and thought that I was in Washington on business. I was required to prove that I had actually attended church by presenting the church bulletin when I got back to the halfway house.

Thanksgiving decorations were bountiful in the neighborhood when I got word from Shaughnessy that my court hearing had been scheduled two days before my release date of November 25, 1998. I would finally learn if I could return to Poland for the next two years. I prayed with all my heart for God's divine intervention.

FORTY-ONE

End of the Ordeal

I met Shaughnessy at his office and we drove across the Potomac River to the Federal Courthouse in Alexandria. We both knew how important this day was going to be.

This time the courtroom was virtually empty, and there was only one case before mine. Special Agent Core did not show up. Prosecutor Frank was present. He was alone. We did not speak.

How I dreaded facing Judge Ellis again. He was about to decide on my future and the future of my family for the next two years. He didn't know or care about me or my family. I had high hopes and low expectations.

My case was called: "The United States vs. William C. Chasey."

Shaughnessy stood and summarized my motion, requesting

that I spend the remainder of my sentence, two years of supervised release, in the Republic of Poland.

Judge Ellis tersely asked Frank what was the government's position on my motion.

Frank stood and nonchalantly said, "We have no position."

I almost fell out of my chair.

Judge Ellis looked directly at me and said, "Motion granted."

"Ms. Simpson, make arrangements for Mr. Chasey to return to the Eastern District of Virginia every six months for the next two years to meet with his probation officer. See that his passport gets delivered to the halfway house in time for his release and his trip home to Poland."

He banged his gavel and instructed the baliff to call the next case.

That was it. Six years of hell was over. I was free!

Having failed in every way to bring me to my knees and to get me to play their dirty game, the U.S. government was now done with me.

I had been wronged. Nevertheless, Virginia and I had fought the good fight. We had been decidedly outnumbered, vastly outspent, and greatly outgunned. Through it all, and with God's special blessings, our love and support for each other had only grown stronger.

We now knew firsthand what President Ford meant when he said, "A government big enough to give you everything you want is strong enough to take everything you have away."

I could look myself in the mirror knowing that at no time had I compromised my principles or my values.

I left the halfway house as early as possible on the morning of November 25, 1998, and returned to Warsaw to begin my new life with Virginia and Katie.

Epilogue

Bill Chasey returned to Poland where for the next fourteen years he re-established himself as a businessman, educator and philanthropist. At the urging of the Federation of the Red Cross in Geneva, Switzerland, Dr. Chasey spent three years as a full-time consultant to the Polish Red Cross. With the financial support of the American Red Cross in southeast Europe, he spent three years as a part-time consultant to the Bulgarian Red Cross.

Concurrently, he served as an adjunct professor of entrepreneurship and corporate social responsibility at the Business School of the American University of Bulgaria, Sofia, Bulgaria. He was a visiting professor of entrepreneurship at the Leon Kozminski Academy of Entrepreneurship in Warsaw, Poland, and a lecturer at the Warsaw School of Economics in Warsaw, Poland.

Dr. Chasey founded the Foundation for Corporate Social Responsibility in Warsaw, Poland, and serves as its president and CEO. The nine-year-old non-governmental organization (NGO) is composed of ninety multinational companies, and has fed over 5 million meals to needy Polish children. You can find more information about the organization on the Internet at *www.fcsr.pl.*

Polish President Aleksander Kwasniewski honored Dr. Chasey for his humanitarian work with the Polish Red Cross. He received the "Child's Friend" Honorary Medal, given to individuals and institutions involved in social work for the benefit of children in the Republic of Poland. He was awarded the Polish Educational Association "Integracja" Award for his work in educating and shaping the lives of young disadvantaged children in Poland, and was awarded the Bulgarian Red Cross "Gold Medal of Honor" for his humanitarian work on behalf of the poor children of Bulgaria.

In 2009 he was diagnosed with multiple myeloma, an incurable blood cancer. He received a stem-cell transplant the same year, and is now under the expert care of his medical team at the Moores Cancer Center at the University of California in San Diego.

Dr. Chesey divides his time between his foundation responsibilities in Poland, and his home in Southern California.

Virginia Chasey retired in 2011 after fourteen years as a high school world history and literature teacher at the American School of Warsaw, a private, not-for-profit educational institution, associated with the U.S. Embassy, serving the international community of Warsaw. Today, she divides her time between Poland—where she continues to work with her husband to improve the lives and education of needy Polish children, in her position as a volunteer member of the foundation's management board—and California, where she enjoys caring for her family and being involved in local charities and her church.

Katie Chasey remained in Poland for a numbers of years, becoming fluent in the Polish language and subsequently teaching English to Polish speakers. She was involved in helping her dad establish the Foundation for Corporate Social Responsibility, while attending the Leon Kozminski Academy of Entrepreneurship in Warsaw. She has since returned to the U.S. where she is completing her university studies.

Congressman Carroll Hubbard pled guilty to violations of federal campaign finance laws, and served two years in prison from 1995 to 1997. In 2006 and 2008, Hubbard was unsuccessful in attempts to seek re-election to the Kentucky Senate. He lost by only fifty-eight votes in the 2006 race. Hubbard's wife, Carol Brown Hubbard, was placed on probation for five years for illegally using her husband's congressional aides to work on her failed campaign for Congress. Hubbard and his wife divorced, and he practices law in Paducah, Kentucky.

Last reports had **Youssef el-Debri** running a communications company in Cairo.

After two decades of work as a full-time federal district judge, **Judge T.S. Ellis, III** took senior status in April 2007. He continues to hear cases in the Eastern District of Virginia, and also has been empowered to hear cases in the Western District of Virginia.

Special Agent Robert Core retired from the FBI. He operates a one-man law office in Washington, D.C.

Omar Mustafa al-Muntasir served as Libya's foreign minister from 1992-2000. He died in Libya on January 23, 2001.

Since leaving the U.S. Senate in 1997, **Senator Larry Pressler** has pursued a business and teaching career. His business pursuits have largely centered on a telecommunications law practice, lobbying, and serving on corporate and advisory boards of several companies.

A panel of three Scottish judges sitting in a special court in the Netherlands found accused Lockerbie bombing suspect **Lamen Khalifa Fhimah** not guilty on January 31, 2001, of 270 counts of murder in the Pan Am 103 bombing trial. He returned to live in Libya.

The same court found Fhimah's co-defendant, **Abdelbasset Ali Mohammed al-Megrahi,** guilty and sentenced him to life imprisonment. Suffering from advanced prostate cancer and given three months to live, he was released on compassionate grounds and returned to Libya on August 20, 2009. As of February 2012, he was still alive, residing in his family compound in Tripoli.

Col. Muammar el-Qadhafi's forty-two-year reign of power in Libya ended on October 20, 2011, with bullet wounds to his head and chest after his failed attempt to escape from the fighters of the Libyan National Transitional Council. Qadhafi was buried in an unmarked grave in the Libyan desert.

After an investigation lasting nearly four years, the Scottish Criminal Cases Review Commission ruled that **Abdelbasset Ali Mohammed al-Megrahi,** jailed for the 1988 Lockerbie bombing, might have been wrongfully convicted, and was the victim of a "a miscarriage of justice."

Bill Chasey with his boss, President Ronald Reagan

President George Bush with Bill Chasey in San Diego

Dr. Chasey bids farewell to Gov. John B. Connally
and joins Ronald Reagan for his 1980 Presidential Campaign

President Ronald Reagan appoints Virginia Chasey, Chair of the Rancho Santa Fe Republican Women, to a six-year term on the U.S. Selective Service System Board

The family photo Bill gave to Libyan Chief of National Security, Youssef Debri, 1992

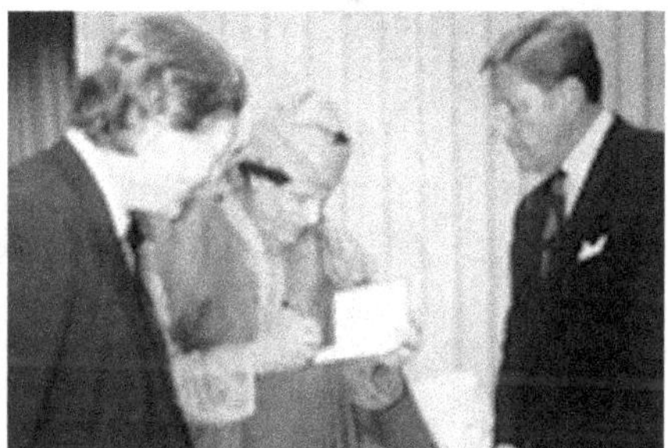

Col. Qadhafi signs copies of his Green Book for Gerrit Bovenkamp and Dr. Chasey, 1992

Bill and Virginia Chasey at the Seattle Cancer Care Alliance, one day post Stem-Cell Transplant, 2009

Bill and his PromiseKids sing "What a Wonderful World"
at the Foundation's 7th Annual Dinner Dance
at the Warsaw Hilton Hotel

Bill with a few of the 3,000 PromiseKids his Foundation
feeds each school day in 15 Polish schools

Endnotes

1 Ten months later, in April 1999, Col. Qadhafi finally relented under the pressure of stringent international sanctions. He ordered the transfer of Megrahi and Fhimah to the Netherlands to stand trial for mass murder under Scottish law.

2 Mancini wrote the music for hundreds of songs for film and television, including "Moon River," the theme for *The Pink Panther*, and the theme for the *Peter Gunn* TV series.

3 The Marine Corps Commandant's home is the oldest continuously occupied residence in Washington, D.C. In 1812, the British set fire to the White House, which President Madison was forced to abandon. The British commander occupied the Marine Corps Commandant's home, which was not set on fire, when the British subsequently withdrew from the city.

4 On April 5, 1986, Libyan agents bombed a Berlin nightclub, frequented by American soldiers, resulting in three deaths and 229 wounded. Ten days later, President Reagan launched a retaliatory air strike against several targets in Libya, including Qadhafi's residence in the Bab al-Azizia compound in Tripoli.

5 In 1985, as a special envoy for the Church of England, Terry Waite travelled to Lebanon to negotiate the release of four Western hostages held by Islamic Jihad. On January 20, 1987, Waite himself was taken hostage. After nearly five years in captivity, most of it in solitary confinement, he was finally released on November 18, 1991.

6 The former dean of Agriculture at the American University of Beirut, Thomas Sutherland was kidnapped by Islamic Jihad on June 9, 1985. He was released, along with Terry Waite, on November 18, 1991.

7 The Iran-Contra Affair was a notorious political scandal, exposed during the Reagan presidency in November 1986. Senior administration officials secretly and illegally sold weapons to the terrorist state of Iran. The profits were secretly and illegally funneled to the Nicaraguan Contras.

8 My response to Ms. Bullman appears in an article I wrote in 2006, which can be found on *www.truthneverdies.com*

9 There were later reports that Hannah did not die in this raid and works in Libya as a physician. Other reports say that she never lived at all.

10 ABSCAM was an FBI string operation , which resulted in the 1981 bribery convictions of Sen. Harrison A. Williams (D-NJ), along with five Members of the House of Representatives: John Jenrette (D-SC), Richard Kelly (R-FL), Raymond Lederer (D-PA), Michael "Ozzie" Myers (D-PA), and Frank Thompson (D-PA). Sen. Williams was sentenced to three years in prison. When my friend, Sen. Larry Pressler, was offered a bribe during this FBI sting, he refused. Pressler—the first Vietnam vet elected to the Senate—was later called a hero for doing so. To which he retorted, "I do not consider myself a hero. What have we come to if turning down a bribe is heroic?"

11 In 2004, a federal court ruled that a section of the 2001 Patriot Act was unconstitutional:

Beginning in 2004, giving expert advice or assistance to groups designated as foreign terrorist organizations is legal.

12 The account was never unfrozen.

13 The book was originally published as, *Foreign Agent 4221: The Lockerbie Coverup.* When the second edition was released in the fall of 1995, the title was changed to *Pan Am 103 The Lockerbie Coverup.*

14 The book was originally published as *Foreign Agent 4221: The Lockerbie Cover-up.* When the second edition was released in the fall of 1995, the title was changed to *Pan Am 103: The Lockerbie Cover-up.*

15 According to a 2006 Leadership Conference Report, plaintiffs won acquittals in federal trials only 15 percent of the time between 1979 and 2005. The chances of beating the IRS were even worse at 10 percent.

16 What's worse is that in the fall of 2005, *The New York Times* reported that over 25 percent of all convicted rapists and murderers, later exonerated by DNA evidence, had pleaded guilty! In other words, prosecutors are so corrupted by their own power that they often intimidated innocent people into pleading guilty to crimes that someone else committed, simply so the prosecutors could score another conviction. And, of course, what about all of those innocent people, whom prosecutors intimidated into pleading guilty, whose cases did not involve evidence that could be overturned by DNA evidence?

17 Genesis Hotels failed a couple of years later. Apparently, Harder ran afoul of the Polish justice system. He couldn't make it in Poland without me and ended up losing his entire investment.

About the Author

Dr. William C. Chasey is the founder, president and CEO of the Foundation for Corporate Social Responsibility in Warsaw, Poland. The nine-year old non-governmental organization (NGO) is composed of 90 multi-national companies, and has fed over 5 million meals to needy children in the Republic of Poland. The foundation presently feeds 60,000 meals each month to 3,000 poor kids in fifteen Polish schools. For more information, go to *www.fcsr.pl.*

Dr. Chasey was a founder of the cause marketing concept, and he continues to be a leading proponent of cause-related marketing around the globe. He has created, consulted with, or directed nineteen different NGOs and/or charities during his career. He consulted and advised twenty-three national Red Cross societies and served for over three years as principal consultant to the Polish Red Cross, where he created a major cause-related marketing campaign called the "Care Partners Network." With the financial support of the American Red Cross in southeast Europe, Dr. Chasey served for three years as a part-time cause-marketing consultant to the Bulgarian Red Cross in the development of a "Care Partners Network," which still provides hot meals to poor Bulgarian children each school day.

He received his B.S. degree in 1962 from Springfield College, a master of arts degree in 1965 from East Carolina University, a doctor of philosophy (Ph.D.) degree from the University of

Maryland in 1969, and an honorary doctor of humane letters (LH.D) from National University in California in 1985.

He served with distinction as a United States Marine Corps infantry officer with the 2nd Marine Corps Division, Camp Lejeune, North Carolina, from 1962-1965. He was awarded the National Defense Service Medal. This medal was awarded for honorable active military service during a time of war or conflict as a member of the United States Armed Forces, (Vietnam War Period).

He completed a distinguished academic career at a very young age, having served on the faculties of six major universities in the United States. He began his academic career as an instructor at the University of Maryland, served as an assistant professor at Delta State University and the University of Texas at Austin, and was awarded the only named professorship in his field, The John F. Kennedy Professorship at Peabody College of Vanderbilt University. He also served as an adjunct professor at The George Washington University and at The Ohio State University.

While living in Europe, he served as a professor of entrepreneurship and corporate social responsibility, and director of the Center for the Advanced Study of Entrepreneurship (CASE), School of Business, American University of Bulgaria, Sofia, Bulgaria (2003-2005). He was also a visiting professor of entrepreneurship and corporate social responsibility at the Leon Kozminski Academy of Entrepreneurship in Warsaw, Poland from 2003-2005, and a lecturer at the Warsaw School of Economics in Warsaw, Poland, from 2004-2005. He is the author of over 100 research investigations, books and inventions.

Dr. Chasey invented a number of research instruments for measuring psychomotor functions of mentally retarded children.

Dr. Chasey was a registered lobbyist with both the clerk of the United States House of Representatives and the secretary of the United States Senate. He was a registered foreign agent with the United States Department of Justice. He represented some of the world's most prestigious business clients, and twenty-three foreign governments and businesses before the United States Congress. He was the lead lobbyist for one of America's largest lobbying efforts, the Caribbean Basin Initiative (CBI), in which he represented eighteen Latin countries and 164 U.S. corporations.

Dr. Chasey's successful lobbying career was based on his direct, personal relationships with, and access to members of the United States Congress. Known for his insightful political knowledge and his command of legislative tactics, he was uniquely qualified to guide his clients through the bureaucratic maze of Capitol Hill. He lobbied for such issues as health care, banking, taxation, biotechnology, telecommunications, defense, trade, education, and all aspects of foreign relations. *Congressional Quarterly* selected Dr. Chasey as one of Washington's "Insider Lobbyists." Dr. Chasey also chaired the Ethics Committee for the American League of Lobbyists.

He served as director of domestic policy for Gov. John B. Connally's presidential campaign, 1979-80, and then became a principal advisor to the presidential campaign of Ronald Reagan and George Bush in 1980. Lou Harris attributed the Reagan-Bush victory to the Christian voter program and registration block directed by Dr. Chasey.

Dr. Chasey was featured on NBC's primetime magazine program, *TV Nation* with Academy Award-winner Michael Moore. This program, a joint venture between NBC and the British Broadcasting Corporation (BBC), played to over 40 million viewers around the world.

He was listed in the Compendium of Persons of Eminence in the Field of Exceptional Children, Who's Who in American

Education, and is a Fellow of the American Academy of Mental Retardation, American Academy of Sports Medicine, and the American Academy of Sports Psychology. He was listed in Outstanding Young Men of America, Who's Who in America, and Who's Who in Washington, D.C.

Dr. Chasey is married to Virginia Chasey, his wife of thirty-two years. Bill and Virginia have one daughter Katie. He also has two adult daughters from a previous marriage. Bill and Virginia divide their time between their foundation responsibilities in Warsaw, Poland and their home in Southern California.

To contact Dr. Chasey please visit:

www.TheTruthNeverDies.com

Other Books by Bettie Youngs Book Publishers

On Toby's Terms

Charmaine Hammond

On Toby's Terms is an endearing story of a beguiling creature who teaches his owners that, despite their trying to teach him how to be the dog they want, he is the one to lay out the terms of being the dog he needs to be. This insight would change their lives forever.

Simply a beautiful book about life, love, and purpose. **—Jack Canfield, Chicken Soup series**

In a perfect world, every dog would have a home and every home would have a dog like Toby! **—Nina Siemaszko, actress, *The West Wing***

This is a captivating, heartwarming story and we are very excited about bringing it to film. **—Steve Hudis, Producer**

ISBN: 978-0-9843081-4-9 • $14.95

The Maybelline Story—And the Spirited Family Dynasty Behind It

Sharrie Williams

Throughout the twentieth century, Maybelline inflated, collapsed, endured, and thrived in tandem with the nation's upheavals. Williams, to avoid unwanted scrutiny of his private life, cloistered himself behind the gates of his Rudolph Valentino Villa and ran his empire from a distance. This never before told story celebrates the life of a man whose vision rocketed him to success along with the woman held in his orbit: his brother's wife, Evelyn Boecher—who became his lifelong fascination and muse. A fascinating and inspiring story, a tale both epic and intimate, alive with the clash, the hustle, the music, and dance of American enterprise.

A richly told story of a forty-year, white-hot love triangle that fans the flames of a major worldwide conglomerate. **—Neil Shulman, Associate Producer, *Doc Hollywood***

Salacious! Engrossing! There are certain stories, so dramatic, so sordid, that they seem positively destined for film; this is one of them. **—*New York Post***

ISBN: 978-0-9843081-1-8 • $18.95

Blackbird Singing in the Dead of Night

What to Do When God Won't Answer

Gregory L. Hunt

Pastor Greg Hunt had devoted nearly thirty years to congregational ministry, helping people experience God and find their way in life. Then came his own crisis of faith and calling. While turning to God for guidance, he finds nothing. Neither his education nor his religious involvements could prepare him for the disorienting impact of the experience.

Alarmed, he tries an experiment. The result is startling—and changes his life entirely.

In this most beautiful memoir, Greg Hunt invites us into an unsettling time in his life, exposes the fault lines of his faith, and describes the path he walked into and out of the dark. Thanks to the trail markers he leaves along the way, he makes it easier for us to find our way, too. **—Susan M. Heim, co-author, *Chicken Soup for the Soul, Devotional Stories for Women***

Compelling. If you have ever longed to hear God whispering a love song into your life, read this book. **—Gary Chapman, *NY Times* bestselling author, *The Love Languages of God***

ISBN: 978-1-936332-07-6 • $15.95

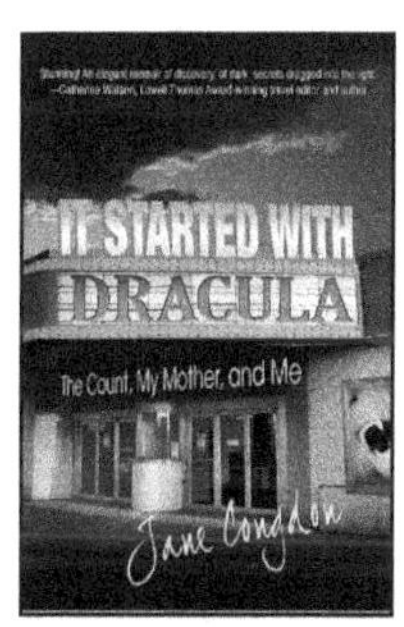

It Started with Dracula

The Count, My Mother, and Me

Jane Congdon

The terrifying legend of Count Dracula silently skulking through the Transylvania night may have terrified generations of filmgoers, but the tall, elegant vampire captivated and electrified a young Jane Congdon, igniting a dream to one day see his mysterious land of ancient castles and misty hollows. Four decades later she finally takes her long-awaited trip—never dreaming that it would unearth decades-buried memories, and trigger a life-changing inner journey. A memoir full of surprises, Jane's story is one of hope, love—and second chances.

Unfinished business can surface when we least expect it. *It Started with Dracula* is the inspiring story of two parallel journeys: one a carefully planned vacation and the other an astonishing and unexpected detour in healing a wounded heart. **—Charles Whitfield, MD, bestselling author of *Healing the Child Within***

An elegantly written and cleverly told real-life adventure story, proving that the struggle for self-love is universal. An electrifying read. **—Diane Bruno, CISION Media**

ISBN: 978-1-936332-10-6 • $15.95

Diary of a Beverly Hills Matchmaker

Marla Martenson

Marla takes her readers for a hilarious romp through her days in an exclusive matchmaking agency. From juggling the demands of out-of-touch clients and trying to meet the capricious demands of an insensitive boss to the ups and downs of her own marriage with a husband who doesn't think that she is "domestic" enough, Marla writes with charm and self-effacement about the universal struggles of finding the love of our lives—and knowing it.

Martenson's irresistible quick wit will have you rolling on the floor.
—Megan Castran, international YouTube Queen

ISBN: 978-0-9843081-0-1 • $14.95

Hostage of Paradox: A Memoir

John Rixey Moore

A profound odyssey of a college graduate who enlists in the military to avoid being drafted, becomes a Green Beret Airborne Ranger, and is sent to Vietnam where he is plunged into high-risk, deep-penetration operations under contract to the CIA—work for which he was neither specifically trained nor psychologically prepared, yet for which he is ultimately highly decorated. Moore survives, but can't shake the feeling that some in the military didn't care if he did, or not. Ultimately he would have a 40-year career in television and film.

A compelling story told with extraordinary insight, disconcerting reality, and engaging humor. **—David Hadley, actor, *China Beach***

ISBN: 978-1936332-37-3 • $24.95

DON CARINA

WWII Mafia Heroine

Ron Russell

A father's death in Southern Italy in the 1930s—a place where women who can read are considered unfit for marriage—thrusts seventeen-year-old Carina into servitude as a "black widow," a legal head of the household who cares for her twelve younger siblings. A scandal forces her into a marriage to Russo, the "Prince of Naples."

By cunning force, Carina seizes control of Russo's organization and uses her skill and savvy to control the most powerful of Mafia groups. Discovery is inevitable—and, Interpol has been watching as well. Nevertheless, Carina survives to tell her children her stunning story of strength and survival.

978-0-9843081-9-4 • $15.95

Living with Multiple Personalities

Christine Ducommun

Christine Ducommun was a happily married wife and mother of two, when—after moving back into her childhood home—she began to experience anxiety, panic attacks, and a series of bizarre flashbacks.

A mesmerizing journey inside the mind and life of a victim of dissociative identity disorder (DID). Christine Ducommun eloquently shares her story of her descent into madness, struggling to regain her sanity as four personalities compete for control of her mind and protect her from the demons of her childhood. A story of courage, healing, identity, hope, and love.

> Reminiscent of the Academy Award-winning *A Beautiful Mind*, this true story will have you on the edge of your seat. Spellbinding! **—Josh Miller, Producer**

ISBN: 978-0-9843081-5-6 • $16.95

Amazing Adventures of a Nobody

Leon Logothetis

Tired of his disconnected life and uninspiring job, Leon leaves it all behind—job, money, home even his cell phone—and hits the road with nothing but the clothes on his back. His journey from Times Square to the Hollywood sign relying on the kindness of strangers and the serendipity of the open road, inspires a dramatic and life changing transformation.

A gem of a book; endearing, engaging and inspiring. **—Catharine Hamm, *Los Angeles Times* Travel Editor**

"Leon reaches out to every one of us who has ever thought about abandoning our routines and living a life of risk and adventure. His tales of learning to rely on other people are warm, funny, and entertaining. If you're looking to find meaning in this disconnected world of ours, this book contains many clues." ***—Psychology Today***

ISBN: 978-0-9843081-3-2 • $14.95

The Rebirth of Suzzan Blac

Suzzan Blac

A horrific upbringing and then abduction into the sex slave industry would all but kill Suzzan's spirit to live. But a happy marriage and two children brought love—and forty-two stunning paintings, art so raw that it initially frightened even the artist. "I hid the pieces for 15 years," says Suzzan, "but just as with the secrets in this book, I am slowing sneaking them out, one by one by one." Now a renowned artist, her work is exhibited world-wide.

A story of inspiration, truth and victory.

A solid memoir about a life reconstructed. Chilling, thrilling, and thought provoking. **—Pearry Teo, Producer, *The Gene Generation***

ISBN: 978-1-936332-22-9 • $16.95

Out of the Transylvania Night

Aura Imbarus

Forty-one-year-old Aura Imbarus eloquently details her escape from the Communist regime in Romanian, and comes to America to rebuild her life. "Achieving the American dream is a matter of goals, hard work, and luck," she says. "But 'being an American' is arduous beyond imagination."

Aura's courage shows the degree to which we are all willing to live lives centered on freedom, hope, and an authentic sense of self. Truly a love story! **—Nadia Comaneci, Olympic Champion**

A remarkable account of erasing a past, but not an identity. ***—Todd Greenfield, 20th Century Fox Studios***

ISBN: 978-0-9843081-2-5 • $14.95

Fastest Man in the World

The Tony Volpentest Story

Tony Volpentest

Foreword by Ross Perot

Tony Volpentest is a four-time Gold Medalist and five-time World Champion sprinter. He carried the Olympic flame at the 1996 Atlanta Olympics. But it is not so much the medals he sports that make him admirable; it is the grit and determination that got him there. Though born without hands or feet, he is the fastest runner in the world. Tony shares his incredible journey, from the feet that Ross Perot built for him, to his 2012 induction into the Olympic Hall of Fame.

This inspiring story is about the thrill of victory to be sure—winning Olympic Gold—but it is also a reminder about human potential: the ability to push ourselves beyond the ledge of imagination, and to develop grit that fuels indefatigable determination. Simply a powerful story. **—Charlie Huebner, United States Olympic Committee**

ISBN 978-1-936332-00-7 • $16.95

Crashers
A Tale of "Cappers" and "Hammers"

Lindy S. Hudis

The illegal business of fraudulent car accidents is a multi-million dollar racket, involving unscrupulous medical providers, personal injury attorneys, and the cooperating passengers involved in the accidents and who also receive a portion of the illegal proceeds.

Newly engaged, Nathan and Shari are blissfully happy—but their joy is tempered by the dark cloud of mounting debt. Seduced by an offer from a stranger to move from hard times to good times in no time, Shari takes the carrot offered her, and finds herself acting as a "stuffed passenger"—the "victim" in a staged auto accident. Shari gets her payday…but breaking free of this dark and dangerous underworld will take nothing short of a miracle.

A riveting story of love, life—and limits. A non-stop thrill ride. **—Dennis "Danger" Madalone, stunt coordinator for the television series, *Castle***

ISBN: 978-1-936332-27-4 $16.95

In bookstores everywhere, online, Espresso, or from the publisher, Bettie Youngs Books:

www.BettieYoungsBooks.com

Bettie Youngs Books

We specialize in MEMOIRS

. . . books that celebrate

fascinating people and

remarkable journeys

www.ingramcontent.com/pod-product-compliance
Lightning Source LLC
Chambersburg PA
CBHW050456270326
41927CB00009B/1779

* 9 7 8 1 9 3 6 3 3 2 4 6 5 *